WHY NEW SYSTEMS FAIL

REVISED EDITION

AN INSIDER'S GUIDE TO SUCCESSFUL IT PROJECTS

With a Foreword by
Bruce F. Webster

Phil Simon

Course Technology PTR
A part of Cengage Learning

COURSE TECHNOLOGY
CENGAGE Learning™

Australia, Brazil, Japan, Korea, Mexico, Singapore, Spain, United Kingdom, United States

COURSE TECHNOLOGY
CENGAGE Learning™

Why New Systems Fail, Revised Edition: An Insider's Guide to Successful IT Projects
Phil Simon

Publisher and General Manager, Course Technology PTR:
Stacy L. Hiquet

Associate Director of Marketing:
Sarah Panella

Manager of Editorial Services:
Heather Talbot

Marketing Manager:
Mark Hughes

Acquisitions Editor:
Mitzi Koontz

Project/Copy Editor:
Karen A. Gill

Interior Layout Tech:
Bill Hartman

Cover Designer:
Luke Fletcher

Indexer:
Valerie Haynes Perry

Proofreader:
Sara Gullion

For product information and technology assistance, contact us at **Cengage Learning Customer & Sales Support, 1-800-354-9706.**

For permission to use material from this text or product, submit all requests online at **cengage.com/permissions**. Further permissions questions can be e-mailed to **permissionrequest@cengage.com.**

All trademarks are the property of their respective owners.

All images © Cengage Learning unless otherwise noted.

Library of Congress Control Number: 2009942396

ISBN-13: 978-1-4354-5644-0

ISBN-10: 1-4354-5644-0

Course Technology, a part of Cengage Learning
20 Channel Center Street
Boston, MA 02210
USA

Cengage Learning is a leading provider of customized learning solutions with office locations around the globe, including Singapore, the United Kingdom, Australia, Mexico, Brazil, and Japan. Locate your local office at: **International.cengage.com/region**.

Cengage Learning products are represented in Canada by Nelson Education, Ltd.

For your lifelong learning solutions, visit **courseptr.com**.

Visit our corporate Web site at **cengage.com**.

Printed in the United States of America
1 2 3 4 5 6 7 12 11 10

Foreword

If you're reading this Foreword to see if you are buying (or have bought) the right book, then let me quickly assure you: if you or your organization is thinking about licensing and installing enterprise-level software–enterprise resource planning (ERP) systems, accounting/payroll packages, human resource packages, and the like, you absolutely want and need this book.

Since 1994, my main professional focus has been on why large IT projects so often get into trouble or fail outright. I have written books and articles and have given lectures on the subject. I have gone into large corporations to review massive IT projects and to make recommendations on how to get them back on track. I have read hundreds of thousands of pages of documents, memos, e-mails, and transcripts regarding disputed and failed IT projects as a testifying expert in litigation.

With that background, I can tell you that Phil Simon knows exactly what he is talking about. This is no theoretical or academic text, no pie-in-the-sky, let's all-hold-hands idealistic manifesto. Phil knows where the bodies are buried. Through this book, he not only digs them up, he conducts a public autopsy so that you can avoid the same fate.

Yes, plenty of other authors have written about IT project challenges and pitfalls. But almost all of those books focus heavily (and often exclusively) on software engineering—that is, specifying, designing, writing, and testing actual software. This book is different: it focuses on the largely neglected category of buying and installing large, complex software packages from third-party vendors. Such projects account for some of the largest IT failures out there, yet no one has really focused on how to avoid those particular disasters.

Right now, you hold in your hand the key to successful enterprise IT selection and deployment. But it's up to you to read it, believe it, and apply it—and then convince those with more authority than you (if such exist) to do the same.

Good luck.

Bruce F. Webster
http://www.brucefwebster.com

Acknowledgments

I am grateful to Michael DeAngelo, Brian Morgan, Michael West, Rob Metting, Scott Berkun, Ben Lewis, Jason Horowitz, and Thor Sandell for their years of sage advice and friendship.

A tip of the hat to Mark Hayes, John Henley, Teri Watkins, Wayne McDermott, Bruce F. Webster, Bob Charette, Shiri Amram, and Jake Wyant.

Mitzi Koontz and Karen Gill of Cengage Learning took this book to the next level.

I also would like to thank my long-time Carnegie Mellon friends David Sandberg, Michael Viola, Joe Mirza, and Chris McGee. Shouts out also go to the following people: Craig Heyrman, Scott Erichsen, Greg Dolecki, Andrew Botwin, Rosalinda Cifuentes, MJ Stabinski-Heckman, Jeremy Rothschild, Ellen French, Alex Saint-Victor, Marc Paolella, Jenifer Simon, Naynish Jhaveri, Tom Bardzell, Steve Katz, Rose Aulik, Jim Harris, and Phil Brown.

My heroes from Dream Theater (Jordan, John, John, Mike, and James) and Rush (Geddy, Alex, and Neil) have given me many years of creative inspiration through their music. Keep on keeping on.

Special thanks go to my parents, Linda and Sandy Simon.

Finally, I would like to thank you, the reader, for buying this book. I'm an independent author and consultant without a marketing team getting my name out there. I rely on people like you to make a living.

If you enjoy this book, please recommend it to a friend; post your thoughts on Facebook, LinkedIn, Digg, or Twitter; or contact me at my Web site: http://www.philsimonsystems.com.

About the Author

Phil Simon is an independent technology consultant and the author of *The Next Wave of Technologies* (John Wiley & Sons, 2010). He writes about the intersection of technology and business.

He began consulting in 2002 after six years of related corporate experience. He has cultivated more than 30 clients from a variety of industries, including health care, manufacturing, retail, and the public sector. Phil has assisted both domestic and international organizations in every aspect of system implementations, activations, and ongoing maintenance.

While not consulting, he speaks on matters related to organizations' use of different technologies and writes for a number of technology-oriented media outlets. He has a bachelor's in policy and management from Carnegie Mellon University and a master's in industrial and labor relations from Cornell University.

To find out more information about Phil and his company, visit his Web site: http://www.philsimonsystems.com.

Phil lives in northern New Jersey.

Contents

Part I: Deciding to Take the Plunge

Chapter 3
Why Organizations Implement New Systems 31

Chapter 4
The Replacement System 41

Part II: System Selection

Part III: The System Implementation

Chapter 12
Testing Issues 157

Chapter 13
People Issues, Roles, and Responsibilities 173

Chapter 14
Reports and Interfaces 195

Chapter 15
Documentation Issues 209

Part IV: The Brave New World of Post-Production Life

Chapter 16
Ongoing System Maintenance **223**

Chapter 17
Operational Changes and Risks **233**

Part V: Maximizing the Chance of Success

List of Figures

List of Tables

Preface

I originally published *Why New Systems Fail* in February 2009. For a variety of reasons, I felt that the time was right for the book. Having worked on so many poorly conceived and terribly run projects in my career, it was painfully clear to me that there was something fundamentally wrong with most organizations' attempts to implement enterprise systems. In more than a decade of working on different IT projects in different countries and industries, I almost invariably saw the same outcome each time: some type of IT project failure.

However, in a way, the title was a bit of a misnomer. The book referenced systems that were, for the most part, actually very mature; they were only "new" to the organizations implementing them. By way of contrast, social networking is truly new. It is a relatively recent phenomenon with a corresponding lack of implementation methodologies and examples from which to learn. A high failure rate on these types of projects can be understood, if not expected, at least for the near future.

Projects involving organizations' implementation of "replacement" systems utilized applications and methodologies that have, in large part, been in existence for more than 20 years—an eternity in the world of technology. Many enterprise system implementations failed despite the presence of many attributes conducive to success: generous IT budgets, relatively mature applications, consulting firms with significant expertise, and thousands of previous projects to serve as examples and cautionary tales. Yet most of these projects continued to fail.

Against this backdrop, I could no longer claim that I just had a string of bad luck as a consultant. Something was broken, and I wanted to see if I could write a jargon-free, generally well-received book demystifying a process plagued by a 60 percent failure rate. While the first edition was certainly not perfect, I believe that I succeeded in that regard.

Since I began writing the first edition in the summer of 2008, much has happened that makes a revised edition of the book timely. For one, IT budgets have continued to decrease in response to the financial crisis and global recession. Many organizations have moved way beyond trimming the fat; some have cut into the bone. Organizations face new IT challenges, in particular doing even more with fewer financial and human resources. This revised edition addresses these challenges to a greater extent than did the first.

There have also been many changes, developments, and advancements in the software world. It is anything but a stable place. Software as a service (SaaS) and open source software (OSS) have continued to gain footing and no longer can be considered on the fringe. This revised edition gives more attention to these topics. Chapter 4, formerly titled "The Make, Buy, or Rent Decision," has been significantly reworked in light of these changes. Now titled "The Replacement System," this chapter expands upon the options available to organizations intent on replacing their legacy systems and enhancing their use of different technologies.

Chapter 20 has been enhanced as well. Formerly titled "Build in a Margin for Error," it now focuses more broadly on "Contingency Planning." I have outlined several other ways for organizations to minimize risk with their new systems.

As a result of the recession, many software vendors have become creative in attempting to enhance future revenue streams. A few have attempted to extract additional maintenance fees from their clients. I've added content that will provide additional options for cash-strapped organizations looking to minimize these costs.

On a different level, I admittedly wrote the first edition in a bit of a bubble. I have since stepped out of it. This revised edition incorporates valuable content from many of the articles, blogs, and books that I have read over the past year. This book is considerably richer for the contacts I have made since the book's initial publication. I have had many intriguing conversations with industry experts, practitioners, and academics who have given me a more rounded perspective on many subjects, including project management and organizations' adoption of different technologies.

I have also removed the majority of Wikipedia citations and replaced them with ones from physical books, e-books, well-regarded blogs, and magazine articles. I have reorganized a good bit of the content, placing a few sections in more natural places. For the sake of easy reference, the book now contains a glossary of commonly used terms.

On an editorial level, there are two groups of changes. Despite my best efforts, an uncomfortable number of errors snuck past my team of editors and my own eyes back in February 2009. (Note that I define "uncomfortable" as anything greater than zero.) Although they did not undermine the book's central tenets, I have corrected the transposed words, minor omissions, and missing prepositions.

This revised edition clarifies some subjects that, while not previously confusing, could have been articulated better in its initial publication. In my defense, I quote Leonardo da Vinci: "Art is never finished, only abandoned."

The revised edition is more current and better written than its predecessor, but one thing has *not* changed: my sense of humor. Case in point: comparing myself to da Vinci in this Preface.

Phil Simon
January 2010

Chapter 1

Introduction

> Trying is the first step to failure.
> —*Homer Simpson*

- Book Layout
- Fantasy World: The Theoretical System Implementation
- The Anatomy of a Typical System Failure
- The Four Major Types of System Failures
- Consequences of a Typical System Failure
- The Expectations Gap
- Risks for Mature Organizations
- A Balanced Approach: Theory, Case Studies, and Examples
- Who Should Read This Book?
- Topics
- Avoiding Death Marches
- So, Why Do New Systems Fail?

In 2006, California nonprofit Public Health Foundation Enterprises (PHFE) decided that enough was enough. The organization's legacy financial, HR, and other systems were essentially silos of information. Its end users could not easily access accurate enterprise data that they needed for their jobs. PHFE lacked integration among its different systems and began looking for a single, unified replacement.

PHFE hired external consultants to list all the organization's current business processes and develop functional requirements for the new system. PHFE ultimately requested proposals from Microsoft, SAP, Lawson, and other software vendors. After some deliberation, in August 2007 PHFE selected Lawson, purchasing software and consulting services worth in excess of $1M.

Fast forward to 2009. Only two years after signing the contract, PHFE initiated litigation against Lawson over its failed system implementation, according to documents filed in U.S. District Court for the Central District of California.[i] The complaint alleged that "PHFE has spent more than $1,000,000 on various programs, rather than one integrated program as promised, that do not work."

Because this is a recent case and the facts have not been established or made public, it is inappropriate for me to pass judgment. I just don't know who's responsible. Based on my experience on these types of IT projects, however, I doubt that Lawson shoulders all the blame. There is *probably* plenty to go around.

Organizations do not initiate lawsuits over botched IT projects every day. Lamentably, however, system failures are common. With regard to IT projects, Homer Simpson's quote at the beginning of this chapter is usually spot-on.

The statistics bear this out. More than three in five IT projects do not do what they were supposed to do for the expected costs and within the expected timeline. More gloomy stats include the following:

- 49 percent suffer budget overruns.
- 47 percent result in higher-than-expected maintenance costs.
- 41 percent fail to deliver the expected business value and ROI.[ii]

And, as we have seen, sometimes lawyers and judges get involved.

Ouch. Or, as Homer is so fond of saying, "D'oh!"

The process of implementing enterprise systems can hardly be called a recent business development.[1] If it were, perhaps the process's high failure rate would be understandable. It is not. Organizations have been implementing major enterprise systems for decades but, as a percentage, few have met their original goals and promises. Reflecting on more than a decade of implementing systems in many countries, industries, and organizations, I have come to one conclusion:

The previous statistics are probably understated.

I have many reasons to question the veracity of these numbers. For one, many executives do not want to admit that their pet projects ran over budget or missed deadlines. What's more, the simple time and money criteria mask less obvious system failures. The project that "makes its date and hits its numbers" may still not give the organization the expected bang for its buck. Many end users fail to use the new system's enhanced functionality and revert to old habits. The average CIO probably does *not* have the following in mind prior to spending upward of $1M or more on implementing a new system:

- Spending an enormous amount of money
- Replicating the problems of the previous system
- Failing to take advantage of most of the system's new functionality

Speaking from years of personal experience, I have been involved with few system implementations that could be categorized as unqualified successes. This begs the obvious questions:

- Why do so many system implementations fail so spectacularly?
- What can be done to increase the chances that organizations' use of new technologies will be successful?

In a nutshell, those two questions drive this book.

---

1. This book addresses types of systems, software vendors, consultancies, and implementation methodologies that have, in large part, been in existence for more than 20 years. Indeed, nascent ERP companies such as SAP and PeopleSoft were founded in 1972 and 1987, respectively, although Gartner Research is credited with introducing the term *ERP* in 1990.

Book Layout

This book is divided into five Parts:

I Deciding to Take the Plunge

II System Selection

III The System Implementation

IV The Brave New World of Post-Production Life

V Maximizing the Chance of Success

This method of organization allows readers to focus on only the sections and individual chapters that interest them. For example, a CIO whose organization has already selected her company's new system may want to skim Parts I and II and focus on Part III. Conversely, a decision maker in an organization yet to implement a new system would be wise to start from the beginning, only focusing on Parts III through V after beginning her IT project in earnest. Those in the midst of a project should pay particular attention to Part III. Finally, someone who has a "30,000 foot" level of interest in these projects should focus on the book's final Part—and, in particular, the final chapter.

Fantasy World: The Theoretical System Implementation

At the onset of a project, senior managers usually believe that their organizations will implement and activate new systems as follows:

1. The system is selected.

2. The system is implemented, during which time all issues are found and promptly addressed.

3. The system is activated.

4. Consultants remain onsite for a few weeks of "post-production" support, ensuring complete end-user knowledge transfer.

5. IT and functional end users can independently maintain the new system after consultants leave.

Based on this expected sequence of events, executives approve these massive projects. Unbeknownst to them, however, the process of implementing and activating a system is almost never this easy. After more than a decade in the field, I have *never* come across a system implementation that has gone this smoothly.

This book does *not* attempt to list every possible cause of system failures. Too many factors are at play: type of system, industry, size of organization, budget, timeline, dates, and so on. Rather, this book delves into the "usual suspects," to borrow a phrase from one of my favorite films. To the extent that each implementation is different—if not unique—the causes of system failures can and do vary on each project. For example, consider data issues: one organization may have pristine data in its legacy system, whereas a second may have wildly divergent data. Still, a third may have minor data issues.

This book focuses on the most common reasons for system failures. Many of the examples stem from projects I have worked on in the enterprise resource planning (ERP) arena. An ERP system stitches together an organization's back office. Specifically, these systems create and store data related to the following types of transactions: manufacturing, supply chain management, finance and accounting, HR, and customer relationship management (CRM). Of course, this depends on what individual organizations choose to utilize.

The Anatomy of a Typical System Failure

Although the specifics vary quite a bit based on the industry, the type, and the scope of the new system, many system failures have similar root causes, issues, costs, and, ultimately, consequences. The similarities do not end there. Organizations also tend to experience these problems and disappointments whether they purchase and implement an existing system or build a system internally or via an independent software vendor[2] (ISV) such as Infosys.

Table 1.1 represents a typical step-by-step failure of Bonham Software at The Page and Plant (P&P) Company.[3]

---

2. Independent software vendors (ISVs) make all types of software for all types of companies. Because organizations have increasingly sought the external expertise of ISVs in creating applications, it should not be surprising that companies such as Infosys have prospered. (The company's stock grew 3,000 percent since its IPO in 1993 to 2007, absent dividends.)

3. Astute readers will notice many 70s rock references throughout this book. There are five *really* good reasons for this. First, I really doubt that I could have used the names of real companies and individuals and I am entirely too impatient to have even asked. Second, I don't like lawsuits. Third, I had to keep myself interested as I wrote. Fourth, I thought that constantly using generic examples such as XYZ, Inc. would hide my considerable panache. Fifth, I figure that at least a handful of people will get them.

TABLE 1.1 The Typical System Failure

Task	Notes
System Selection	
The senior management of P&P decides that it needs to buy or build a new enterprise system.	
Vendor selection begins. Formal RFIs (requests for information) and RFPs (requests for proposals) are sent to major vendors or ISVs.	
Vendors or ISVs send formal responses, hoping to make the final cut.	
P&P personnel evaluate vendor/ISV responses. Decisions about "next steps" are made and communicated to these organizations.	P&P neglects to provide key business requirements that will come back to haunt the project.
Vendors and ISVs make formal presentations to key P&P constituents.	
P&P personnel evaluate proposals and references that vendors or ISVs provide.	
P&P narrows its selection to two vendors or ISVs based on perceived functionality, cost, time to implement, references, track record in the industry, and so on.	
P&P selects Bonham Software as its future enterprise system. For the sake of simplicity, assume that Bonham wins the consulting business as well.	Typically, Bonham will also attempt to win the consulting business. Many times, however, vendors such as Bonham recommend certified partners for the work if P&P deems Bonham too expensive or Bonham does not have the resources to complete the implementation.
System Implementation	
The implementation of Bonham Software formally begins.	
Unanticipated data and conversion issues manifest themselves, causing significant project delays. The climate becomes adversarial among key internal and external players.	The project begins to fall behind schedule.

Task	Notes
Testing is consequently delayed, and additional "parallel" tests are added to see if fixes have resolved identified issues.	Delays mount. P&P end users alert the team about previously omitted requirements.
Delays and "rework" typically feed into employees' previously approved vacation time or key deadlines (month-end, quarter-end, year-end closing, W-2 printing, and the like). The net result is that delays of two weeks can quickly become two months.	Management should not take these delays lightly, because key players may be unable or unwilling to move their personal commitments.. Often, these delays do not receive adequate attention.
Because of certain hard deadlines such as January 1 or the beginning of a new quarter, P&P devotes less attention and fewer resources to properly document current and future business processes.	The downstream impact of this can be enormous, especially if a key resource leaves the organization without sufficiently documenting or training others in how to conduct a key business process.
Functionality and features promised for Phase I of the implementation are pushed to later dates.	
Data challenges cause issues with interfaces to vendors. Vendor delays in returning test files exacerbate the problem, because they typically have a multitude of clients and cannot focus exclusively on P&P.	Interfaces may include health coverage for employees, direct deposit for employee checks, employment verification, and so on. These must work upon going live; there's no room for error here.
A "go/no-go" meeting is held, at which point key players determine if they are ready to proceed with system activation.	Despite the objections of several key players, P&P forges ahead, ostensibly aware of the risks.
P&P activates its new system.	Unfound and unsuspected functional, data, training, and interface issues manifest themselves, causing emergency "patchwork" or corrections.
Post-Production Support	
P&P end users are unprepared for issues that may arise. They still have much room for improvement in error correction, reporting, and so on.	
Bonham consultants plan to remain at P&P for two weeks to ensure a smooth transition and to address any system issues.	Ultimately, Bonham's stay lasts months afterward (at considerable additional expense to P&P).

The Four Major Types of System Failures

Not all failures are created equal, and there certainly are *degrees* of failure. This book defines four major types of system failures, one of which may not become apparent until months after an organization has activated a new system. Each case study is classified in terms of the following failure scale:

- The Unmitigated Disaster
- The Big Failure
- The Mild Failure
- The Forthcoming Failure

The Unmitigated Disaster

The most egregious failure occurs when an organization spends millions of dollars implementing a system and misses deadlines repeatedly. It ultimately junks the new system for a different one altogether or reverts to the legacy system. Relationships between system integrators (SIs) and clients are often severed. Lawsuits in such cases are not completely out of the question. Fortunately, these abominations are atypical.

The Big Failure

These types of failures are less severe but more common. Perhaps an organization initially budgets $2M and one year on an implementation and ultimately spends $4M over the course of three years, getting much less functionality than expected in the process.

The Mild Failure

Very often, a system failure is so mild that one can hesitate to even call it a failure, especially relative to the two types just mentioned. By comparison, these are rousing successes! For the sake of consistency, however, this book uses the term "failure." An example of the Mild Failure is the company that initially budgets $2M and a year on an implementation and ultimately spends $2.2M over the course of fifteen months, getting slightly less functionality than expected in the process.

The Forthcoming Failure

Sometimes a system failure is not immediately apparent. At first, this notion may seem perplexing. If an organization has met its goals with respect to both its budget and deadline, how can it consider the system a failure?

Budget and deadline are only two criteria for a system failure, as the statistics at the beginning of the chapter illustrate. The answer to this question lies within the organization's data, documentation, processing, and people. Examples of latent failures include the following:

- The implementation team has made a key mistake that will come back to haunt the organization down the road.
- End users may not completely understand the system and, as a result, make significant errors or revert to "old ways," negating one of the major benefits of the new system.
- The organization is vulnerable to employee attrition on two fronts:
  - End-user documentation is deficient and, if key staff members leave, their replacements will need significant time or training to do their jobs.
  - Knowledge is not dispersed; only a few employees understand the system in sufficient breadth and depth.

These are failures waiting to happen. Organizations are not prepared for shocks to their systems. This has become more likely as companies have trimmed headcount in response to the worst recession in decades.

I am reminded of an organization, Oates Health Care[4], that activated its ERP in 2003 with a fundamental but unknown problem with the way in which it calculated employee overtime. No one identified this issue during setup or testing. Only when an ex-employee filed a lawsuit did the problem come to light, five years *after* Oates had gone live.

For Oates, fixing the problem in the system involved two things: one simple and one difficult. The first merely entailed changing some flags in the system, allowing it to begin calculating overtime correctly *from that point forward*. However, checking those flags did not retroactively go back and recalculate overtime for all employees paid incorrectly over the past five years. A breakdown of those errant employee records is presented in Table 1.2.

Let's be clear about the enormity of this task: recalculating employee overtime for each employee over 52 weeks over a period that may be as long as five years. Such a task was well beyond the time and skill of Oates' existing end users (arguably a failure in itself). Even if an internal super-user knew *how* to do this on over 10,000,000 records, he or she would *not* have been able to do it. For *ad hoc* analyses, Oates provided its end users only with Microsoft Excel, a valuable tool but one not nearly robust enough to handle a task of this magnitude. As a result, Oates hired Bishop Consultants to perform this task at considerable expense.

---

4. Yes, this is another 70s rock reference.

TABLE 1.2 Breakdown of Payroll Records Requiring Analysis at Oates Health Care

Item	Value
Employees paid per year	6,500
Average types of pay per week per employee	6
Weeks per year	52
Checks per year	338,000
Payroll records per year	2,028,000
Years of data requiring analysis	5
Total records (over a five-year period)	10,140,000

Had Oates' end users or its SI properly tested its system prior to going live, it may have avoided its current state of affairs. To be sure, it would not have had to spend the time, internal resources, and funds on Bishop to fix the problem. Bishop recalculated employee overtime pay, but Oates' end users were mostly unavailable during the remediation project. This prohibited Bishop's consultants from transferring knowledge to Oates' end users during the error-resolution process.

Ironically, Oates did not learn from its mistakes. Despite the recommendation from Bishop, Oates did not seriously consider adding a more powerful reporting tool for end users to conduct similar kinds of analyses, such as Crystal Reports, Microsoft Access, or Business Objects. Oates also failed to actively recruit more technical end users to use these very tools, should it one day have decided to purchase them. If Oates encounters a similar problem in the future, it will be at the mercy of external consultants such as Bishop once again.

Consequences of a Typical System Failure

The consequences for a failed implementation go beyond mere dollars and cents. Let's return to the P&P example in Table 1.1. Bonham Software may forever have a tarnished reputation within P&P among both end users and employees who actually do not even use the system on a regular basis. Bonham may always be known as "that system that screwed up payroll." Data could be lost or altered in such a way that it would be impossible to retrieve. Due to lack of training or documentation, employees' jobs may actually become *more* difficult than they were with P&P's legacy system.

For Bonham Software, as a company, the project was a disaster. Bonham now has a tarnished reputation in the industry resulting from this highly publicized failure. It may have difficulty collecting the hundreds of thousands in accounts receivable from P&P and lose key consultants. P&P may also refuse to provide a reference for its new partner.

As stated before, many types of issues haunt system implementations. Although each of the case studies detailed in the book differs in terms of the way in which the organizations employed technology and even in the technologies themselves, there is considerable overlap among the issues encountered.

The Expectations Gap

Table 1.1 illustrates that system implementations typically leave many parties disappointed in the ultimate outcomes. Senior management expects the new system to be implemented smoothly, on time, and within the planned budget. Client end users expect to learn how to properly use the new system and be self-sufficient when consultants leave. SIs expect strong client references. For each party, these expectations are often unmet, many times by a significant degree.

Disappointments often give way to disasters. A less-than-inconsequential number of these projects have their plugs pulled mid-implementation. Organizations sometimes go live when they are wholly unprepared to do so. Issues abound, and the benefits and cost savings once promised by the vendor and SI may be significantly less pronounced than what clients ultimately see. In retrospect, after system activation, many clients opine that the new system is a far cry from what they expected when senior management signed the original contracts.

Risks for Mature Organizations

Although this book focuses on organizations implementing new systems, most of the content applies to the maintenance, enhancement, and support of existing systems as well. Mature systems are hardly immune to failure. Successfully activated systems often begin to show signs of future problems. Moreover, a Mild Failure could easily become either a Big Failure or, in extreme cases, an Unmitigated Disaster. Just because a new system goes live on time and under budget does *not* mean that an organization is out of the woods. There is still significant risk, discussed at length in Chapter 17, "Operational Changes and Risks." Systems can and often do begin to experience major difficulties after even successful activation, attributable to the following:

- System upgrades and the decommissioning of older versions of the application
- The introduction of additional functionality within a system
- Changes to business processes
- Acquisition of a company and the integration of additional legacy systems
- Unwise expansion
- Key employee turnover (voluntary)
- Staff reductions/layoffs

This last risk has increased significantly over the past two years, as organizations have had to deal with the worst economic crisis in the past 75 years. Often, companies were already lean and lacked appropriate backups in the event of employee departures. Recent cutbacks in IT budgets—and related personnel—have left many organizations even more exposed to system failures.

A Balanced Approach: Theory, Case Studies, and Examples

Throughout this book, theory and practice are given equal weight. Consider system testing for a moment. This book does not simply espouse the virtues of system testing; to do so would be facile. After all, all consultants and implementation teams intend to run proper parallel tests.[5] How, then, should the importance of—and frequent missteps associated with—testing be illustrated? By drawing upon extensive examples and detailed case studies, this book manifests the *essential* questions that cause testing to be compromised. These include

- What causes system testing to produce unexpected results?
- What are the effects of failed testing on the project's timeline, budget, and ultimate outcome?
- Most important, what specifically can an organization do from the beginning—and during—a project to promote accurate, timely, and comprehensive testing?

---

5. In a parallel test, identical data is loaded or entered into two disparate systems for testing purposes. The results are then compared. In theory, the output should be very similar, if not identical. Legitimate system differences often persist, however, as no two systems are exactly the same.

What's more, the book covers the entire life cycle of a system implementation: from an organization's initial decision to go down this road until system activation and beyond. Topics such as project management are certainly covered, but not in an abstract manner. This is not a book about project management in a vacuum.

A NOTE ON CASE STUDIES

The examples and case studies in this book stem from actual system implementations and IT projects. However, the names of the organizations, SIs, and individuals have been changed. Specific names are not nearly as important as the lessons they provide. As we will see, many ostensibly different organizations face similar—if not identical—challenges implementing systems.

It's commonly been said that one learns more from failures than from successes. To that end, this book's case studies and examples will examine in great detail projects that failed, identifying the specific individuals, decisions, and events responsible for the outcomes.[6]

The book's eight detailed case studies are listed in Table 1.3.

TABLE 1.3 List of Case Studies in Book

Case Study	Chapter	Description	Result
Costanza	9	A Flexible Client and a True Consulting Partner	Averted Failure
Lifeson	11	Replicating the Old in the New	Unmitigated Disaster
Portnoy	11	A Square Peg and a Round Hole	Unmitigated Disaster
Elton	13	The Stubborn Client	Big Failure
Julian Marketing Partners	15	Building Its Own System	Mild Failure
Wilson	15	Good Design but Lack of Resources	Big Failure
Petrucci	18	Trying to Boil the Ocean	Big Failure
Tate	22	Adding on to a Poor Foundation	Forthcoming Failure; Became Unmitigated Disaster

---

6. Although, again, the actual names are fictitious.

We often hear IT project failure statistics similar to those cited at the beginning of this chapter. Lamentably, we rarely hear the specifics that cause so many IT projects to fail.[7] Absent these details, how will organizations learn how to avoid them? A few things come to mind:

- SIs and consultants
- Academic studies
- Conversations with peers

To be sure, consultant advice is essential. Also, the value of quantitative studies and formal and informal discussions regarding IT failures should not be minimized. Still, these mechanisms are often not able to fully answer many critical questions. Consider for a moment digital health records, a topic that will get much play with $19B in stimulus money earmarked for it.

Specific questions include these:

- What challenges have hospitals faced digitizing their health records?
- How did they overcome those challenges?
- What can other hospitals learn from these successes and failures?

Organizations of all sorts try to hide their system failures and often are successful in doing so. In the rare event of a lawsuit, it's not uncommon for parties to settle confidentially, perhaps with the help of a third party. When the results of failed IT projects do become public, key players often attempt to minimize the damage for obvious reasons. Software vendors are less likely to sell new licenses and services if word gets out that their applications do not work as advertised or require heavy customization. SIs face similar concerns from discerning clients.

For their part, clients rarely want to air their dirty laundry about issues faced during the implementation. These include petty internal politics, inadequate mainframe systems, messy data, end-user resistance, and other major blunders that caused projects to exceed their budgets, miss their deadlines, and result in suboptimal functionality. People don't want to look bad and subject themselves to public scrutiny. Clients are not above reproach, however. Not everything can be blamed on consultants and vendors.

On IT projects, organizations of all types make avoidable mistakes because Company A didn't know that Company B encountered the same issue. The fundamental problem reflects broader societal trends and economic

---

7. Relative to IT project failures, general business blunders are much more commonly documented. For an absolutely outstanding account of many of these corporate mishaps, check out *Billion-Dollar Lessons: What You Can Learn from the Most Inexcusable Business Failures of the Last 25 Years* by Paul B. Carroll and Chunka Mui.

incentives mentioned in books such as *The Cheating Culture* by David Callahan and *Freakonomics* by Steven D. Levitt and Stephen J. Dubner. In this case, what's best for one vendor or client (lack of bad public relations) is not best for others or for the industry at large.

Who Should Read This Book?

This book has no one intended audience, and I have yet to read a book that can be everything to everybody. This book is no exception. Still, I have written with three primary audiences in mind.

As a full-time independent consultant, I wish that I had known many of the things in this book when I started working with systems back in the mid-1990s. (Maybe I wouldn't have gone into the field, but that's a separate matter!) Many current and aspiring consultants would benefit from the advice dispensed in this book, both on a general level as well as in terms of any specific projects on which they may be working.

Beyond consultants, this is a book for end users at all levels within an organization. At the top, CIOs and CTOs thinking about implementing a major new system could probably use a reminder about the implementation challenges *before* plunking down hundreds of thousands or millions of dollars on a questionable project.[8]

Underneath the C-level, many organizations are already somewhere in the middle of such a project. The subject matter, if applied properly and in a timely manner, may help project managers, end users, and implementation teams avoid many of the outcomes detailed in the case studies and examples. Regardless of the stage of the implementation, the practical tips have the potential to right the ship. Understanding the causes of system failures may help organizations avoid them, although there are no guarantees.

Topics

At a core level, this book is about three fundamental processes in the life cycle of enterprise systems: selection, implementation, and maintenance. Each of these processes consists of many different activities, tasks, and other subprocesses. In other words, this book is *not* exclusively—or even predominantly—about any one topic, although it does cover quite a few.

---

8. Certain chapters are not intended for C-level executives. For example, rare is the CIO who writes custom reports. As such, they can probably skip Chapters 12 and 14, which deal with testing issues and reports and interfaces, respectively.

Consider project management, for example. Plenty of good books on the market are devoted to that subject.[9] However, one of the central tenets of this book can be stated as follows:

> Certain projects are fundamentally easier to manage than others. An ill-conceived project with inadequate resources, poor documentation, internal resistance, and the like has a low chance of success even if run by Jack Welch himself.[10]

This book provides a holistic approach to selecting, implementing, and maintaining systems. It does *not* look at any one topic, such as project management, in a vacuum. Although project management is important, it is no elixir to a project gone wild. Every topic in this book is important and can derail an otherwise well-managed project.

Avoiding Death Marches

Implementing new systems is *not* like baking a cake. Organizations *cannot* follow a recipe with the following ingredients: three consultants, six weeks of testing, two training classes, and a healthy dose of project management. Nor do projects bake for six months until complete, after which time everyone enjoys a delicious piece of cake. For all sorts of reasons, a well-conceived and well-run project may fail, whereas a horribly managed project may come in under budget, ahead of schedule, and do everything that the vendor promised at the onset.

Successfully implementing new systems is as much an art as a science. As such, this book makes no guarantees about outcomes. Ideally, this book's content will help organizations avoid project "death marches." (Note that avoid is not the same as prevent.) In his seminal book *Death March*, Ed Yourdon writes the following:

> Quite simply, a death march project is one whose "project parameters" exceed the norm by at least 50 percent. In most projects, this means one or more of the following constraints have been imposed on the project:
>
> - The schedule has been compressed to less than half the amount estimated by a rational estimating process.
> - The staff has been reduced to less than half the number that would normally be assigned to a project of this size and scope.

---

9. I have really enjoyed *Making Things Happen: Mastering Project Management (Theory in Practice)* by my friend and annual basketball teammate, Scott Berkun.

10. Jack Welch was the CEO of General Electric (GE) between 1981 and 2001. He is widely considered to be one of the greatest leaders in U.S. business history.

- The budget and associated resources have been cut in half.
- The functionality, features, performance requirements, or other technical aspects of the project are twice what they would be under normal circumstances.

So, Why Do New Systems Fail?

Many people ask me this question. The short answer is "people." The slightly longer answer is that software vendors push, and organizations choose a new system lacking a solid understanding of the four basics for implementing any major technology: data, people, processes, and technology. For the really long answer, keep reading this book.

Summary

The reasons typically vary, but the outcomes of many IT projects are sadly the same. Many differ only to the degree to which they have disappointed or outright failed. Rare is the implementation that meets its deadline at or under budget and gives end users the functionality promised from day one. Quite simply, this is a book about why these failures happen and what can be done to avoid them.

Endnotes

i. http://www.pcworld.com/businesscenter/article/170600/nonprofit_sues_lawson_over_alleged_erp_failure.html

ii. http://advice.cio.com/remi/two_reasons_why_it_projects_continue_to_fail

PART I

Deciding to Take the Plunge

This Part focuses on an organization's decision to retire its legacy system. It starts with the reasons that many organizations are loathe to even consider an undertaking of this magnitude. Many ultimately reach a tipping point and decide that the benefits of a new system finally outweigh their costs—in other words, the status quo is unsustainable.

2 Why Organizations Maintain Legacy Systems

3 Why Organizations Implement New Systems

4 The Replacement System

Chapter 2

Why Organizations Maintain Legacy Systems

> Humanity is acquiring all the right
> technology for all the wrong reasons.
> —*R. Buckminster Fuller*

- The Technology Adoption Life Cycle
- Legacy Systems
- Eight Reasons That Organizations Maintain Legacy Systems

Many legacy systems have long outlived their usefulness. It's not uncommon that a mature organization purchased and implemented its accounting, inventory, or payroll system—more likely, system(s)—well before the advents of the Internet, e-mail, and other automation and communication tools. To say that a system is antiquated, however, is not to say that it will be retired anytime soon. Many systems remain active for years beyond their heyday. The opening quote holds quite a bit of meaning for many seasoned executives at mature organizations.

The Technology Adoption Life Cycle

Very few individuals and organizations implement new technologies right after their introduction and development, a phenomenon that has been termed the Technology Adoption Life Cycle (TALC).[1] Applied to organizations, TALC can be graphically represented as shown in Figure 2.1.

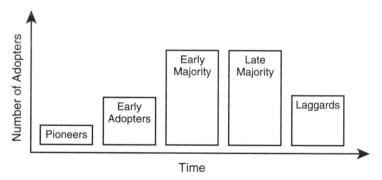

Figure 2.1 *TALC.*[i]

A full discussion of why and when organizations adopt technologies is not warranted here. Suffice it to say that TALC has three major applications for the purposes of this book:

- The majority of organizations waits until a new technology has become pervasive and mature before deciding to use it—if at all.

- Few tend to be "on the left side of the curve" for reasons that will become apparent in this chapter.[2]

---

1. In *Business Innovation and Disruptive Technology: Harnessing the Power of Breakthrough Technology for Competitive Advantage*, Nicholas Evans writes that "the traditional curve took shape because communications channels were constrained and even the innovations themselves were not immediately widespread or accessible." He goes on to write that this is changing, but that's a subject for a different book.

2. This is not to say that they should be. Few organizations have a business need to immediately adopt an unproven technology and be "on the bleeding edge."

- Although TALC applies to all technologies, the focus in this book is on enterprise systems.

Before we explore the reasons for purchasing, implementing, and activating new systems, let's answer two fundamental questions:

- What is a legacy system?
- Why do organizations maintain them for so long?

Legacy Systems

The term *legacy system* has many definitions. Most reflect the antiquated nature of the technology. Many people associate legacy systems with the following:

- Clunky mainframes
- Difficulty in extracting information
- Heavy IT involvement
- "Green screens" as opposed to user-friendly graphical user interfaces (GUIs)
- Keystroke- and code-based navigation as opposed to the mouse
- An inability of individual end users to customize their own experience — that is, one size fits all

In *An Executive's Guide to Information Technology: Principles, Business Models, and Terminology*, Robert Plant and Stephen Murrell write that "...a system needs to be considered in terms of its ability to support the current and future processes of an organization; an inability to support changing process requirements is now taken as the definition of a legacy system." This is an excellent definition of the term and explains, at a high level, the decision to purchase and implement a new system.

As such, legacy systems are *not* necessarily confined to the old clunkers of the past. A system implemented in 2002 might have been contemporary until recently. However, because of changes in business needs, that system is no longer adequate for the organization; it is now a legacy system for the purposes of this book.

Eight Reasons That Organizations Maintain Legacy Systems

Now let's delve into eight specific reasons that organizations maintain legacy systems.[3] Many of the following reasons are completely reasonable.

- Living in oblivion
- If it ain't broke, don't fix it
- The cost of action
- All functions are not created equal
- Fear of the unknown
- Fear of the known: horror stories and risk aversion
- Insufficient time and people
- Change agents and employee turnover

Living in Oblivion

Many organizations maintain their legacy systems for a simple reason: certain executives honestly—and incorrectly—believe that their organizations already have at their disposal systems that allow end users to do their jobs efficiently and effectively.

For example, at one large organization in the late 1990s, a senior VP of HR remarked that her company's systems were actually wonderful, because they produced nice-looking, "actionable" reports. She did not know, however, that many end users needed to cobble together those reports from disparate sources of data over the course of several weeks.

Executives may lack knowledge of their systems' limitations because of true ignorance or denial. Regardless of the reason, the net effect is the same: senior management at these organizations is unlikely to consider a superior system because no one with the necessary power will push for it. Not only has the need for a new system not been identified, *the contrary belief exists*. For the idea of a new system to gain traction, someone or some event has to convince senior management of each of the following:

- The current system is deficient and cannot meet the organization's current or future business needs.
- Systems currently exist in the market that would meet the organization's current or future business needs.

---

3. I have no illusions that this is the complete list. In my experience, however, these are the most common reasons. (Subconsciously, I am probably happy that these reasons don't conveniently fall into a "top ten" list.)

- The benefits and savings of a new system more than justify the time, cost, and effort involved in purchasing and implementing it.

Such a system can be successfully implemented in the organization.

Collectively, this is usually a tall order. Many executives mistakenly believe that their business needs are unique. They may stumble on any one of the preceding points. If that happens, any momentum for a new system would die right then and there. However, let's delve a bit deeper into some of the dynamics within an organization to explore the case that needs to be made for a new system.

Consider Eric, the head of HR at a fictitious company with deficient systems. Eric understands that many companies have similar business needs and processes— annual open enrollment, government reporting, and so on. He is open to investing the financial and political capital necessary for a new system to become a reality. Before taking that leap, however, he takes a step back. Eric knows that certain pockets of the organization represent considerable political obstacles. Sofia, the head of IT, and Eva, the head of finance, quickly come to his mind. Eric knows that it is premature for him to make his case for a new system. With that in mind, he does the following:

- Based on the quality of the data in the legacy systems, Eric starts a massive data cleanup project within the organization.
- He recruits technology-savvy staff. He knows that the new system will require more "data" work than has traditionally been the norm for his staff.

In short, Eric knows that these two important steps will help him make the case for a new system and lay the groundwork for a successful implementation. For these reasons, Eric is a wise man. It is much better for him to take interim steps *before* suggesting that management spends money on a new system.

When the time is right to broach the subject of a new system, Eric has already essentially negated two potentially lethal arguments from Sofia and Eva. By cleaning up his department's data and hiring more technical personnel, he has robbed his opponents of some fairly potent ammunition. Sofia and Eva may still object for many reasons, not the least of which is cost. However, at least they cannot claim that HR and payroll data is too inconsistent to be successfully loaded into a new system. Further, they will not be able to argue that Eric's staff—which would undoubtedly play a key role— does not have the technical skills to handle a new system. Eric is getting his ducks in a row and will make the push when the time is right.

The case studies and examples in this book will show how infrequently executives display Eric's kind of wisdom and foresight.

If It Ain't Broke, Don't Fix It

Using a similar line of reasoning, many decision makers have framed the argument for a new system in terms of the lowest common denominator. The criterion for a new system is not whether the legacy system has the latest bells and whistles. Rather, the current system has to be broken or will imminently break. For instance, "Why do I need a new payroll system?" the director of finance may ask. "We are paying employees correctly now. Why should I spend all of this money to pay them more correctly?"

This mentality is certainly prevalent in many organizations, particularly in mature ones run by "lifers." Truth be told, this is a tough challenge to overcome for the change agent. It is difficult for anyone to make the case for change if senior management perceives no upside and the affected area is a cost center, such as HR.

The Cost of Action

Although the next chapter provides greater detail about the specific costs of implementing a new system, suffice it to say for now that they are substantial in any economic climate, much less a recession. Even executives who recognize the need for a better system may very well concede that it is not the organization's top priority. Organizations only have so many dollars to spend. Quite simply, even a system universally recognized as deficient may not make the cut during budget time.

A progressive executive can argue (much like a vendor) that the new system will pay for itself over a number of years. Reduced administrative or personnel costs, coupled with increased access to vital information and analytics, may sway reluctant senior management. Lamentably, the short-term costs are often too high to justify murky, long-term benefits.

All Functions Are Not Created Equal

Functions of a business that generate revenue tend to have, on average, superior systems. If an organization's sales system is inadequate or cumbersome, the bottom line suffers. Rest assured, financial systems that make reporting difficult or inaccurate will receive quick attention from a CFO. In these instances, the data-mining opportunities from a superior system may yield increased revenue and profits.

On the other end of the spectrum, many departments such as HR have yet to make the jump to strategic partner, and their systems typically reflect that.

Consider payroll systems. Businesses do not realize a competitive advantage from paying their workers. Key employees do not remain with an employer because of paychecks. In all likelihood, an organization will replace its Human Resource Information Systems (HRISs) only if it believes it can dramatically cut administrative costs related to HR, benefits, and payroll, with two exceptions:

- Support for the current system will soon expire.

- Support for the current system will become prohibitively expensive.

Fear of the Unknown

Let's consider Roma Industries, a company pondering the purchase and implementation of Oracle applications throughout the enterprise. Roma's finance director, Richard, has 20 years of experience with the legacy system and knows it like the back of his hand. Although Richard admits that the legacy system is clunky, he knows how to enter journal entries, run profit and loss statements (P&Ls), and extract and manipulate data. He may publicly object to Oracle for financial considerations, but his real objection is that he has neither the time nor the desire to learn a new system while performing his day job.

Richard will not admit this, however. He uses a different approach: what if Oracle turns out to be no better than the current system? What if it's actually worse? Sure, Oracle's demo looked impressive, and the system *may* make life easier at Roma. However, what if the company does not realize the benefits promised by Oracle's salespeople? Roma could not easily "unring" this bell. Organizations that decide to implement new systems rarely revert to their legacy systems. If Roma's implementation of Oracle is not successful, it will probably not try again with another application, such as SAP. Organizations almost always get one bite at the apple.[4]

The required financial commitment and political capital of a new system are just two of the reasons that virtually guarantee that an organization will get just one bite at the apple.

Fear of the Known: Horror Stories and Risk Aversion

Many system implementations fail disastrously and publicly. As a result, many organizations on the fence about implementing a new system are reluctant to repeat the mistakes of their counterparts. These projects almost always have high profiles within organizations, and disasters have resulted in many executives being shown the door.

---

4. I do know of a few companies that have actually tried again with a different vendor. These are the exceptions that prove the rule.

One of the most memorable horror stories occurred a few years back with The Hershey Company.[ii] Its implementation of a new SAP supply chain system caused significant delays in production during its two busiest times of the year (Halloween and Christmas). Things got ugly, and lawyers got involved. It is understandable that executives do not want to expose their organizations to that kind of risk.

Along with horror stories, many organizations are risk-averse with respect to tinkering with their back office systems. On some level, they may believe that new systems can reduce costs and provide superior functionality, two arguments typically cited by vendor salespeople. Senior managers may still not want to risk missing payroll, losing track of inventory, or being unable to run key financial reports. Perhaps they have seen firsthand how problematic, costly, and time- and resource-intensive these projects can become. Many are aware of other dirty little secrets:

- Vendor and consultant promises often go unfulfilled.
- Many end users do not take advantage of the new system's increased capabilities.

As a result, many senior executives may believe that, for all the bells and whistles of a new system, there is relatively limited actual upside. If payroll and inventory are accurate now, the best case scenario is that they will still be accurate in the new system. The worst-case scenario is absolute chaos, enough to scare executives from retiring their legacy systems on their watch.

Insufficient Time and People

Consider OSI Medical Instruments, a company with the requisite budget and desire to retire its mainframe-based accounting system. Senior management is dying to enter the 21st century. What would give it pause? For one, OSI may not have the human bandwidth necessary to implement the new system. The project may result in a financial and operational catastrophe. Perhaps some key employees have recently left the company, so OSI is scrambling to make do in the interim.

Senior management at even properly staffed organizations should think long and hard about implementing a new system. Such a project is no small endeavor for any organization, and daily end-user workloads will increase substantially, often for six months to a year. A perfectly legitimate question is, "Do our employees have the time to devote to this project and make it successful?" The answer may very well be "no."

Change Agents and Executive Turnover

With executive turnover at an all-time high,[iii] newly anointed CXOs may well have different priorities than their predecessors. Very rarely will new senior VPs and COOs bring the same visions as their predecessors. Given the amount of money involved in a new system implementation, a new CIO may want to review any major IT initiative upon being hired. As this CIO gets the lay of the land, she may well decide that the current system may not be ideal but the organization certainly should spend its limited dollars elsewhere with better bang for the buck.

Finances aside, politics in organizations also drive the perceived need for new systems. For instance, Keaton Financial hires Mallory as its new VP of HR. Mallory comes from a progressive company with a powerful HRIS. She is full of energy and wants to immediately improve Keaton's systems, taking the function into the new millennium. Upon entering her new role, she encounters antiquated systems, poor data, and resistant internal forces. After two years of fighting uphill, she leaves Keaton for a similar role with an organization that shares her philosophy. The momentum that Mallory generated for a new system at Keaton will probably leave with her.

Summary

For a number of reasons, organizations often face significant hurdles in even recognizing the basic need for new systems. People, political, technical, financial, and data issues often prevent organizations from retiring legacy systems. However, most organizations eventually reach an inflection point: the perceived advantages of new systems finally justify their costs.

Endnotes

i. Figure taken from Evans' book, *Business Innovation and Disruptive Technology: Harnessing the Power of Breakthrough Technology for Competitive Advantage.*

ii. http://www.financialdirector.co.uk/financial-director/news/2048644/erp-disasters-bet-company-lose

iii. http://www.strategy-business.com/press/16635507/20306

Chapter 3

Why Organizations Implement New Systems

If you think there's a solution, you're part of the problem.
—*George Carlin*

- The Costs of Inertia
- Accounting Advantages/Capitalization
- Organizational Growth
- Acquisition
- Business Imperative
- Desire for Consolidation and Simplicity
- Cost-Effectiveness
- System Envy
- Vendor Dissatisfaction

For a number of reasons, even the most risk-averse organization has incentives to retire its legacy system. For one, the amount of risk associated with maintaining antiquated technologies increases over time. Also, as the functionality of new systems increases, the perceived—and, in fact, real—benefits that an organization can expect to realize from new technologies also increase.

Let's look at COS Entertainment, a company that originally implemented its legacy system in 1980. In 1998, COS management looked at new systems. COS determined that the costs and functionality of new systems did not justify retiring its legacy system. However, new systems have since matured and added functionality—to be discussed later in this book. As such, COS revisited the possibility of implementing a new system in 2008. The costs of the legacy system have increased while its benefits have decreased, demonstrated by Figure 3.1.

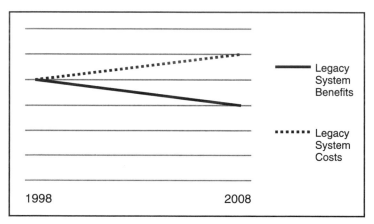

Figure 3.1 *Relative costs and benefits of legacy systems over time.*

> **NOTE**
> Many organizations ultimately reach an inflection point at which they must seriously consider replacing their disparate legacy systems with a single, unified, integrated alternative. The expected benefits of these new systems, more often than not, must exceed their expected costs by a wide margin.

In the COS example, note that the company was not ready to implement a new system at the precise moment at which the costs of its legacy system exceeded its benefits.

Executives cannot look at their legacy systems in isolation and ask, "Does our current system work for our organization?" That question is too simplistic. Rather, systems must be considered within the context of their feasible alternatives.

TIP

Senior managers should always ask a fundamental question before attempting to activate a new system: "Does our organization currently possess the human and financial resources and political wherewithal to successfully implement a new system?"

To answer the financial aspect of this question, let's first look at the costs that organizations can expect for a new system. Although not a definitive list, Table 3.1 represents expected costs that a relatively large organization can expect to incur during a new system implementation.

TABLE 3.1 Ballpark Costs of Implementing a New Tier 1 or Tier 2 System

Item	Cost: Lower End	Cost: Upper End
Purchase of Vendor Software License	$200,000	$500,000
Annual Support	$44,000	$110,000
External Consultants	$300,000	$1,000,000
Internal Resources' Time	$300,000	$1,000,000
Totals	$844,000	$2,610,000

Note that Chapter 5, "The Sounds of Salesmen," will examine software tiers in more detail. Also note that additional implementation-related costs may include the following:

- Recruiting, hiring, and training personnel with skills required by the new system

- Modifying previously functioning interfaces to and from different vendors

- Training current employees on how to use the new system

- Taking care of unforeseen costs stemming from typical activation issues, such as correcting employee paychecks, underpaying or overpaying vendors, and so on

> **CAUTION**
> If the organization cannot stomach these costs, the political climate is not right, or the resources are not available, the organization would be best served by waiting until those obstacles can be overcome. Unless there is some overarching business imperative, the organization should stop immediately.

So, let's return to the question of the costs and benefits of a new system. Is there a sufficient margin between the two such that the organization can make the case for change? For many reasons, particularly in mature organizations, the gap between costs and benefits typically needs to be fairly significant. Again, senior management will rarely pull the trigger when expected benefits marginally exceed costs. COS was no exception to this rule.

Let's consider a number of other factors that drive the need for new systems. The goal here is to understand organizational decisions to retire legacy systems and move to more contemporary—and superior—alternatives. Although there is certainly some overlap among the following reasons, they are listed as follows:

- The costs of inertia
- Accounting advantages/capitalization
- Organizational growth
- Acquisition
- Business imperative
- Desire for consolidation and simplicity
- Cost-effectiveness
- System envy
- Vendor dissatisfaction

The Costs of Inertia

At some point, an organization may no longer have the option of maintaining its legacy system. In other words, a mature organization with no burning desire to purchase or build a new system may be forced into doing so because:

- It becomes prohibitively expensive for the organization to maintain its legacy system.
- The vendor of the legacy system is going out of business.
- Relatively few individuals actively support the legacy system.

For whatever reason, sometimes organizations just don't have a choice. Whether they like it or not, they have to depart from the past and embark on a costly and time-consuming journey.

Accounting Advantages/Capitalization

Many organizations can realize certain tax advantages by virtue of implementing a new system. Certain IT costs can be capitalized, impacting the overall net cost of the project. Capital expenditures (CAPEX) create future benefits for the organization. According to the U.S. Census, capital expenditures "…include all expenditures during the year for both new and used structures (excluding land) and equipment chargeable to asset accounts for which depreciation amortization accounts are ordinarily maintained."[i]

Although CAPEX alone is typically not the main driver for a new system, it is a nice side benefit for the bean counters and helps make the case for organizational change.

Organizational Growth

Perhaps a company has run a small system that served it well while it had 400 employees and $20M of revenue. However, after four years of massive growth, the company is no longer so small. It requires a much more powerful back office system to handle increased transactions. Not only can the front end become insufficient, but it requires a more robust database or back end to meet its business needs. In this case, the company can easily justify the costs of the new system.

Acquisition

Sometimes a system can be cost-effective, well-functioning, and integrated but is still replaced. Typically, this takes place during an acquisition. For example, Theismann Apparel acquires Rypien Clothing. Theismann runs Oracle applications, whereas Rypien runs Lawson for the same functions. Theismann wants to keep all transactions in a central place and minimize support costs. As a result, Theismann converts Rypien data into Oracle applications and terminates its relationship with Lawson.

Business Imperative

Back in the late 1990s, many organizations purchased and implemented new systems because their legacy systems faced Y2K risks. Although Y2K is not a concern today, there are instances in which an organization has a compelling need to pursue a new system. These organizations may be able to continue using their legacy systems but would have to significantly tweak them to support recent regulatory or business developments. A good example of this is the 2002 passage of the Sarbanes-Oxley Act (SOX). From a systems standpoint, SOX compromised the utility of many older financial systems conceived well before the accounting scandals of the late 90s and early 2000s, such as Enron and Tyco. Legacy systems simply could not handle the SOX requirements for enhanced audit capability.

In other words, as discussed in Chapter 2, "Why Organizations Maintain Legacy Systems," many legacy systems can no longer meet organizations' basic needs. For example, a recent study conducted by The Hackett Group found that four in five companies cannot accurately forecast midterm cash flow—that is, cash flow two to three months out[ii]. This is arguably the single most important metric for an organization. The same study found that "about 70 percent of all companies surveyed rely almost exclusively on standalone spreadsheets as their primary cash forecasting tool, with few turning to best-of-breed applications or enterprise resource planning (ERP)-related systems."

Spreadsheets playing such a critical role in so many organizations is scary. Now, don't get me wrong here. Replacing spreadsheets with a superior enterprise system alone will by no means automatically guarantee improvements to the following:

- Quality of valuable enterprise information
- Access to that information
- Use of that information

A new system merely provides the *opportunity* for organizations to achieve these outcomes. Rather, the bottom line is this:

CAUTION
Spreadsheets have their limits, and many organizations require better technology to compete.

Desire for Consolidation and Simplicity

Many organizations have added disparate applications to their core legacy system(s) over the years. As a result, many have been left with an eye chart of disconnected systems that operate in isolation, contain redundant or inconsistent data, or require excessive maintenance. Widespread frustration from the end-user community over the inability to pull basic and accurate data is sometimes sufficient for an organization to "blow up" the mess that has accumulated and move to a single, integrated system.

Cost-Effectiveness

Even the organization that can survive under its existing legacy system may opt to take the plunge. Although certain businesses can continue with the status quo, at some point critical mass may be reached. There comes a time at which it is more cost-effective to adopt a new system. A perfect example of this is the company that pays an outsourced service provider such as Automatic Data Processing (ADP) to print employee checks.

ADP "is one of the largest payroll and tax filing processors in the world, serving more than 585,000 clients. Employer services account for the majority of the company's sales; ADP also provides inventory and other computing and data services to more than 25,000 auto and truck dealers. Other offerings include accounting, auto collision estimates for insurers, employment background checks, desktop applications support, and business development training services."[iii]

Although ADP offers different pricing models, most of its clients tend to pay for each employee transaction. Larger organizations that need to print thousands of employee checks receive larger bills from ADP than do smaller organizations.

Let's say that Bonds Construction employs 1,000 people who are paid biweekly. Bonds pays ADP $2 per check, equating to $52,000 per annum. (This amount does not include ADP's creation of custom reports, typically costing clients about $175 per hour.) Now, if Bonds' population grows to 2,000, the annual fee doubles to $104,000. That amount may start to look excessive compared to what the company could expect to spend if it processed its own payroll internally. The annual cost of employing a full-time payroll manager (say $50,000 per year) may prompt Bonds to cut its own checks.

Similarly, consider Rutherford Music, an organization paying three separate support and licensing fees each year to different vendors, each of which is $50,000 per year. Rutherford management may not feel that $150,000 in annual maintenance is cost-efficient. Its GL, Payroll, and HR systems are stitched together by interfaces, making the system cumbersome. Rutherford figures that it can save considerably on annual maintenance costs by implementing an integrated system.

Note that not all new systems are more powerful and expensive than their predecessors. Sometimes organizations shrink due to economics or divestitures and opt to purchase and implement a less robust, less costly system.

System Envy

Keeping up with the Joneses is not confined to cars and houses; many times organizations want to mimic the technology of their competitors. Let's look at Portis, a maker of fine china. Its existing EVP of HR and newly hired COO develop system envy and decide that the company needs the same system that its main competitor (Riggins) now has. Portis's existing systems may be cost-effective and even sufficient for its end users. However, Portis's current systems lack the "wow" factor—that is, the bells and whistles of other applications.

Vendor Dissatisfaction

Although not common, organizations sometimes purchase and implement new systems because of a frayed relationship with their existing vendors. Specific reasons may include these:

- Inadequate system functionality
- Excessive support costs
- Forced upgrades

To be sure, supplanting one system for another is a complex and expensive endeavor for the reasons described in this book. As a result, rarely has vendor dissatisfaction historically been the main reason that organizations have changed vendors. However, this may change in the near future. The flexible pricing models of software as a service (SaaS) vendors and the increasing use of open source software (OSS) applications may put traditional on-premise software vendors on shorter leashes with their clients.

Summary

This chapter explained the major reasons that organizations implement new systems. Organizations have different reasons, although money is almost always one of the most important considerations. Let's move to the next fundamental question: will the new system be bought, built, or rented?

Endnotes

i. Source: http://www.census.gov/econ/aces/faq.html

ii. http://www.industryweek.com/articles/four_out_of_five_companies_cant_forecast_cash_flow_19652.aspx

iii. http://www.hoovers.com

Chapter 4

The Replacement System

It is better to know all the questions
than some of the answers.
—*James Thurber*

- Replacement Options
- Considerations

An organization should not make the decision to retire its legacy system without a plan for its eventual replacement. Fortunately, most do not paint themselves into such a corner. Until recently, organizations needed to ask the classic make or buy question: are we going to build our own system from scratch, or are we going to purchase a mature system that tens, hundreds, or even thousands of organizations currently use? Most organizations realized that their core competencies did not involve building large, complicated enterprise systems from scratch. Rather, they opted for buying a commercial off-the-shelf (COTS) system and hiring system integrators (SIs) to implement that system. For example, in the 1990s, it was not uncommon for a firm to buy PeopleSoft and then hire IBM to implement it.

Times have changed. The traditional make-or-buy decision has been complicated in recent years by the advent—and widespread adoption of—the following:

- Software as a service (SaaS)
- Open source software (OSS)
- Independent software vendors (ISVs)

This chapter addresses the major alternatives to legacy systems available for organizations.

Replacement Options

Organizations not satisfied with their legacy systems can go in a number of different directions.

Option 1: Internal Development and Ownership

Organizations can always build applications from scratch using internal resources. To be sure, there certainly are advantages to building a custom and proprietary system. Specifically, such a system would meet each business need and require no process changes. Not dealing with external parties such as SIs and software vendors may also appeal to senior management.

Advantages aside, organizations should think carefully prior to undertaking such a project.[1] Although this is certainly not a book about software development, organizations considering this route need to remember a few cardinal rules:

---

1. This is not to say that all systems are created equal. A simple application that tracks employee expenses is a much different animal than one that attempts to correctly pay U.S. employees in 48 states with thousands of tax authorities.

- Issues found later in an application's development cycle are exponentially more time consuming and expensive to fix than issues found at the beginning of the cycle.

- Unlike off-the-shelf applications, software developers can essentially build anything. Software engineers and coders do best with pristine development specifications, allowing them to accurately build the applications and functionality desired.

Although exceptional circumstances exist, organizations are almost always better served by avoiding internal development, particularly of more complex systems when cost-effective alternatives already exist in the marketplace. In their oft-cited management book *In Search of Excellence*, Tom Peters and Robert Waterman advise organizations to "stick to their knitting."

Option 2: Contracting an ISV

Many organizations do not possess the internal expertise to build complex applications from scratch and contract an ISV to do just that. ISVs are often able to create custom applications for organizations in a quicker and cheaper manner. Of course, the applications developed by ISVs are only as good as the requirements that clients provide to them. What's more, ISVs merge, go out of business, or acquire others. Translation: there is no guarantee that an ISV today will be around next year.

Option 3: One Vendor

Many organizations in the 1990s and 2000s opted to replace their patchwork of applications with a single enterprise resource planning (ERP). This entailed utilizing all of a single vendor's applications—or at least as many as it needed. These organizations wanted to maximize integration, avoid multiple support and license costs, and issue resolution. To do this, they sometimes needed to change business processes; rarely did Oracle, SAP, or Lawson reflect each organization's status quo out of the box.

Option 4: Multiple Vendors and the Best of Breed Approach

Not all organizations have opted for a single solution—whether buying or renting—for all of their business needs. Some have stitched together multiple best of breed (BOB) applications. A BOB-based strategy is one in which organizations purchase different applications from different vendors. These technologies do not talk to each other out of the box, and organizations almost always stitch together these applications.

To be sure, BOB applications can be integrated with other systems, including ERPs.[2] For instance, a company may buy and implement PeopleSoft throughout the organization, integrating it with Taleo's Talent Management product. Typically, the business need is strong enough to justify the additional expense required to purchase and integrate the BOB application with the rest of the organization's systems. Two case studies detailed in this book (Portnoy and Tate) focus on organizations that attempted to stitch together BOB systems with their ERPs.

> **NOTE**
>
> Organizations rarely implement core systems and BOB systems concurrently. Clients tend to integrate BOB systems after they have activated their core systems and their end users have had ample time to adjust to them.

In his article "The Benefits of the Software-as-a-Service Model," Curt Finch defines SaaS as: "…on-demand software, the ASP model, or hosted software. [It] involves renting Web-based software hosted at the provider's site. For many companies large and small, SAAS is the best way to roll out new technology."[i]

Option 5: SaaS

Vendors like Workday and salesforce.com provide another option for organizations that want to "rent" software.

SaaS has gained quite a bit of traction over the past five years. In fact, salesforce.com founder Marc Benioff has stirred a great deal of controversy by openly talking about the "death of software." Talk like that does not go unnoticed, and many executives of traditional software vendors have dismissed SaaS as application service provider (ASP)[3] revisited.

One such rebuke came from Lawson Software CEO Harry Debes, who returned fire. Debes gave an interview on August 28, 2008 in which he dismissed the long-term viability of SaaS, arguing that SaaS is essentially the

---

2. Note that the integration of different systems is unlikely to be covered by any vendor's support agreement; clients tend to rely on SIs to complete the integration of different systems.

3. ASPs offered a "pre-SaaS" alternative to on-premise software during the 1990s and early 2000s. ASP clients would not have to host their own data. Rather, they relied on external vendors to do that for them. For a variety of reasons, the ASP model did not become as prevalent as its early advocates expected.

ASP model revisited. Nor is SaaS an alternative to a license and support model at the heart of his company's business model. Debes said, "SaaS is not God's gift to the software industry or customer community. The hype is based on one company in the software industry having modest success. Salesforce.com just has average to below-average profitability. People will realize the hype about SaaS companies has been overblown within the next two years. An industry has to have more than just one poster child to overhaul the system. One day Salesforce.com (CRM) will not deliver its growth projections, and its stock price will tumble in a big hurry. Then the rest of the [SaaS] industry will collapse."[ii]

Who knows if either Benioff or Debes is right? In reality, SaaS may be the lesser of two evils for some traditional software companies—the other being open source applications. Already on board with SaaS is Oracle CEO Larry Ellison. He has embraced the SaaS model for many of his company's myriad applications. From his standpoint, it's better that his clients consider the switch to a pay-per-use model to a "free" model, to be discussed next.

Option 6: OSS

Open source applications have matured since their advent and, as a result, become a viable alternative for organizations looking to replace or upgrade antiquated systems. I asked Steve King, the head of consulting and architecture for the DMSBT Group, about a contemporary definition of OSS. Steve says

> OSS is any software product for which the developers of the product have released the source code back to the community; enabling democratized participation in the development and enhancement of the software, and to derive new software or product offerings from the project. Open source is a safe, free alternative to major software vendors who require substantial licensing or subscription fees in order to be able to deliver the solution and continually extend the functionality of a product. Open source developers can extend a product over a weekend, and the modifications can be merged into the main product in the very next release. This type of development cycle means that products can be developed by millions of developers from around the world or by a handful in Oakland. It gives the product an agility above and beyond that of any of the major commercial vendors.

> They can be found at the heart of some of the most popular and powerful systems that are used by billions of people daily. Google, Yahoo, and NASA are among the most content-rich organizations in the world, yet they are powered largely by open source technologies.

OSS offers a unique flexibility to developers and companies who demand software vendors be as robust in their after-sales support and response to feature requests as they are in the development of their product. OSS vendors will deliver the product for free; however, many do offer direct enterprise support, giving organizations the option of using a community edition—free of license and support costs—or an enterprise edition backed by commercial support and service-level agreements.

Companies such as Compiere sell customized applications that organizations not only own, but *control*. Much like SaaS, OSS allows organizations to avoid a number of major drawbacks associated with between-the-firewall software vendors: forced upgrades, dangerous customizations to the "vanilla" product, heavy IT involvement, and paying support on unused applications.

An organization that wants to run an "antiquated" version of a finance and accounting system can do just that—sans the vendor's pressure to upgrade. The organization can simply pay the vendor annual support fees without fear that their system will eventually be unsupported—and be at risk for potential system failure. Expect the adoption of open source applications to continue to rise in the next few years, penetrating previously untapped markets such as ERP.

ERP is not the only sphere in which OSS has made inroads. Open source alternatives have emerged to operating systems (Linux), productivity suites (OpenOffice), and many other COTS applications.

Considerations

Table 4.1 illustrates the six main system options for organizations looking to replace legacy systems and the pros and cons of each.

The pros and cons of each option cannot be considered in a vacuum. Many factors drive an organization's decision to buy, build, or rent. Some of these factors include the following:

- Size of organization
- Number of expected annual transactions (a key in "rental" agreements)
- Budget
- Control
- Timeline
- Security concerns

TABLE 4.1 Advantages and Disadvantages of Different System Options

Option	Advantages	Disadvantages
Internal Development	System is custom-built for organization. No need to pay support to vendor. Full control of upgrades and enhancements. Developers are internally more accountable than external vendors.	A client does all testing. A client cannot rely on other organizations to serve as de facto testers. Involves a great deal of design work; a missed requirement early on is both common and expensive to introduce into the application. There is no available pool of workers with experience in this unique system. Current internal resources may not be best suited for development.
ISV	An organization with extensive experience custom builds a system for a client. Full control of upgrades and enhancements. Typically cheaper and quicker than internal development.	The ISV or client performs all testing. A client cannot rely on other organizations to serve as de facto testers. Involves a great deal of design work; a missed requirement early on is both common and expensive to introduce into the application. There is no available pool of workers with experience in this unique system. Reliance upon external party that may be acquired, merge, or go out of business. Possible communication or cultural issues stemming from developers in different time zones, countries, and so on.

TABLE 4.1 (continued)

Option	Advantages	Disadvantages
Buy-One Vendor	An organization is presumably buying a mature (fully tested) system that should be relatively bug free. Other organizations use the system and act as testers, expediting the discovery and resolution of major issues. Employees can be hired from the labor force with experience using the system.	A generic system may not match end-user business requirements out of the box. Support of the new system typically runs at about 20% of the initial license fee. Customizations come at the organization's expense; support will not cover modifications under the vendor's default agreement. One point of contact for issues; expedited issue resolution. Minimized license and support fees (relative to BOB approach).
BOB/ Multiple Vendors	Each application has superior functionality to a generic ERP. Relative to using all applications from one vendor, less business process change.	Increased integration challenges. Multiple support and license fees. Potential netherworld of issues falling outside the support agreements of each vendor.
SaaS	Potentially quicker activation time. Lower IT involvement, as vendor handles upgrades. Potentially lower cost of ownership (based on number of transactions). Organizations pay only for software used; no money is wasted on shelfware.	Hosted software and data give rise to security concerns in an organization. Vendor may charge considerable amount for custom reports. Potential ability to customize the system.

Option	Advantages	Disadvantages
Open Source	Large development community means that external resources can be hired if needed. Greater ability to customize the system to meet end-user needs. Less change to internal processes to meet limitations of the system.	Many OSS apps are not entirely mature yet. Greater risk that customizations will lead to unexpected errors. Possible security concerns because the source code is available to anyone who wants it.

Size of Organization

As a general rule, a small organization—in terms of employees and revenue—is much less likely to purchase and implement a large, expensive system than a large organization. For example, not too many 200-employee companies poised for modest growth can justify a $500,000 outlay for a new system such as SAP. For these organizations, relatively small-scale solutions like Abra, PeachTree, Sage's MAS90, and QuickBooks are probably sufficient for the time being. If not, the rental option may be appealing for simple cost reasons.

On the other end of the spectrum, it is unlikely for a large, 40,000-employee multinational corporation to justify the expense of building its own ERP. In this case, building a back-office system is often just plain silly. For example, pharmaceutical companies should make enterprise systems about as often as network security companies should manufacture their own aspirin.

Number of Expected Annual Transactions

Many SaaS agreements are transaction based: the organization that enters more sales or pays more employees will receive larger bills from their vendors than will companies with fewer transactions. Thus, a small organization would be more amenable to a pay-as-you-go system. At the end of the year, if the organization pays more, it probably had a stellar year.

A large organization will typically not rent software, at least throughout the enterprise. Certain pockets or departments might go this route, perhaps on a trial period. Consider a company that expects to conduct 4M financial or employee transactions at 50 cents per transaction. It is facing $2M in annual expenses, an amount often large enough to sway that organization toward buying its own system.

Budget

Budget is a primary driver of the make, rent, or buy decision. ERP vendors know that it is expensive and time-consuming for organizations to build comprehensive payroll, GL, and procurement systems from scratch. They also know that many prospective clients' legacy systems have long outlived their usefulness. Major vendors are competitively priced. One might be a bit more expensive than another on any one deal, but it is fair to assume that comparable vendors' prices will be in the same ballpark.

Control

Renting or purchasing software from a vendor may restrict a client's ability to tinker with that software. An organization with the desire, knowledge, and resources to customize its system probably wants no part of renting. The organization that builds a system from scratch or "gets under the hood" of a purchased system controls that system. These viable options present their own challenges to be discussed at length in Chapter 16, "Ongoing System Maintenance."

Timeline

The organization that needs to go live in a relatively short period may be tempted to rent, thinking that it does not have the time or budget to endure a traditional soup-to-nuts implementation. For example, perhaps a small startup has recently received funding and is looking for a "quick fix." The thinking here is that employees are probably too busy to participate in a full-blown implementation. All else being equal, a SaaS solution *may* have a shorter ramp-up time than that of an on-premise application. As discussed previously, however, there are no guarantees.

Security Concerns

Certain executives are not comfortable with key employee, GL, or sales information lying outside of their control. Although SaaS vendors like salesforce.com and Workday claim to house their hosted information in a secure manner (and I certainly cannot claim that they do not), a CIO simply might feel uneasy about not "owning" her company's information. On the OSS side, because anyone can download the application, it's theoretically easier for someone to find the holes.

Summary

There is no simple or correct answer to the question of whether organizations are best served by renting, buying, or building systems. The factors discussed in this chapter differ for every organization. As a general rule, however, absent a compelling business need, organizations should purchase or rent a tested, proven solution rather than build one from scratch. From a business perspective, the amount of time, money, and effort required to build a new GL, supply chain, or payroll system will dissuade all but the most naïve or stubborn senior managers. As a last resort, an organization determined to create a new back office system—and incur the related risks—should consider this: these systems result in no sustainable business advantage.

For smaller organizations, renting may be a more viable option, particularly if the application addresses a relatively common business need (such as accounting, sales, or payroll) and will result in relatively few annual transactions. These organizations do not tend to have the budget for a large, expensive ERP unless they project massive short-term growth. They generally do not have the resources to start from scratch and build their own core systems.

The case for building is perhaps strongest for organizations that have an immediate and niche need with no apparent software application on the market, at least at a reasonable cost. Although this is not a book on software development, suffice it to say that many custom applications suffer from poorly defined design specifications. As such, an ISV or internal developer may need to make certain leaps of faith that turn out to be incorrect. This hinders development and causes delays and cost overruns.

Endnotes

i. http://www.computerworld.com/s/article/107276/The_Benefits_of_the_Software_as_a_Service_Model?taxonomyId=014

ii. See http://seekingalpha.com/article/93066-lawson-s-harry-debes-saas-industry-will-collapse-in-two-years

PART II

System Selection

This Part will focus on an organization's selection of partners for their new systems. Vendors and system integrators (SIs) submit formal proposals to prospective clients in an attempt to win their business. We will see how many projects start off on the wrong foot.

Chapter 5

The Sounds of Salesmen

The salesman knows nothing of what he is selling save
that he is charging a great deal too much for it.

Oscar Wilde

- Disclaimer
- Tools of the Trade
- Software Tiers and Costs
- A Note on SaaS and Tiers
- System Convergence and the Software Industry
- Type of Industry: Does It Matter?
- Should an Organization Rent or Buy?
- Contract Language and Distant Early Warnings
- A Pound of Salt
- A Note on Fields

Sadly, I have heard about the sounds of salesmen[1] many times. Here's one variation.

Tim is the head of HR for Shelby and Associates, a medium-sized accounting firm. As his firm grew, the hodgepodge of Microsoft Access databases, Excel spreadsheets, and other disparate sources of employee information made doing business increasingly difficult. Things such as government reporting, annual open enrollment, and tracking of employee turnover became administrative nightmares. What's more, knowing which employees possessed which skills—a key in a service-oriented firm such as his—required quite a few phone calls. Finally, Tim's patience wore out. After a few months of interviewing vendors, he selected a new Human Resource Information System (HRIS) for his company.

A few weeks after signing the contract with the vendor, Tim was aghast. The vendor initially claimed that certain functionality was included in the new application, such as electronically automating the new hire "on-boarding" process. It turned out that these were, in fact, enhancements to the standard application requiring customization. The vendor could build these features into the vanilla product, but the time and expense required would not be covered under the initial contract.

Tim could not believe what he was hearing. Already encountering issues early into the project, he faced the possibility of going back to his senior management and telling them that the project would require more money. He was not too excited with this possibility. Did I mention that he works for an accounting firm?

Unfortunately, this scenario is all too common. Although possibly a bit of an exaggeration, the *Glengarry Glen Ross*[2] mindset of "always be closing" is still quite prevalent in many software companies. Salespeople view making sales as their primary objective, whereas "getting it to work" is typically the consultants' responsibility. Many end users have asked me to demonstrate functionality that they erroneously believed was "out of the box" when, in fact, those features were only possible via some type of system modification.

---

1. I am borrowing the title of this chapter from Simon and Garfunkel's classic song "The Sounds of Silence." My favorite group, Rush, also used this line in their 1980 song "The Spirit of Radio." I figure that if it it's good enough for Rush, it's good enough for me.

2. *Glengarry Glen Ross* is writer David Mamet's award-winning play about a group of desperate real estate agents who must compete in a sales contest where the losers will be fired. The agents work their same tired leads until one hatches a scheme to burglarize the office, steal the leads, and sell them to a rival. (Matthew Tobey, "All Movie Guide")

> **CAUTION**
> I cannot overstate the importance of system selection. A "wrong" or mis-
> guided choice of systems based on poorly understood requirements
> almost always makes its successful implementation extremely unlikely—if
> not impossible—to achieve.[3]

Disclaimer

Of course, project failures are not exclusively the fault of software vendors. Organizations cannot be absolved from blame, because they sometimes set outrageous expectations and unattainable goals for their projects. The Petrucci case study in Chapter 18, "Mid-Implementation Corrective Mechanisms," is a case in point. The point made at the beginning of this book bears repeating: on these types of projects, there is usually plenty of blame to go around.

In other words, just because this chapter focuses on vendors does not mean that SIs and clients are off the hook.

Tools of the Trade

In the 13 years in which I have been working with enterprise systems, I have seen them evolve quite a bit. Organizations used to have three fundamental options when a vendor's offering did not meet its needs:

- Change the business process
- Change the application via customization (discussed in Chapter 9)
- Develop some type of workaround

Times have certainly changed since the mid-1990s. Although hardly a com-prehensive list, vendors have made five major advances resulting in more malleable software better able to meet an organization's needs:

- Add-ons
- E-mail notification
- Database triggers and notifications
- Improved reporting solutions
- Form design tools

---

3. The same holds true for the selection of a consulting partner, covered in Chapter 8, "Selecting Consultants," and planning a project, covered in Chapter 9, "Implementation Strategies and Phases."

Add-Ons

To be completely fair to salespeople, systems are becoming more powerful with "add-on" tools and "extensions" that increase the power of delivered functionality. When a prospective client asks a question about the out-of-the-box functionality of a system, the salesperson will typically say, "Yes, the application can do that." That same individual will often neglect to mention the second part of the answer.[4] For the system to do what the end user wants, the organization would have to purchase—and implement—one or more of the complementary products mentioned.

E-Mail Notification

Historically, end users have relied largely on phone calls and intraoffice mail to do their jobs. Thanks to technology, however, things have dramatically changed. Systems can prompt end users to approve purchase orders (POs) and automatically send e-mails to accounts payable. Along the same lines, systems can automatically send important forms (I-9, W-4, and so on) to new hires.

Database Triggers and Notifications

Database triggers[5] take place when an event is recorded in the database. For example, an HR clerk changes an employee's hire date or an invoice is overdue beyond 60 days in accounts receivable. To the extent that these events can impact a number of things (such as an employee's benefits or a company's financial statements), the trigger prompts end users to take additional steps within the system.

Improved Reporting Solutions

Vendor software typically contains reporting functionality out of the box in the form of standard or "canned" reports. Tools such as Crystal Reports and Business Objects, however, are much more robust solutions that can handle complex reporting requirements. A vendor's canned reports usually do not meet all of an individual client's specific business needs.

---

4. For an excellent and humorous take on enterprise software salespeople, check out Doug Mitchell's e-book, *Confessions of an Ex-Enterprise Salesperson*.

5. In their book *Database Management Systems*, Patricia Ward and George Dafoulas write that "A trigger defines an action the database should take when some database-related event occurs. They are associated with a single table within the database and are specific to an Update, Insert, or Delete operation or a combination of these against rows in the table…They are *automatically* executed whenever a specified event occurs and a condition is satisfied." (emphasis added)

Form Design Tools

The front end of the application, whether Web-based or not, can typically be modified to meet clients' needs. In some cases, the change can be as simple as the name of a field, such as "employee name" becoming "associate name." In other cases, the change involves significantly altering existing forms or creating entirely new fields and forms.

Software Tiers and Costs

Enterprise systems fall into major categories or tiers. Those in the same tiers tend to be more similar than dissimilar, both on technical and functional fronts. Table 5.1 shows each tier, typical clients, and examples of vendors at the time of this writing. Routine expansion, contraction, and consolidation in the software industry makes the table more guide than gospel.

Table 5.2 shows approximate costs by tier.

Note that these are ballpark numbers and do not reflect any one vendor, client, or even proposal. Such numbers may vary considerably.

TABLE 5.1 Software Tier Breakdown[i]

	Tier 1	Tier 2
Description	Software for the large enterprise.	Software for midsized clients; market contains the largest number of potential customers.
Types of Clients	Multisite, multinational corporations. The average Tier 1 customer has revenues in excess of $200M. Clients need licenses for more than 200 users.	Clients have revenue from $20M to $200M and may have a single site or a few sites. Clients need licenses for 100 to 200 users.
Examples	Prior to the recent M&A activity, the players included JD Edwards, Infor, Oracle, PeopleSoft, and SAP. Now that Oracle has purchased PeopleSoft (which had purchased JD Edwards), the map has left only a few primary enterprise resource planning (ERP) vendors: SAP, Oracle, and Infor. One could argue that Lawson (after its recent Intentia merger) is now a Tier 1 app as well.	QAD, Infor's Syteline, Microsoft Navision (Dynamics NAV), ABAS, Glovia, Ultipro, Best's MAS500, and Epicor Vantage.

TABLE 5.1 (continued)

	Tier 3	Tier 4
Description	Software designed for single-site customers.	Basic accounting and HR systems.
Types of Clients	These clients have revenues less than $40M and are looking to expand their capabilities.	Clients include small start-ups or companies with $2M or less in revenue.
Examples	Lily's Visual Manufacturing, Intuitive Manufacturing, Microsoft Great Plains (Dynamics GP), DBA Software, and Best's MAS200.	Examples include Microsoft Great Plains (Dynamics GP), DBA Software, Best's MAS200, Peachtree, Accpac, and QuickBooks.

TABLE 5.2 Approximate First-Year Costs by Software Tier

Tier	License Fee	Implementation Fees	Support	Total First-Year Expenses
1	$400,000	$400,000	$88,000	$888,000
2	$200,000	$200,000	$44,000	$444,000
3	$100,000	$100,000	$22,000	$222,000
4	$20,000	$20,000	$4,400	$44,400

Finding the Right Tier

Organizations may find themselves "between tiers" from a budgetary standpoint. The organization not prepared to spend roughly $1M on total first-year implementation costs should probably look for an alternative to Tier 1 applications. It should not even send a request for proposal (RFP) to vendors such as Oracle, SAP, or Infor. However, at times, the budget range on a project might cause senior management to consider software from multiple tiers.

Consider Gavin Industries, an entertainment company with 3,000 employees, $10M in revenues, and a $600,000 budget for a new enterprise system. It is considering two alternatives:

- A more powerful and expensive Tier 1 application that it could not afford to fully test because of budget considerations. The license fee would eat up too much of the project's budget, forcing corners to be cut throughout the implementation.

- A tested, stable, and less powerful Tier 2 application that Gavin could utilize safely, properly, and consistently throughout the organization. The license fee would allow a proper implementation, with slightly less functionality relative to Tier 1 applications.

What should Gavin do? It most certainly should *not* spend $500,000 for the Tier 1 application's licensing and support. Barring exceptional circumstances, the company cannot successfully implement the product for a mere $100,000. The better alternative is to purchase a Tier 2 solution for $200,000 or so and implement it correctly.

In this case, the second alternative benefits Gavin and its end users much more than the first.

CAUTION

Any perceived or real advantages of a Tier 1 application need to be viewed within the context of the organization and its ability to support that application. If not tested and used properly, superior functionality from a more costly application does the organization and its end users much more harm than good. A more complex, powerful, and expensive system only makes sense if the organization and its end users can properly manage it.

A Useful Analogy

A few years ago, I heard an interesting analogy regarding some of the main ERPs. Consider some of the major systems with respect to building a house. With Lawson (at the time firmly in the second tier), the house comes almost prebuilt, and clients need only to paint and decorate it. PeopleSoft comes with a floor plan and a general design. With SAP, the client has not even picked out the land yet. Organizations would do well to keep this analogy in mind with respect to ERP purchases, time frames, and budgets.

A Note on SaaS and Tiers

As discussed in Chapter 4, software as a service (SaaS)-based companies like Workday[6] and salesforce.com offer an intriguing alternative to on-premise applications. Rather than purchasing, implementing, and paying annual support for a new system, SaaS allows organizations to rent applications and pay a per-transaction or per-end-user fee. Because of their variable cost models, SaaS-based companies transcend tiers. In theory, organizations from 10 employees to 10,000 (or more) can run this software at an affordable cost.

---

6. Workday offers further proof of the long-term viability of SaaS beyond salesforce. com. In April 2009, during the middle of the worst economic downturn since the Great Depression, the company secured an additional $75M in Series E funding led by New Enterprise Associates (which contributed $45M) with existing investors Greylock Partners and Workday CEO and cofounder Dave Duffield also participating. This brought the total funding raised to $150M. (Source: TechCrunch)

Thus, SaaS applications are theoretically "tier-independent" and can be run by any organization. As for cost, Table 5.3 presents approximate first-year costs for the organization using software on a rental basis.

TABLE 5.3 Approximate First-Year Costs for a SaaS Client

Size of Organization	Small	Medium	Large	Global
Annual Transactions	1,000	5,000	20,000	50,000
Implementation Time (Months)	2	3	4	6
Implementation Costs per Month	$10,000	$15,000	$20,000	$30,000
Total Implementation Costs	$20,000	$45,000	$80,000	$180,000
Per-Transaction Cost	$1.00	$0.90	$0.80	$0.70
Annual Transaction Costs	$1,000	$4,500	$16,000	$35,000
Total First-Year Expenses	$21,000	$49,500	$96,000	$215,000

Note that these numbers represent rough estimates, not tied to any vendor, application, potential client, or deal.

System Convergence and the Software Industry

Organizations considering the purchase and implementation of an existing system should understand the following: systems in the same tier tend to have similar functionality and scalability. For example, an organization cannot compare Peachtree's financial software with Oracle Financial's. They are apples and coconuts. Compared to Peachtree, Oracle offers far more across the board, as well it should, given the huge disparity in cost. In the same vein, one cannot realistically compare Ultipro with Lawson's HR and Payroll product; the latter simply offers clients a great deal more integration with other products, such as reporting capability, scalability, and the like.

This is not to say that Ultipro or Peachtree are inferior products on some absolute level; they are not. Systems need to be viewed in relative terms and in conjunction with the business requirements that organizations need them to fill. An organization may only need a small, bare-bones application for 10 end users and may not need to make the requisite financial commitment required from a Tier 1 ERP. A 300-employee domestic publishing house simply would not use items such as multiple currencies in Oracle, for example. Consider a car analogy. One should not compare a $10,000 used station wagon with a top-of-the-line, $250,000 Lamborghini. Yes, both cars will go from point A to point B. However, if the driver requires the ability to go from 0 to 60 in less than 5 seconds and is willing to pay for it, the Lamborghini is the way to go.

The software industry has seen a great deal of consolidation in recent years, and many products unable to find traction in the market have disappeared altogether. Ultimately, the organization looking at software vendors in the same tier will find that, in general, there are many more similarities than true differences in terms of delivered system functionality. Systems have converged a great deal over the past 10 years. An organization would be hard pressed to find a truly distinct product, although one vendor's individual features may be temporarily unique, at least until its competitors develop and integrate similar features.

A few examples of this convergence among many applications are instructive.

- Lawson's HR/Payroll application had long used employee groups to facilitate reporting, benefits administration, employee vacation and sick accruals, and so on. A single vacation plan could encompass employees in the different departments, divisions, and employment statuses (full-time, part-time) and apply different accrual rates to those groups. An organization would not have to set up and maintain 10 different plans for 10 different groups. PeopleSoft (prior to being acquired by Oracle in 2005) realized that this was useful functionality and, in fact, a potential differentiator at the point of sale. Thus, years ago it added the equivalent of employee groups.

- While researching Oracle's 11i Benefit application a few years ago, I was struck by the number of similar batch programs with Lawson equivalents. To be sure, the names of the programs are different, and they access different tables on the back end. Still, the programs have the same fundamental purposes: they facilitate the administration of benefits and update records en masse.

On a more general level, all the major Tier 1 players (SAP, Oracle/PeopleSoft, and Infor) provide features[7] such as the following:

- Web-based versions of their products—no longer must the client support a traditional client-server configuration

---

7. Note that many of the names of these features vary and change on a routine basis. Self-service has given way to "portals," for example. Changing the name of the application does *not* change that application's purpose and features. Of course, don't tell that to the marketing folks at software companies.

- Forms of self-service for employee open enrollment, time entry, and so on
- Batch processing
- Regulatory, compliance, and financial reporting
- Standard reports and *ad hoc* reporting tools (although the latter tend not to be as robust as add-on products such as Crystal Reports and Business Objects)

This is a far cry from saying that all systems (even in the same tier) are identical in terms of absolute functionality, scalability, and cost. Large organizations from different industries with diverse needs and populations run PeopleSoft, SAP, and Infor, as the salespeople from each vendor will certainly mention.

This is important to remember during the sales cycle. For example, senior management at Katz International may use an SI to evaluate vendors or go about it alone. Regardless, Katz should not take at face value a vendor's claim that it can uniquely meet its needs. Odds are that another system from the same tier can largely meet those needs as well. Katz's ultimate decision should hinge on items such as the perceived advantages and cost of the new system.

Type of Industry: Does It Matter?

Without question, there are perceived leaders among vendors in certain industries. As discussed earlier in this chapter, an international manufacturing organization is much more likely to go with SAP than a Tier 2 or 3 solution. Conversely, a single-site hospital is unlikely to have the budget (or, frankly, the need) for much of SAP's functionality; to that end, it would give Lawson a strong look.

Truth be told, perceptions may trump reality, especially within tiers. The hospital mentioned earlier could absolutely pay its employees and produce financial statements via SAP. Cost aside, Lawson and SAP are more similar than dissimilar. During system selection, then, the overriding question for an organization should *not* be, "Which is the *best* system?" Rather, executives should ask a similar, contextual question, "Which system is cost-effective *and* allows us to meet our business needs?"

Although this might seem obvious, many times, system implementations start off on the wrong foot because of this disconnect. The specific system and SI selected tend not to be the primary drivers of a system failure. It is more nuanced. Budgets, profit margins, business climates, and organizational politics come heavily into play. To elaborate, consider the following two organizations in Table 5.4: Dickinson Hospital and Harris Apparel.

TABLE 5.4 Comparison of Dickinson and Harris Clients

	Dickinson Hospital	Harris Apparel
Industry	Health care	Retail
Profit Margins	22%	7%
Revenues	10M	10M
Company Founded (Year)	1982	1996
Annual Financial and Employee Transactions	1.5M	4M
Age of Current Systems (Years)	28	14
Employees	4500	4500

These two organizations have decided to purchase and implement a new system and have narrowed their selections to several Tier 1 and 2 prospects. Which one should each select and why? Although there is no one correct answer to such a simplistic scenario, each should consider the following, *all else being equal*:

- The profit margins of each should drive its decision to some extent. Retail is a much tougher and dynamic business than health care, as evinced by the margins and number of annual transactions. For example, Harris probably cannot afford a two-year implementation of a new system for $4M to the same degree that Dickinson can. By virtue of its less frenetic pace, Dickinson could purchase a bigger system and implement more functionality out of the box; it has more resources at its disposal in a more controlled business climate.

- The more hectic business environment will affect Harris's end users more severely than those at Dickinson. During "holiday hire" in retail (in November and December), for example, HR and payroll end users will have virtually no time to devote to consultants. Also, because of the lower profit margins, it's a safe bet to assume that Harris is "leaner" in terms of internal resources than Dickinson. As such, Harris *may* need to use more external consultants for the implementation than Dickinson.

- The more dynamic nature of retail also means that Harris's end users have probably worked there for shorter periods of time than their Dickinson counterparts. Perhaps Harris's current staff has experience with PeopleSoft, for example, and can offer valuable insight during the selection process. If Harris chooses PeopleSoft, its in-house expertise will be a considerable asset, and the organization's learning curve may be less steep.

- Conversely, health care tends to be more rigid and bureaucratic relative to retail. It's quite possible that Dickinson end users will be reluctant to change their business practices due to a system limitation. To the extent that these limitations are often discovered after a system has been selected and the implementation has begun, Dickinson management should gauge two things: 1) the willingness of its internal staff to be flexible and; 2) the ease and cost of each system under consideration to be customized.

- Finally, Dickinson's older legacy system will probably prove to be more problematic than Harris's system. As a general rule, older systems typically contain "tougher" data, much of which may be inaccurate, unobtainable for conversion purposes, or both.

In the end, an organization choosing a system has few absolutes. As this book will illustrate, a system failure is *not* exclusively a function of industry. I have worked on successful and unsuccessful projects in quite a few industries. In general, however, health care and nonprofit or government clients tend to be much more prone to failure than clients in retail and telecommunications. Organizations in the latter industries are usually more adept at handling change than those in the former.

TIP

As a general rule, the older a company's systems and data, the higher the profit margins, and the less dynamic the industry, the more difficult a system implementation will be. Organizations should keep this in mind from the beginning as they select a vendor and an SI, plan a project, and assign timelines and resources.

Should an Organization Rent or Buy?

Tables 5.1 and 5.2 contain important information for organizations considering both the traditional purchase as well as the relatively new rental model. The pricing models of a SaaS-based application may be attractive to many organizations, hinging on their expected annual transactions. This begs the question: is renting better than buying?

The answer is an unequivocal "maybe." The jury is still out on SaaS; it remains to be seen whether it offers inherent time or cost advantages relative to on-premise applications. In theory, SaaS implementations and activations *may* go more smoothly, result in fewer issues, take less time, and cost less than traditional system implementations. The greatest *potential* time and cost savings are realized in the following ways:

- **Software.** Organizations do not need to install, maintain, or upgrade SaaS software; the vendor takes care of all of this.

- **Hardware.** SaaS software does not need to be tied to enterprise-wide databases and servers.

When deciding on whether to rent or buy, senior management typically feels more comfortable using a single software vendor—if possible. Large software vendors typically can accommodate the entire gamut of their clients' systems needs, but some SaaS solutions may not. For example, Employease, one of the early adopters of the SaaS model, provided human resource and benefit functionality but did not handle payroll. Although Employease did have a partnership with ADP to provide that very service prior to being acquired by ADP in 2006,[ii] its clients had to enter into agreements with multiple vendors. Along those lines, the recently launched Workday has a similar relationship with ADP to process payroll. This is not to say that ADP or Workday provide inferior products, functionality, or support. However, one-stop shopping may be inherently more appealing to the organization with a desire to minimize its vendor relationships.

On another note, certain SaaS clients have encountered integration issues with pieces of their system architectures.[iii] Consider the hypothetical example of Stone Construction. Stone begins using Workday—in lieu of its legacy system—for annual open enrollment. Stone still needs to send those enrollments via interface to its benefit carriers. To the extent that different organizations utilize different carriers, Workday does not provide delivered integration to Aetna and MetLife, two of Stone's benefit providers. Stone may employ an integration company such as Cape Clear to create those bridges via service-oriented architecture[8] (SOA) or Web services.[9] Alternatively, Stone's IT department may decide to do this internally. Regardless of which route it goes, SaaS does *not* obviate Stone's effort and expenses related to interfaces and complete integration of its systems.

In the end, there is no silver bullet. To continue with the house analogy from earlier in this chapter, regardless of whether the organization has purchased

---

8. In *Service Oriented Architecture For Dummies,* Judith Hurwitz, Carol Baroudi, Robin Bloor, and Marcia Kaufman describe the SOA world as one in which "business applications are assembled by using a set of building blocks known as components—some of which may be available 'off the shelf,' and some of which may have to be built from scratch."

9. A web service is defined as "a software system designed to support interoperable machine-to-machine interaction over a network." (Source: W3C)

or leased the land, it still needs to know exactly what it wants to build. It still needs to buy the right materials, hire capable contractors, and test the plumbing and electricity before moving in.

CAUTION

Poorly defined business processes, bad data, lack of training for end users, and other implementation issues discussed in subsequent chapters will plague any new system implementation, regardless of the type of arrangement that the organization has with its vendor.

Contract Language and Distant Early Warnings

Although most projects derail over the course of a number of months, occasionally a system implementation implodes immediately after contracts are signed. This was the case in Shelby and Associates, mentioned at the beginning of this chapter. Although last-minute issues are sometimes inevitable, organizations obviously want to avoid immediate project fractures. The question is, "How?"

Prior to signing any contracts with vendors and SIs, senior managers should do the following:

- Painstakingly detail each of its organization's business requirements
- Ensure that the final vendor and SI contracts contain specific line items in relation to each system-delivered feature and service

After signing contracts, no entity—client, vendor, SI—should have a doubt about which features and services each will provide. Clarity minimizes project confusion among the different parties. What's more, detailed contract language eliminates the ability of the vendor or consulting firm to blast a client with expensive change requests. (Note that Chapter 8 extends the discussion of SIs with respect to types of firms, system selection, and types of arrangements.)

Admittedly, this is easier said than done. Clients—especially of the first-time variety—may lack the time and expertise to write contract language with sufficient granularity to sufficiently protect themselves in the event of a dispute. Vendors and SIs will typically not help clients in this regard. To address this issue, organizations should seek the assistance of resources with related expertise. A poorly worded or open-ended contract with a vendor or SI increases the probability of miscommunication, contentious relations, and, ultimately, a death march.

Ideally, meticulous contract language is superfluous during an implementation. Senior management would not need to revert to the formal agreement often—if at all—because all parties are on the same page. As a result, no one on the client side will have had disputes with the vendor or SI surrounding the services or system functionality that each is obligated to provide. However, remiss is the organization that does not plan for this realistic contingency. Absent such language, clients are typically left with the following options when a problem of this nature arises:

- Agree to the requests of clients and vendors for additional funds
- Attempt to reach some type of compromise
- Pull the plug on a project altogether
- Threaten legal action
- Threaten to withhold payments to the vendor or SI
- Indicate an unwillingness to provide a positive reference after the completion of the project
- A combination of all of the above

These alternatives may or may not produce the desired results. To be certain, they will create—or exacerbate—an adversarial relationship between client and partner. By insisting upon comprehensive contract language, however, organizations can minimize the need to pursue these confrontational options.

A Pound of Salt

Many software vendors equip their sales teams with tools to "prove" the value of their products during the sales cycle. These tools quantify the savings that prospective clients can expect to realize soon after purchasing and implementing the vendors' products. One of the most common tools is a return on investment (ROI) calculator that shows how quickly an organization can expect the new system to essentially pay for itself. Typically, a new client can expect to see a positive ROI in only a few years.[10]

For instance, the vendor may present the following business case. A new system costs $1M to purchase and completely implement. However, the benefits of the new application more than outweigh its costs. Specifically, the

---

10. Think about it. All else equal, would you purchase a system that wouldn't justify its costs for twenty years?

new system will allow the organization to see a positive ROI within four years via the following:

- Reduced administrative costs
- Fewer errors and expedited error resolution
- Improved access to analytics and other key business information

Depending on the type of system(s) under consideration, vendors will trumpet the specific benefits of their products to each line of business (LOB). For example, consider the following:

- An HR product will result in reduced employee turnover, recruiting costs, and time to fill key positions.
- The manufacturing module will make the organization "leaner," reducing manufacturing lead time[11] (MLT) and increasing both delivered quality and delivery performance.

A few caveats are in order here. First, vendor claims may or may not turn out to be accurate and justified, so take some salt when considering them. This is not to impugn the integrity of software vendors. In fact, many new systems have resulted in benefits that have more than justified their costs.

By the same token, however, it is foolish for organizations to take vendor claims as gospel. Look at their models. Are the alleged outputs based on realistic inputs and assumptions? It is imperative to look at—and question—these assumptions from the beginning.

NOTE
The success or failure of a new system hinges directly on the acceptance of that system by the organization's end users. Efficiency to senior management may mean job insecurity to a long-time employee scared about his future. Don't assume that there will be no problems on the project just because the vendor's model neglects to include them.

---

11. MLT is the total time that it takes an organization to manufacture a product from beginning to end.

A Note on Fields

Software vendors' claims may or may not be true on some objective level. During sales presentations, they will often mention successful case studies and provide many clients willing to provide references. It is essential to remember the following point:

Not all organizations are created equal.

In other words, the difficulty and cost of implementing a "new" system is easier at a *greenfield site*—that is, an organization that currently has no system. End users at greenfield organizations tend to be happy having any system; usually, they openly embrace the automation and features of whatever system management has decided to put in place. Moving from paper and spreadsheets into the 21st century is widely considered to be a positive thing. Also, from a technology standpoint, greenfield sites pose relatively few obstacles and constraints.

End users at a *brownfield site*—that is, an organization that already has a system with existing issues—tend to be a bit more ingrained in their ways and less open to change. These organizations are used to doing things in a certain way, and the replacement system means that they will have to change certain business practices. From a technology standpoint, brownfield sites often pose significant obstacles and constraints. Together, end-user resistance to change and technological barriers often mean that brownfield sites may become *blackfields*—that is, a scorched earth.

Summary

Winston Churchill once said, "Never trust a man without vices." Applied to software vendors, prospective clients would do well to remember that no application is perfect. Whether renting, buying, or building, executives should remember that salespeople get paid to trumpet the virtues of their software, with an emphasis on "soft" (read: malleable) solutions. Yes, software can be built and customized to meet just about any business need. Sometimes this can be done with relative ease, sometimes not.

Vendor selection is a necessary precondition for an organization to embark on a systems implementation. The choice of a vendor is almost always irreversible. Organizations should take every step possible to avoid a suboptimal decision because the stakes are so high. To that end, the suggestions offered in this chapter should help organizations make better decisions and get their implementations off on the right foot.

Vendor demonstrations can be outright dazzling, but organizations should view them with more than a grain of salt. Prospective clients will never hear the word "no" from a salesperson in response to a question such as "Can your software do this?" To be sure, the answer to this question is typically not a complete misrepresentation of the truth. After all, anything is possible. For the prospective client, the better question to ask the salesperson is, "Does your software do this out of the box?" When the salesperson answers in the affirmative, the follow-up question should be, "Can you please show me how to do that, right now?"

Endnotes

i. Modified with permission from ERP and More. See http://www.erpandmore.com.

ii. http://www.workday.com/partners/partner_directory/adp.php

iii. http://www.informationweek.com/news/services/saas/showArticle.jhtml?articleID =211200952

Chapter 6

Business Processes

Good design can't fix broken business models.
—*Jeffrey Veen*

- The Chicken and Egg Question
- The Symbiotic Relationship Between Business Processes and Systems
- The Limits of Reengineering

Truth be told, when implementing new systems, many organizations miss a fundamental opportunity to improve or reengineer key business processes.[1] This omission can take place during the initial project planning or soon after, as testing uncovers unanticipated issues. This short but crucial chapter examines why this is the case.

The Chicken and Egg Question

Organizations with deficient business processes tend to have deficient systems, begging the question of which comes first. There is often no simple answer to this question, because most systems have evolved over time. In other words, organizations change and augment their systems as their business processes change. For example, Carson Dairy has added several patchwork interfaces and smaller systems to its overall system architecture over the past decade. As a result, Carson end users face delays and lack real-time access to data, situations that senior management certainly did not foresee years ago. The cure may be worse than the disease, but short of "blowing up" its existing system architecture, Carson is stuck with suboptimal systems and processes for the foreseeable future.

The Symbiotic Relationship Between Business Processes and Systems

Based on their experience with legacy systems, end users are accustomed to doing their jobs in a certain way. Lamentably, prior to kicking off an implementation, organizations often do not give sufficient thought as to how they can improve the efficiency of both individual jobs and business processes. Within an organization, the initial level of excitement generated by vendors' dog-and-pony shows often dissipates during the project, as unforeseen problems invariably manifest themselves. It is understandable—but regrettable—that end users often revert to what they know and may attempt to replicate the old system in the new one. As a result, features that many times sold the product in the first place are postponed to Phase II. Even worse, they may never see the light of day. Project teams sometimes set up new systems to essentially mimic their predecessors.

---

1. In their classic management text, *Reengineering the Corporation: A Manifesto for Business Revolution*, Hammer and Champy define reengineering as "the fundamental rethinking and radical redesign of business processes to achieve dramatic improvements in critical, contemporary measures of performance, such as cost, quality, service, and speed."

Organizations often fail to understand that business processes do not exist in a vacuum; they must be viewed against the backdrop of the technology used to enable those processes. Systems and business processes are related in a symbiotic—but not causal—manner.

> **NOTE**
> Organizations with broken systems typically suffer from broken business processes and vice versa.

Consider Opeth Produce, a company with a broken payroll process. Paying employees there is painfully slow and rife with errors. With that in mind, one of the following *must* be true with regard to Opeth's current payroll system:

- The existing system cannot support a better process as currently configured, irrespective of the knowledge of Opeth's end users.
- Opeth's existing system cannot support a better process, regardless of any potential type of configuration.
- End users do not know how to use Opeth's existing system to achieve superior results, including fewer adjustments and manual checks and more accurate government reporting.

So, would a new system improve payroll processing at Opeth? It depends. If Opeth's management is hell-bent on replicating antiquated processing methods in a new system, the answer is an unequivocal "no." If the payroll department can and will learn how to use the system properly, the answer is "yes."

> **NOTE**
> Implementing new systems provides organizations with unique opportunities not only to improve their technologies, but to redefine and improve key business processes. Ultimately, for organizations to consider these new systems successes, the post-legacy environment must ensure that business processes, client end users, and systems work together.

Often, these three levers fail to support each other, as the following three examples illustrate.

A Broken Annual Process

Fenster Electric is a multinational corporation with employees in 40 countries. Each year, it awards employee merit increases, bonuses, and stock options (MIBSO for short). Because of its eye chart of existing systems as well the general level of coordination involved throughout the organization, MIBSO begins in late August of each year, culminating in April of the following year. Alternatively stated, Fenster routinely takes more than half the year to handle employee compensation administration. A high-level representation of the tasks and dates in this process is presented in Table 6.1.

TABLE 6.1 Annual Fenster MIBSO Process

Task	Start Date
Initial data validation of current employee populations and salary data	August
HQ sends personnel files to each Fenster site	September
Budgets announced and communicated	October
Site personnel make preliminary MIBSO determinations, send files back to HQ	December
Senior management begins review of initial site figures	January
Senior management finalizes employee MIBSO figures	February
HQ personnel send final files to central processing unit	March
Bonuses and stock options awarded, and merit increases applied to employee salaries	April

Fed up with such inefficient processing, Fenster executives are considering the purchase of a new enterprise system. Let's return to the "chicken and egg" question at the beginning of this chapter for a moment. Fenster needs to start with its business process, *not* the system. Senior management needs to first ask if and how it can streamline MIBSO, *not* if a new system can support its current and wholly inefficient process. Fenster should not consider employee compensation administration a sacred process with respect to the following:

- The amount of time required each year
- Each step in the current MIBSO process
- The order in which each step takes place

If Fenster implemented a new system that left its current MIBSO process largely unchanged, many in the organization may rightfully ask, "What was the point? It still takes us seven months to manage employee compensation." However, if senior management and experienced consultants determine that

Fenster—via a new system—can successfully condense the entire MIBSO process to two months, that new system will produce tangible results and savings.

A Broken Process

Sanchez Financials receives resumes from applicants via both electronic and snail mail. Its recruiters then manually send letters of acknowledgement to candidates, keeping their resumes on file. Sanchez has no central repository of applicant information and, as a result, posts many jobs multiple times when perfectly viable candidates' resumes exist on individual employees' hard drives and in physical folders.

Sanchez's recruiting costs are excessive. Many applicants complain that they are rejected multiple times for the same job or interview repeatedly for a job. Hiring managers complain that their positions take too long to post and to fill, resulting in out-of-control overtime costs. Recruiters spend way too much time trying to locate acceptable candidates and rely on memory while their time-to-fill (TTF) statistics are well below industry averages.

Sanchez purchases and implements a new applicant tracking system (ATS) delivering the following functionality:

- The electronic receipt of resumes
- Automatic job agents allowing posted jobs to be "pushed" to interested applicants
- More sophisticated search capability for recruiters
- Tracking of recruiting expenses

In this instance, the new technology allows Sanchez to completely reengineer its recruiting process. Sanchez could now essentially eliminate paper and electronically track all applicant correspondence. Hiring managers could use powerful search criteria to find the best applicants for newly posted positions. Recruiting costs could plummet. By virtue of reduced recruiting costs and increased benefits, Sanchez's ATS could basically pay for itself over a three-year period.

For the ATS to be successful, Sanchez's end users must realize that their jobs will significantly change. The possessive recruiter who insists that everything go through him will need to get with the program. Lazy hiring managers who expect HR to do their jobs for them will need to accept and embrace their new responsibilities. Although Sanchez's legacy system did not contain many bells and whistles, its new ATS does. However, that fact alone does not guarantee the results that Sanchez expects. Just because a new system can do all the wonderful things promised by the vendor does not mean that it will.

In this example, the new ATS itself does not guarantee a thing. For the benefits of the new ATS to be realized, Sanchez's end users need to get on board.

The preceding example was fairly dramatic. A broken recruiting process can be completely reengineered, and few would argue that Sanchez's status quo is optimal in present-day corporate America. However, let's look at a less obvious situation. Consider an organization with a suboptimal business process that could be improved.

A Suboptimal Process

Spencer Seafood is implementing a new enterprise system but wants to keep paying its vendors or employees every two weeks. In this sense, Spencer's new system needs to reflect the same business processes as its legacy system. Specifically, system rules need to enable biweekly payments. This is not to say that "everything should be the same" or that "the new system should mimic the old across the board." Alternatively stated, Spencer may still be able to make quantum leaps with its new system vis-à-vis:

- Reporting
- Automation
- Audit capability
- Increased data tracking
- Self-service

Although Spencer maintains the same business procedures with its new system, end-users' jobs do not have to remain unchanged. Yes, the AP director might still want to pay vendors herself, and the payroll manager may be reluctant to turn the new system's payment print program over to a clerk. Consider the specific improvements that Spencer could still realize from its new system:

- Employee time records could be automatically generated, thus dramatically reducing the following:
  - The need for payroll clerks to manually enter data.
  - The number of related data-entry errors.
- Invoices could be automatically matched via batch program.
- Access to the data could be democratized; no longer would end users need to formally request reports from a central IT function.
- Benefit automation rules could enable new employee premiums to be calculated once employees change status. Terminated employees' benefits automatically could cease at the end of the month, no longer requiring manual intervention.

The Limits of Reengineering

The Portnoy and Lifeson case studies discussed in Chapter 11, "Setup Issues," detail the perils associated with refusing to change *any* business process during a system implementation. For now, suffice it to say that these case studies describe organizations significantly altering their new systems because they were afraid of change, wasting millions of dollars in the process. However, the opposite problem is just as potentially dangerous. Sometimes senior management attempts to introduce *too many* changes to business processes, along with a new system. Possible causes of this type of overreaching include

- An ambitious management team falling victim to vendor or SI promises and attempting to do too much too soon
- Business necessity
- A new executive attempting to transform an organization not willing to embrace a new system and way of doing things

In his analysis of Nike's nine-year struggle with its new i2 supply chain system, Chris Koch of CIO.com writes that "Blank sheet reengineering can lead to unrealistic business process designs that can't be implemented through enterprise software."

In other words, there are limits to how much change an organization and its end users can stomach at once. Concurrently changing everything that a key business function does—and how its end users do it—can lead to failures of spectacular proportions.

Koch goes on to state, "Deep discussions of how business is conducted can lead to something invaluable: a clear, performance-based goal for the project."[i] Koch is absolutely correct, but key individuals need to be willing to make changes for the overall good of the project. Remember that new enterprise systems are by and large integrated, unlike many of their predecessors. "Squeaky wheels" who refuse to alter how their departments do things can cause significant delays for areas of the project.

Summary

The organization that wants to realize the benefits and cost savings of a new system must be willing to consider reengineering its core business processes. Doing so makes that organization more likely to succeed. The new system may, in fact, do many of the things promised by the vendor. A new system merely provides organizations with *the opportunity* to do things better and more efficiently. Organizations that revert to antiquated methods maximize the likelihood that their new systems will be just as cumbersome as their predecessors.

Endnotes

i. http://www.cio.com/article/32335/Five_Lessons_Learned_from_Nike_s_i2_Debacle

Chapter 7

Support for the New System

Complain to one who can help you.
—*Yugoslav Proverb*

- Types of Support
- Vendor Agreements
- Recent Vendor Tactics

An organization should decide early in a project (either during vendor selection or, at the very latest, the planning phase) what type of support it requires. Doing so allows it to staff the project appropriately as well as prepare for life after system activation.

In this context, support does *not* mean external consultants or partners who will guide the organization through the implementation. They are the focus of the next chapter. Rather, support here means ongoing assistance with system troubleshooting *after* system activation.

Types of Support

There are at least four main types of support available for organizations that have purchased systems. (Options are likely different for organizations that build and rent systems.) These are detailed below, along with a brief description of the advantages, disadvantages, and risks associated with each.

Support from the Vendor

By far, this is the most common and most expensive form of support. Typically, at about 20 to 22 percent of the initial software license fee, vendor support allows clients to access the vendor's support site, knowledge base, application and technical troubleshooting, and other online tools. Clients can access patches and other "fixes," as well as open a case if the vanilla—that is, unmodified—application is not working as designed. For example, a payroll close program does not update history. If the client has not altered that program's underlying code in any way, a support representative will fix—or help the client fix—the issue. However, if that same client modified that payroll close program by "getting under the hood," that client would not qualify for support under the terms of the agreement. Typically, in this scenario, the vendor will offer to assist the client to the tune of about $200 per hour.

Many organizations have historically opted for the standard level of support (although recent developments to be discussed later in this chapter have caused different organizations to reconsider their options). It is important for organizations to understand that standard vendor support does not cover items such as setting up the general ledger, processing payroll, or assisting with the writing of custom reports, even if the vendor also sells the reporting tool. For example, support representatives are not going to sit with clients for three hours figuring out why a custom purchase order report does not work properly. Again, for this type of assistance, the client has to pay the vendor's hourly rate.

Note that the single notion of direct vendor support is giving way to different levels of support. Under this emerging phenomenon, clients can pay more to get more. A basic level of support might entitle clients to 8 a.m. to 6 p.m. support Monday through Friday. More advanced and costly levels of support might entail 24/7 coverage, on-demand access to live product specialists, and support with system customization.

An organization should know beforehand the specific items that will and will not be covered under its individual support agreement long before going live. Armed with this knowledge, the organization can then make intelligent decisions about customizations, setup, reporting, and so on. What's more, the organization can then allocate the right resources throughout the project and after system activation. Clearly, if an organization has activated a new system without appropriate internal resources to properly support that system, it has significantly increased its chances for failure.

Years after its system activation, an organization may consider an option typically called "sunset support." In this scenario, a client pays the vendor above and beyond its annual support fee for a relatively limited time while it runs a less-than-current version of the vendor's software. Typically, the client has to work out a separate deal with its account manager. The organization usually weighs the cost of remaining on the older version of the software against the cost of upgrading. To the extent that it is far easier for software vendors to support one or two major releases of their products, these agreements tend to be quite costly for clients.

Support from a Vendor-Sanctioned Partner

Because of strategic partnerships or a lack of resources, a vendor may direct clients to other companies for sanctioned support. Alternatively, a client may go this route because the partner charges less than the vendor. This support may be technical, functional, or both. Note that the support is typically for out-of-the-box functionality, not for changing the code of the software. There are instances in which a client may purchase "total" support for delivered functionality and system modifications. However, such support tends to be expensive.

Support from a Third Party

Typically the least expensive but riskiest option, organizations can opt for support from a third party not sanctioned by the software vendor. For example, Chicago Bagel Emporium (CBE) runs Lawson version 7.2.4 and is considering third-party support for several reasons. First, CBE management may simply think that it can save a considerable amount relative to its annual support contract with Lawson. Second, and arguably more common, CBE may opt for this type of support because Lawson is forcing clients to upgrade from one major release to another—for example, from version 7 to 8. For whatever reason (current resources or expense of upgrade), CBE wants to remain on version 7.2.4 indefinitely without incurring the aforementioned and typically pricey "sunset" support costs.

Vendors typically discourage clients from purchasing unsanctioned support for a number of reasons, including these:

- The supposed lack of expertise of the independent support company
- The need for the client to stay relatively current
- Vendor enhancements to newer version of the software

Regardless of vendors' pleas, some organizations decide to remain on older versions of applications indefinitely and are more than satisfied with their level of support.

Many third-party support companies have done well in the current economic climate, probably because organizations are looking to save on vendor maintenance costs. One of the major players, Rimini Street, offers alternative maintenance and support contracts for Oracle and SAP customers. It recently reported the following:

> For the first half of 2009, Rimini Street's sales bookings more than quadrupled compared to the first half of 2008, and revenue and invoicing approximately tripled for the same period. In the second quarter alone, sales bookings jumped by more than six times quarter-over-quarter, while revenue and invoicing each more than tripled compared to the second quarter of 2008. Rimini Street's tremendous growth for the first half of the year follows record growth in 2008, when sales also more than quadrupled from the previous year.
>
> Other key achievements in the first half of 2009 include these:
> - Launched SAP support service and announced signing of first SAP R/3 4.x and ECC 6.0 clients
> - Expanded U.S.-based operations infrastructure and increased staff by nearly 25 percent
> - Expanded physical global support operations to Europe and Asia-Pacific
> - Announced 400 percent year-over-year increase of JD Edwards customer base
> - Named a "Hot 100" Private Software Company by JMP Securities

- Achieved over 90 percent client contract renewal rate and 98 percent client satisfaction rating

- Continued timely delivery of extensive tax and regulatory updates ahead of the software vendor's planned release date for similar updates[i]

Although independent support may not be right or cost-effective for every organization, it cannot be dismissed outright as a legitimate option. Client savings may be significant with a potentially superior level of support relative to its vendor.

Informal Support Mechanisms

Organizations looking for informal support can always go to a little place rife with information on just about every major system: the Internet. Many Web sites, blogs, and newsletters exist for just about every application. The lone exception is the home-built application, although software developers exchange advice and best practices in many online forums as well. Support here is much less structured than it is for organizations that build their own applications, however. For example, the firm that contracts an independent software vendor (ISV) to build a custom inventory control system in .NET cannot expect Microsoft to troubleshoot that application; the company would have to purchase support, typically from the same ISV.

Aside from the online world, user groups are enormously helpful resources for networking and learning best practices. End users from different organizations meet to discuss common issues and solutions. This is the perfect place to go to learn firsthand about everything from client experiences with upgrades to the new features of an enhanced application. Other benefits include meeting end users from other organizations to exchange best practices, reporting tips, or even business cards for future networking.

For a number of reasons, it is essential for organizations to fully understand that which their support agreements do and do not cover. It's a matter of when—not if—issues present themselves in a production environment. Organizations that fail to understand what to expect from support specialists significantly increase risk, time to resolve key issues, and the severity of the problem itself.

We are far from finished discussing support. Chapter 12, "Testing Issues," revisits support during the system testing process, examining how to most effectively log a call. Also, Chapter 16, "Ongoing System Maintenance," looks at vendor support once organizations have gone live. We will see that, although vendor support may be infrequently used, there are ways to expedite error resolution during times of crisis.

Vendor Agreements

Many CEOs or CIOs purchasing enterprise software for the first time do not carefully read—or fully understand—their vendors' end-user licensing agreements (EULAs). Much like the rest of this book, the intent of this section is *not* to demonize software vendors. My objective here is simply to advise organizations of a few things that they often overlook while selecting, purchasing, implementing, and maintaining new systems. These omissions may well have unexpected and dire consequences at some point in the future.

Vendors sell their products on an as-is basis. This means that vendors are *not* responsible for any undesirable results stemming from their products. In many—if not most—cases, vendors' lack of accountability for system-related problems is completely reasonable. The analogy of an automobile manufacturer is an apt one. In the event of an accident, should a car maker be held liable if the driver goes 85 mph, ignores traffic lights and stops signs, and never takes his car in for maintenance? By the same token, vendors cannot be held responsible for the mistakes of their clients' end users.

Returning to Oates Health Care in Chapter 1, "Introduction," its management could not have held its vendor responsible for the incorrect calculation of employee overtime. Oates' system actually worked as configured; it was just configured incorrectly, and the issue was never identified during testing. Put another way, the system *would have worked* if it had been set up correctly. As such, Oates could *not* expect to recoup from its vendor the costs of the external consultants required to resolve the issue. Perhaps Oates might have had a better case against its original system integrator (SI), but that's a separate discussion.

Another point often lost in a contract's fine print bears mentioning. According to most EULAs, organizations do not actually buy the vendors' software, *per se*. Rather, they only purchase *licenses* to use that software. These licenses often are nontransferrable; organizations are typically prohibited from reselling any unused licenses to other organizations. Also, senior management should make sure to review vendor agreements during any M&A activity. Simply assuming that a new organization or partnership will fall under the existing EULA is ill advised.

Recent Vendor Tactics

Software vendors have been creative in attempting to extract extra revenue from their clients over the past two years. In one example, Lawson Software offered a window in which its clients could enroll in a Value Improvement Program (VIP). On his blog, John Henley of Decision Analytics writes that the company's program induced its clients to "…purchase additional products in exchange for extending their current maintenance and/or locking in future fees [This would] increase the adoption of Lawson's add-on products. Who wouldn't purchase a $50,000 add-on in order to save $60,000 in fees?"[ii]

More than a few clients agreed with this sentiment and took advantage of Lawson's VIP. Perhaps these organizations were motivated by the program's burning plank. While benefitting its clients was a nice side benefit, Lawson's management was able to accomplish a more pressing objective: to maximize the company's short-term revenue.

SAP took a slightly different tack. In early 2008, the company announced that its clients could now purchase different levels of support. Support had previously been a binary: SAP clients either paid for it or did not.[1] Under the new arrangement, SAP Standard Support would continue to cost roughly 17 percent of a client's initial license fee. The number for the newly announced Enterprise Support was 22 percent.[2] Under premium support, SAP clients received a greater range of services as well as more hours of coverage during the day.

This arrangement may be mutually beneficial to both SAP and its clients. I would argue that greater client choice is certainly a positive development. Forcing all clients to be supported under a one-size-fits-all plan doesn't make much sense; different clients have different needs. It seems silly that an organization that relies extensively on a vendor's support should pay the same as the organization that uses it occasionally. From SAP's perspective, the company locked in additional revenues from willing clients.

The potential increases in support costs—whether or not they were justified and even beneficial—came at a less-than-opportune time for IT departments. Many CIOs have recently looked at their IT budgets in an attempt to spend less, not more. Two of the potential items on the chopping block have

---

1. However, those that did not could have purchased independent support.

2. SAP was certainly not alone in charging more for premium support. Lawson and Oracle have also introduced similar programs. Note as well that Oracle support has always been a necessarily complicated animal, given the company's track record for acquiring vendors with established customer bases.

been software license and maintenance costs. On his well-trafficked blog "Software Insider's Point of View," former Forrester Research associate R "Ray" Wang identifies ways for organizations to reduce shelfware. Wang concedes that this is easier said than done, because many vendors impose the following constraints on their clients:

- **Enterprise wide agreements.** These all-you-can-eat agreements incentivize customers to buy more than they need at a "good" discount.
- **Repricing clauses.** Many contracts contain language that imposes list price recalculations when users choose to return their licenses to the vendor.
- **Bundled contracts.** Contractual language often prevents clients from unbundling their software as needed. In addition, vendors have initiated focused programs to bundle licenses.

To reduce shelfware, Wang advocates that clients try to do the following:

- **Return unused licenses.** Vendors agree to take back licenses and proportionately reduce maintenance costs. Customers lose future rights to those licenses.
- **Park unused licenses.** Vendors agree to hold unused licenses and not charge maintenance. Customers still have rights to the licenses and will pay for maintenance when licenses are deployed.
- **Apply credit to purchase of new licenses.** Vendors agree to assign a value to shelfware. Credit on used licenses will be applied to future purchases. Customers lose rights to the original software but gain rights to new software and functionality.[iii]

Depending on the contract language between vendor and client, some of these options may not be possible.

Note that some software vendors have been playing "good cop" during the economic malaise. For example, Oracle has held the line on support increases, telling its clients that, "We understand your hardships and, as your partner, are willing to work with you." Whether this stance stems from benevolence or fear is an interesting question. Certain vendors may be spooked by the ongoing threats of software as a service (SaaS) and open source software (OSS)[3]; they may not want to risk alienating their clients.

---

3. And if they're not, they should be.

> **NOTE**
>
> For the foreseeable future, software vendors—especially publically traded ones—are likely to continue tinkering with their support agreements in an attempt to solidify future revenue streams. In this sense, vendors are like every other company in a free enterprise economy. It's incumbent upon client senior management to run the numbers and see if money spent on support increases could be better deployed elsewhere in the organization. For instance, is $180,000 (a $60,000 increase in support for three years) better spent on a combination of employee training, additional internal or external resources, or employee retention bonuses?

Summary

The type of support that an organization requires should vary in direct proportion to the complexity of its system, its internal resources, and its business environment. A relatively small, stable, well-staffed organization with a rigorous internal auditing process has different support requirements than a large, dynamic, chaotic one staffed with insufficient internal resources. Higher-level (read: more expensive) support does not negate the possibility of an issue manifesting itself. It can, however, expedite its resolution.

Endnotes

i. http://www.riministreet.com/news.php?id=827

ii. http://blog.lawsonguru.com/2009/04/27/cue-09-descends-on-san-diego/

iii. http://blog.softwareinsider.org/2009/07/21/tuesdays-tip-3-approaches-to-return-shelfware/

Chapter 8

Selecting Consultants

Help me help you.
—*Tom Cruise*, Jerry MacGuire

A friend of mine once compared the relationship between the client and the system integrator (SI) to a marriage. My friend is a fellow consultant with many years of experience. In his view, clients "court" prospective SIs after selecting a system and ultimately decide to "walk down the aisle" with one of them. Things tend to go well at first, but cracks inevitably appear in the armor. Either the two work through the issues (remaining married), or one, usually the client, seeks a divorce.

Beyond this notion of matrimony, organizations may employ consultants in a variety of ways as they march down uncharted paths. This chapter explores an organization's basic need for consultants throughout an implementation, the types of SIs and arrangements available, the pros and cons of each, and several general warnings.

Pre-System Selection

Although hardly the norm, organizations sometimes use an SI to assist them in selecting a new system (pre-implementation). I have been involved in several of these engagements. Under this arrangement, the client engages a consulting partner that may or may not actually implement the systems currently under consideration. SIs may be hired to accomplish any of the following tasks:

- Assist a client in articulating the needs of the business
- Assist a client in preparing requests for proposals (RFPs) or requests for information (RFIs)
- Evaluate vendor proposals
- Interview vendors and participate in vendor sales demonstrations
- Refine the pool of vendors
- Ultimately, assist the organization in making its final decision
- Negotiate license fees and consulting rates

Sometimes an organization that seeks guidance from an SI before deciding on a new system already has a relationship with that SI. Obviously, the organization is placing a great deal of trust in its partner to help it select the "right" system. Although the decision is ultimately the client's, the SI is in a position of considerable power. For example, if Synchronicity Consulting specializes in PeopleSoft implementations, it is probably predisposed toward recommending PeopleSoft to its clients, regardless of whether that system is the best fit. There are two reasons for this. First, Synchronicity probably wants the business. Second, Synchronicity probably knows from personal experience that PeopleSoft can work for its clients. SAP or Lawson may work as well as, if not better than, PeopleSoft, but Synchronicity cannot vouch for those systems. As a result, it may very well recommend PeopleSoft without fully considering comparable systems.

If an organization elects to use an SI to manage its selection of a new system, it would be well advised to ensure that its partner has no inherent biases toward any particular vendor. As discussed in Chapter 5, "The Sounds of Salesmen," there are many similarities among off-the-shelf systems, particularly those in the same tier. Although some true differences exist among applications within the same tier, organizations that use an SI for system selection should adhere to the all-or-nothing principle. Clients should utilize partners with experience either with a number of different applications or no specific application.

Implementation Consulting

After selecting its new system, an organization must address the extent to which it needs external consultants to implement that system. Truth be told, consultants are *not* absolutely essential for a new system to be implemented. However, experienced consultants have "been there and done that." Organizations considering implementing systems with minimal assistance from external consultants should do so only if they have sufficient internal resources that have previously participated in similar—if not identical—projects. To the extent that most organizations cannot meet this criterion, they should use external consultants. Alternatively stated, for good reason most organizations use external consultants to lead or at least assist with system implementations. The next question is, "Which type of SI should be used?"

A company's selection of a vendor will, to some extent, drive its selection of an SI. Remember that not all SIs do the same thing. Indeed, a client's options run the gamut from small, boutique SIs that specialize in the software selected to large firms, such as IBM, that can do anything.

Although not all consultants are equally knowledgeable, experienced ones have been in the trenches before and are in the best position to assess the requisite trade-offs that clients will invariably have to make during the implementation. Fundamentally, consultants should be able to tell their clients honestly whether desired system outputs justify their inputs. Of course, clients need to ask that question first, not just plow ahead with some preconceived notion of what they want. Clients often fail to ask their consultants this question or listen to the answer, often resulting in issues, delays, and exceeded budgets.

Sometimes a client is familiar with the work of a particular consultant. Consider Satch Services, a company that hires Merchant Consulting to lead its implementation. Satch management is particularly impressed with a consultant named Gary, a rock star with strong procurement and GL experience. Satch feels that Gary is the perfect match for its project. However, Merchant cannot realistically guarantee *which* of its consultants will work on the Satch project. Although Merchant can attempt to accommodate Satch's request, a consultant's individual circumstances (work or personal) may make that impossible. Translation: unless specifically outlined in the contract, Satch management should not ink the deal with Merchant expecting to work with Gary. Ideally, Merchant employs other strong consultants besides Gary.

Type of Consulting Engagements: Fixed Bid Versus Time and Materials

Some organizations ask SIs to submit fixed-bid contracts. In general terms, this is an estimated cost based on the project plan. A fixed-bid contract specifies a flat amount of money to be paid to an SI for configuring and testing a system within the client's time frame and budget. It does *not* hinge on total consulting hours worked.

A fixed bid is fundamentally different from a time and materials (T&M) contract. Under a T&M arrangement, an organization agrees to pay, say, $175 per hour per consultant, plus expenses, throughout the duration of the project. Although there is no minimum or maximum on the amount of money that the organization will pay the SI, a T&M deal is rarely a blank check. The consulting firm typically proposes some type of time frame to allow the client to estimate total consulting expenditures.

This begs the question, "Which is best?" Of course, it depends. On a fixed-bid contract, the SI has the incentive to finish the work as quickly as possible. Ideally, the sooner that an SI can activate a client's system, the sooner that it can deploy the same consultants on a new assignment. On a T&M contract, however, the SI may have the opposite incentive: to extend the time that its people are onsite for as long as possible because each hour of time results in additional revenue.

On a fixed bid, organizations should expect resistance from an SI's project manager over any type of application enhancement. Implementation team members will hear the term "scope creep"[1] quite a bit from SIs, because they

---

1. Scope creep takes place when the project initially sets out to accomplish X. However, based on a number of factors, the project now must accomplish X, Y, and Z. For projects sold as fixed bids, the SI will avoid scope creep like the plague.

are incentivized to finish projects as quickly as possible. Conversely, clients will rarely hear about scope creep from SIs on T&M projects. Their partners have strong financial incentives to maximize the duration of any given project.

Two Warnings

The majority of organizations implementing a new system choose a consulting partner at least in an advisory capacity, if not for the entire project. There are a few reasons for this. First, rarely does the organization have the internal expertise in the application(s) being implemented. Second, end users have their day jobs and cannot focus exclusively on the implementation; the SI is devoted to the success of this project and, in theory, can help ensure that its clients meet their goals. Third, and sometimes most important, is the political consideration. If the project should start to derail, consultants are the easiest to blame. By hiring experts who promise a smooth ride during the sales cycle, organizations can hold external consultants accountable for issues, irrespective of whether they are the true cause of those issues.

With that in mind, clients would be well advised to heed the following advice.

Consultant Temperament: Be Aware of the Path of Least Resistance

All too often, organizations select only the SIs that appear to be the most malleable and obedient. This is an enormous mistake. Companies should certainly *not* choose partners who are rigid, irritable, and outright rude. External consultants will be around for a considerable period of time (typically about a year from start to finish, depending on the project). To be sure, poor personal relations among team members do not move things in a positive direction.

Organizations should hire consultants who insist on doing their fundamental job throughout the duration of the project: being the product experts. There are limits to the malleability of applications, despite what salespeople often tell clients. The consultant who steers the reluctant client toward a particular configuration or business decision is not necessarily being difficult. Especially if the client selected an SI with experienced personnel, the consultant probably knows the negative outcomes of suboptimal decisions.

Cost: Be Aware of the Lowest Number

Consider Vernon Manufacturing, a company that has decided to implement an ERP. Table 8.1 shows responses to an RFP from two different SIs: CMU Consulting and Cornell Partners. Both are alleged experts in implementing the ERP. Note that both bids are for T&M.

TABLE 8.1 Comparison of Two SIs' Responses to Vernon's RFP

Resource	CMU Consulting	Cornell Partners
Consultants Required	4	3
Hourly Rate	$175	$175
Hours/Week	40	40
Weeks Onsite	32	28
Total Cost	$896,000	$588,000

At first glance, Cornell Partners may appear to be the better SI; it seems to be able to do the work for a considerably lower fee compared to CMU. However, Vernon is quite foolish if it stops right there and signs with Cornell Partners. Some SIs try to lowball clients with initial bids containing some interesting fine print. The contracts of some deals have language similar to the following:

> The Vernon proposal reflects all current business requirements and future configuration, reporting, customization, and interface needs. Any deviation from the above will be considered out of scope and will constitute a formal change request, not covered by the initial project budget. Work performed outside the scope of the engagement (as defined by the contract) will be performed at the rate of $175 per hour.

Translation: the number submitted from Cornell ($588,000) is *not* comprehensive. Changes will be billed separately. Note that CMU's bid contains no such language.

If Vernon selects Cornell, it should be absolutely certain that it has properly and completely defined *all* of its business requirements related to reporting, interfaces, and so on. Note that this is exceptionally difficult for organizations to do prior to the beginning of a project. Vernon's failure to do so—and lack of understanding of the initial contract will likely result both in contentious conversations with Cornell about "scope creep" and Vernon spending money not included in its initial budget.

For the moment, let's assume that Vernon selects Cornell. Throughout the project, Cornell's project manager tells Vernon senior management that the client's constant barrage of "change requests" is adding up. Cornell and Vernon personnel have many spirited debates about the project and its burgeoning cost. From Cornell's standpoint, Vernon personnel did not adequately define all of its business requirements prior to beginning the engagement. By charging more for the additional work required, Cornell is simply following the contract. The bickering between SI and the client has left the project running considerably behind schedule and over budget. Cornell's revised costs are listed in Table 8.2, along with CMU's original estimates.

TABLE 8.2 Comparison of Two SIs' Actual Costs

Resource	CMU Consulting	Cornell Partners
Consultants Required	4	5
Hourly Rate	$175	$175
Hours/Week	40	50
Weeks Onsite	32	32
Total Cost	$896,000	$1,400,000

As evinced from the table, CMU's initial bid was both accurate and lower in absolute terms. Alternatively stated, the ostensibly less expensive consulting firm turned out to cost significantly more money. Organizations considering multiple consulting proposals should ask themselves the following questions:

- What is covered/not covered by the contract?
- Are the business requirements sufficiently defined so that a strictly scoped T&M contract is viable?
- Is the organization postponing a long-term headache for short-term savings?

Clients should ask these questions as early as possible, certainly before any contract is signed with an SI. Many projects have become quite adversarial over contract language.

Which Type of Contract Is Best?

Generally speaking, T&M contracts tend to have fewer issues than do fixed bids. Rare is the overall positive experience for clients who hired an SI on a low, fixed-bid arrangement. Unfortunately, some SIs sell deals intentionally on the low side to increase project revenue via change requests. This often promotes an adversarial work environment, contentious relations between client and consultants, and system failures.

Types of Consulting Arrangements

Given how much consultants cost, many clients might question the need to have a team of three or more highly paid hourly resources on staff for 40 hours per week. To be sure, there is more than one way to deploy consultants in a cost-effective manner. As a general rule, the quality and number of required external resources varies indirectly with the quality and number of available and experienced internal resources, as evinced by Figure 8.1.

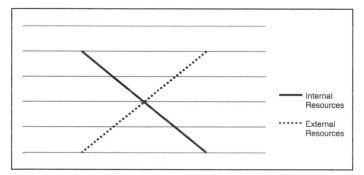

Figure 8.1 *Trade-off between internal and external resources during a system implementation.*

An organization with extensive internal resources and expertise needs *fewer* external consultants.[2] Of course, those internal resources still have to do their day jobs for the organization to conduct business. For example, a payroll manager cannot set up, test, and document the future payroll system at the expense of paying current employees. By the same token, the head of IT cannot configure security for the new ERP while neglecting to fight the fires of the current system. This rule can alternatively be stated as follows:

> If an organization wants to minimize the number of external consultants on an implementation, it must ensure that the end users on its implementation team 1) are devoted regularly and significantly to the implementation of that new system; and 2) have sufficient expertise in that system.

The organization that extensively employs external consultants still needs its internal resources to be heavily involved in the implementation from the beginning until the end of the project. Organizations that do not staff their implementations sufficiently—that is, in a manner conducive to making key

---

2. Fewer does not mean zero. Organizations cannot expect to successfully implement major systems exclusively with consultants or end users. Although not necessarily advisable, note that organizations may be able to handle upgrades and enhancements in a consultant-free manner.

end users available throughout the project—essentially guarantee a bevy of issues, including these:

- Lack of knowledge transfer from consultant to client
- Increased project costs stemming from consultants remaining months after the organization goes live

Minimal consultant input and resources does not mean zero. On just about every major system implementation, organizations need to utilize external application experts, technical resources adept at installing the application, and seasoned project managers who have dealt with many of the issues likely to face the client. To that end, clients' consulting options include the following:

- Traditional consulting
- Milestone consulting
- Multiple consulting partners
- Rapid deployment
- Creative arrangements

Traditional Consulting

In a traditional consulting arrangement, a firm deploys a team of full-time individuals at a client site for 40 hours per week, typically 4 days at 10 hours per day per consultant. SIs typically prefer this arrangement for a number of reasons. First and foremost, traditional consulting maximizes billable time and revenue. Second, and there is more than a bit of truth to this, consultants on the ground can better steer clients in the right direction throughout the project, manage issues, and ensure an overall smoother implementation than if they were not present.

On the downside, traditional consulting tends to be the most expensive option for clients. Also, many organizations face end-user availability issues. Client end users are often overworked and too busy to spend time with consultants. Remember, end users on project teams have day jobs, whereas consultants work exclusively on implementing the new system. Although consultants can work independently, at certain points, client input is imperative. Consultants onsite are billing regardless of whether their skills are being used efficiently. If a project is actually running ahead of schedule, rare is the SI that attempts to move dates up or suggests that its consultants do not need to be onsite for several weeks.

Milestone Consulting

Under this arrangement, a client employs a consulting firm to check in on a regular basis. The goal: to ensure that the project is both meeting its individual goals and, from a broader perspective, remains on track. A client often utilizes a hybrid consultant—equal parts project manager, techie, and application expert—to visit onsite every two weeks or so.

Benefits of this approach include keeping costs to a minimum. Also, to the extent that the consultant's arrival is known well in advance, end users can focus on their day jobs during the week knowing that they will devote certain days to the new system, coinciding with the arrival of the consultant. In theory, this can be more efficient.

This method should be used judiciously, because it is rife with potential disadvantages. For one, there may be no one keeping an eye on the implementation on a daily basis, allowing goals and dates to fall by the wayside. Issues may not be broached in time to address them without impacting a go-live date. Also, the flow of the project may suffer. Projects that constantly start and stop often lose momentum. Projects with more interruptions have a greater chance of failure, and milestone-based approaches tend to have this limitation.

Multiple Consulting Partners

Most of the time, organizations choose a single SI for implementation. However, it is not completely unprecedented for a client to hire several SIs concurrently. For example, let's say that Keel Event Management hires RTB Consultants and FBN Consultants at the same time for the same implementation. Keel senior management believes that it can split responsibilities between its two partners.

The obvious question here is, "Why?" Perhaps Keel believes that RTB and FBN bring different areas of expertise to the table. Maybe it believes that RTB and FBN can "keep each other honest." Perhaps neither RTB nor FBN is large enough to supply the required resources.

Speaking from years of personal experience, this arrangement is almost always a bad idea. At least one of the following outcomes is likely to occur from this type of arrangement:

- RTB and FBN will each neglect to perform an important task based on the honest belief that each thought the other was responsible for it.
- RTB and FBN will each work on the same task in the belief that each thought it was responsible for that task.

- RTB and FBN will each use the project to try to win more work from Keel, undercutting the other in the process.

- RTB and FBN will view the work completed by the other as inferior and attempt to discredit it.

- Even in the unlikely event that RTB and FBN can table any kind of rivalry, the coordination of their work adds administrative costs and delays to the project and increases the chances for miscommunication.

In the end, Keel will suffer from the intercompany conflict.

If a client does not believe that a single SI can meet its needs, it should simply find one that can, with one exception: the client has significant legal or audit-related reasons for one SI to audit the other. Absent this, separating responsibilities is almost always a recipe for failure. In this case, the whole is much less than the sum of the parts.

Even in the event of an audit requiring multiple consulting partners, organizations should take heed of the following example, again based on a true story.

I once worked on a system triage project with a highly respected SI. Let's call this SI Satriani Consulting Group (SCG). SCG was one of two SIs hired by the client, Porcupine Medical. The other—and lesser known—SI subcontracted me. SCG needed consultants to write a series of intricate reports against its disparate systems to solve a complicated business problem. Porcupine's years of inconsistent business practices, bad data, poor documentation, and a complete dearth of internal audits resulted in a major problem with respect to employee pay; it was processed incorrectly for years, and it was time to pay the piper.

By way of background, SCG is a large firm and had at its disposal individual consultants with years of experience using Porcupine's systems; SCG could have deployed consultants who would have actually been worth the $200 per hour or so that it was charging. For some reason, however, SCG chose to send two smart but green consultants without experience in *any* of Porcupine's systems—or knowledge of the business practices that caused the payroll problem in the first place.[3]

Porcupine needed both SCG and me to *independently* arrive at results. SCG and I would then need to reconcile any differences. SCG's role sounded like an audit to me, especially because I began working on the project one month before SCG even arrived onsite. SCG maintained otherwise. In the words of the SCG's project manager, the company needed to "reperform" my work.

---

3. Examples such as these are the main reason that, if I ever again take a full-time client position, I will use independents and boutique firms if I have any say in the matter.

To this day, I do not understand what that term means. Whatever this meant, SCG's consultants did not have anywhere near the knowledge required to solve Porcupine's problem and do the work that it was contracted to do. By way of comparison, I had nearly a decade of experience using Porcupine's specific systems, and this project hurt my brain.

SCG attempted to have it both ways on this project: it attempted to independently arrive at the results while requesting access to—and actually mimicking—the very methodology that I employed to arrive at them. This is analogous to getting a little bit pregnant. SCG consultants would frequently ask me how to derive rates of pay, weekly and pay period employee totals, and the like. Not only did this violate any remote appearance of independence, but answering their questions disrupted my momentum and ultimately increased the number of hours that I worked on the project. Porcupine was essentially paying me to teach SCG consultants who themselves were billing Porcupine to learn how to solve Porcupine's problem. This is not exactly a recipe for a successful project.

In the end, SCG consultants merely copied my work, made a few minor changes, and claimed that they independently validated my work. Porcupine spent more than $250,000 on the project, the majority of which went to SCG consultants who essentially rubber-stamped my work without any idea about its accuracy. Porcupine could have done the project for 25 percent of its final cost. At a bare minimum, Porcupine could have requested that SCG provide consultants with the requisite experience to do an independent analysis.

Rapid Deployment

In recent years, some SIs and vendors have proposed an alternative to the traditional consulting arrangement. They have offered budget-conscious clients a rapid implementation designed to take anywhere from three to six months from soup to nuts. In return for the reduced consulting time and expense, clients relinquish some traditional decision making concerning application flexibility and setup.

For example, rather than spend a month determining with end users which GL accounts or benefit plans to configure, consultants arrive onsite with these items essentially decided in advance. This does not mean that consultants force clients to erroneously use a petty cash account or start enrolling employees in a 403(b) plan that does not exist. Rather, consultants will quickly configure the client's system with predesigned templates. If the system configuration and business process cannot coexist, the client has to change its practice to conform to the new system.

Results of rapid deployment have been mixed. On the positive side, some clients have realized considerable savings, particularly on consulting fees. Efficiency also increases, because end users cannot debate which codes the organization will use or how it will conduct a major business process; the SI essentially makes these decisions for the client. Obviously, this approach will not work across the board, because a change in business process may be too severe for a client to stomach. Alternatively, the delivered functionality of the vanilla system may result in significant reporting or security gaps.

Creative Arrangements

Clients may pose alternate arrangements to minimize consultant cost during the project. Assuming that an organization has sufficient internal expertise, it may want to have consultants assist only with the setup or testing of the application. A client may want to independently handle items such as custom report writing.

This approach can potentially minimize consulting costs. Also, much like the milestone approach, client end users can theoretically schedule their work to maximize knowledge transfer while consultants are onsite.

Although costs may be minimized, client risk may very well increase with creative approaches. Consultants not involved in the setup of an application, for example, might point out issues in the middle of an implementation that end users should have flagged at the beginning. The impact on testing may be significant enough that the go-live date is jeopardized. Some SIs may be reluctant to take on projects such as these, citing a lack of total ownership. Boutique firms—discussed later in this chapter—are often afraid of bad business and may consider these types of arrangements excessively risky. After all, how can a client expect an SI to routinely jump into an implementation at critical points and hit the ground running? What if individual consultants must rotate in and out of the project due to scheduling issues?

This last question is perhaps the most pragmatic and compelling argument against approaches predicated on occasional consultant involvement. SIs make money by deploying their employees on a full-time basis, not two days per week. Thus, the client that entrusts an excellent consultant with a key role during system implementation will, in all likelihood, not be able to secure that consultant's services on an intermittent basis. The risk is that new consultants will have to routinely review project-related documentation before being brought up to speed. At critical points of a project, the time required for this assimilation simply does not exist. Also, all consultants do *not* have the same skills, even if they have comparable backgrounds and certifications. Clients that opt to have consultants visit infrequently run the risk that the new consultant is not as knowledgeable as his predecessors.

Which Is Best?

There are too many factors to determine the best type of consulting arrangement for a client. Certainly, all approaches have potential drawbacks. To be sure, most organizations do not have the expertise that SIs can provide. As such, organizations benefit from knowledgeable, onsite consultants who ensure that the project stays on course, issues are reported and resolved, and individual objectives are met.

Types of SIs

Organizations have at least four different options with respect to types of SIs. Clients that do not have the requisite internal bandwidth and expertise to independently undertake a massive implementation can employ the following types of SIs:

- The vendor
- Large firms
- Boutique firms
- Independents

DISCLAIMER

I have worked with all sorts of SIs in my career but, before continuing, I should admit that I am admittedly slightly biased toward boutique firms and independents based on my own experience. This is *not* to say that there are not dedicated, knowledgeable, and talented consultants working for vendors and large SIs. Rather, as a general rule, I have found that consultants working for themselves and for smaller firms tend to justify their hourly rates better than consultants working for vendors and large SIs.

Despite my predisposition, I have done my best to remain objective in both this section and this book. We will soon see that there are no guarantees, regardless of the type of SI contracted. With that out of the way, let's explore each type of SI in detail.

The Software Vendor

Organizations buying Oracle, for example, can certainly hire Oracle consultants—that is, full-time Oracle employees that implement the company's applications for a living. From a billing and accountability standpoint, things *may* be simpler for the organization that opts to go this route.

First-time clients often do not understand, however, that the specific consultants implementing the system did not design that system. Clients discovering Oracle "bugs" cannot expect Oracle consultants to magically fix them.[4] Now, there are instances in which some vendors may provide their own consultants with superior documentation relative to that which they would provide to partners and clients. This is sometimes the case during application upgrades.

A vendor's consultants may be less willing to call a spade a spade. Translation: a client should not expect a vendor's employees to freely admit to the shortcoming of their employer's product. Also, from a cost perspective, vendor consultants are typically the most expensive of the lot. This does not mean that they are necessarily better than the other SIs discussed in this chapter. Vendors can justify above-average rates for their consultants via name and brand recognition.

Most major vendors have partnerships with large and boutique firms. Vendors that do not have enough available consultants to staff a project will commonly reach out to these partners and rent consultants, marking them up accordingly. A client might sign with Oracle only to have a consultant from another firm (an Oracle partner) working on the actual implementation.

Large Firms

Large SIs such as IBM and Deloitte and Touche (D&T) employ hoards of consultants supporting just about every major enterprise system. Their businesses each have multiple revenue streams; they hedge their bets by playing in multiple sandboxes. If revenue from the PeopleSoft line of business (LOB) suffers, they will attempt to compensate for that with additional revenue from another LOB, say SAP. Compared to boutique firms, large SIs are diverse: a relatively small percentage of total company revenue emanates from any one system.

---

4. I'm not picking on Oracle here. All systems have bugs or, euphemistically, "undocumented features."

Large firms offer the auspices of credibility, hence the old adage, "No one ever got fired for hiring IBM." Rate-wise, organizations can expect to pay in the ballpark of $200 per hour per consultant. Aside from cost, name and brand recognition are high for these firms. Like vendors, large firms "rent" additional consultants for projects as needed. Also similar to vendors, large firms tend to employ a range of consultants, from the highly experienced to the neophyte, often staffing large projects with a combination of both so that new hires gain valuable experience. Right, wrong, or indifferent, it is not uncommon for these firms to deploy consultants currently "on the bench" for engagements for which they might not be a pure fit. For example, a large firm may send to a client implementing Oracle Financials a consultant skilled primarily in Lawson Financials, particularly for a low-visibility assignment. Remember from Chapter 5 that these systems are similar. The logic here is this: if a consultant can write reports or run test scripts from one system, he should be able to do it from another.

Like vendors, large SIs rarely turn down "bad" business. If these firms do not have the requisite consultants to staff any one project, they do one or more of the following:

- Hire more consultants
- Enter into subcontracting agreements with independents or partners
- Put consultants from different LOBs on projects for which they might not be qualified[5]

A project that appears to be problematic will usually not dissuade the large SI from pursuing it, regardless of probable pitfalls. Remember that individual LOBs in large firms typically constitute a small portion of overall revenue; the partner or salesperson in that firm that passes up a sale—regardless of any red flags—is probably going to be reprimanded or asked to leave the firm, absent a really compelling reason. As we will see in the Portnoy case study in Chapter 11, "Setup Issues," large SIs often ignore substantial project risks under the guise of "pleasing the client." This mentality almost always leads to system failures and the occasional double Jack Daniels for consultants on the project.

---

5. This is my single biggest gripe with large SIs and, to be fair, not all of them do this. I consider myself a pretty smart guy but I know my limits. For example, if asked to contribute in a meaningful way on a SAP Procurement project, I wouldn't know where to begin. I have never worked with SAP or any procurement module of any major system. As such, I would have to research most basic client questions, never mind more involved ones. Large SIs sometimes put consultants in these untenable positions because the latter are often available or "on the beach" in consultant-speak. In my view, this is really shortsighted and ultimately inimical to everyone involved—the client, the consultant, and the SI.

Boutique Firms

Unlike their larger brethren, boutique firms specialize in the system that the client is implementing. These firms do *not* offer a vast array of services or cover the same range of systems as their larger counterparts. Boutiques' main selling point is their often-exclusive focus on one particular system. They tend to employ only experienced, knowledgeable consultants, not newly minted ones. Boutique firms are apt to contract seasoned independents as needed because their business models tend to be sensitive to clients' sales cycles. They simply cannot afford to have full-time consultants "on the bench" for long periods of time because they have nowhere to put them. Unlike their larger counterparts, boutiques do not employ nearly as many consultants, in terms of sheer numbers or variety of applications and technologies. For these reasons, boutiques do not place available consultants currently on engagements for which they are not suitable.

Boutique firms typically work with only a few clients concurrently and are averse to project failures. They tend not to be "chop shops" in the eyes of their own consultants and clients. These firms sometimes do what larger firms usually consider unthinkable: turn down "bad" business. Management at boutiques knows red flags when they see them and often do not want to risk sullying their companies' reputations with botched implementations. As a result, established boutique firms tend to have high client retention rates.

During the sales cycle, both boutiques and large firms often trumpet their ability to bring certified consultants to the table. To be sure, all else being equal, a certified consultant is better than an uncertified consultant. However, vendors often play games with the certification process for partners. I have met more than a few consultants—although technically not certified—who knew twice as much as their certified counterparts. Translation: certified does not mean "better."

Independent Consultants

Finally, organizations can go the independent route either by contacting known independents directly or by using a recruiting agency to find them. If an organization uses an agency, then that agency typically marks up independents anywhere from 30 to 60 percent.

Like the other consulting options, independents have their pros and cons. On the cost side, independents tend to cost significantly less for a number of reasons. They almost never maintain a proper business office because they actively try to minimize overhead. This allows independents to charge rates typically 40 percent lower than those of established firms. Even with a reasonable markup by an agency, the final cost to a client is often considerably lower than a large or boutique firm. On the downside, independents do not have the same name recognition and network of a larger consulting practice. If an implementation implodes, an executive has to defend the ostensibly risky decision to hire a single, independent consultant.

As a general rule, independents tend to be a knowledgeable bunch. Most have "graduated" from larger organizations and enjoy the autonomy of working for themselves, choosing projects that make the most sense for them. Ironically, many clients use independents whether they know it or not. As stated before, often vendors and SIs augment their staff with independents as their business and staffing needs mandate.

Let's consider a detailed example of an organization in need of staff augmentation. Pratt University is in the midst of its PeopleSoft implementation. Pratt's SI—LLD—just lost its lead procurement consultant and does not have a suitable replacement immediately available. Other LLD consultants are engaged at Pratt at the rate of $175 per hour.[6] Pratt turns to Townshend Recruiters to augment its staff, whereas LLD attempts to backfill the position. Townshend finds two suitable consultants.

First up is Joe the Independent, to borrow from the 2008 presidential campaign. Joe has more than 12 years of experience as a consultant in PeopleSoft procurement and financials. Aside from being a certified functional consultant, he knows how to make some basic technical tweaks and has extensive reporting knowledge in a number of mainstream reporting tools. His rate is $120 per hour.

Next is Rena, an independent relatively new to PeopleSoft. She has three years of experience and is much less technically savvy than Joe. Her rate reflects her comparative lack of experience: $80 per hour.

Townshend marks up independents 50 percent, making Joe's hypothetical hourly rate to Pratt $180 and Rena's rate $120. Townshend knows that rate will be an issue with Pratt and asks Joe to "be flexible" and move into Rena's ballpark. In all likelihood, Joe will not drop his rate by one-third. Townshend needs to understand (as does Pratt, for that matter) the additional costs associated with being independent, detailed in Table 8.3.

The costs in Table 8.3 do *not* factor in the additional risks that independents like Joe and Rena incur, including billing issues and the potential difficulty of finding work. Independents are not on a company's payroll like the LLD consultants in this example. Joe faces the real risks of both not finding work and not being paid by a company that owes him for wages and expenses. In

---

6. Note that hourly rates fluctuate based on many factors, including the economy, the geography, the length of the project, and the type of skills required by the client.

total, Joe must deal with much more risk and significantly higher expenses (see bold items in Table 8.3) than regular W-2 consultants, both of which justify his higher hourly rate. Reward should be proportional to risk.

TABLE 8.3 Estimated Annual Revenue and Costs of an Independent Consultant

Item	Cost
Hourly rate	$100
Hours worked per year	1,500
Total gross revenue	$150,000
Extra Social Security taxes because an independent is often an employee *and* an employer, based on the 2008 $102,000 wage limit	**$6,324**
Annual medical insurance (based on full family coverage)	**$8,000**
Annual Errors and Omission Insurance	**$2,000**
Total Revenue (pre-federal, state, and local taxes)	$125,370

One of the many positives of being independent is that Joe can write off more business expenses than a W-2 employee. Table 8.3 does *not* reflect his net income. The following point is critical: Joe needs a compensating wage differential to justify being independent. If Joe could only make, for example, $60 per hour (roughly $100,000 per year, gross) as an independent, he would be taking unnecessary risks. Joe can easily earn this much as a full-time employee of an SI, given his vast experience.

Let's return to the Pratt example. Townshend submits the profiles and final rates of Joe and Rena to Pratt, whose senior management strongly prefers Joe over Rena but balks at Joe's rate. Townshend attempts to negotiate Joe down, but he will move to only $110 per hour. Townshend agrees to reduce its markup as well, making Joe's final rate $150 per hour, an amount acceptable to Pratt.

In this scenario, everybody wins:

• Pratt gets an experienced consultant who can hit the ground running. The delay to the project is minimized, especially if Joe can work effectively with other LLD staff.

• Townshend makes $40 per hour on Joe's work for the duration of the project.

• Although Joe's risks and costs are substantial, locking down a long-term assignment for $110 per hour is probably a smart business decision.

> **NOTE**
> The bottom line with independents is that organizations get what they pay for. An independent's rate is a direct reflection of the experience that he brings to the table. The organization that opts for the less expensive independent should not expect the same level of performance that it would receive from a more seasoned—and expensive—one.

Which Type of SI Is Best?

The "best" SI is largely a function of the individual consultants placed on a given project. To that extent, client senior management often overrates the name recognition of larger SIs. Paramount considerations are the experience, knowledge, and quality of the individual consultants on the project, regardless of the name on the SI's stationery. Firms of *all* sizes have run unsuccessful projects; no one has a perfect batting average. A client that hires a large, well-known firm in no way guarantees the successful activation of its system. In fact, a smaller firm may provide a better chance to succeed.

> **NOTE**
> In the end, an organization should not make the mistake of assuming that all SIs are equal. They are not. Nor should it choose a partner solely on the basis of cost. The skills of consultants from a more expensive SI may, in fact, be worth a premium.

As stated earlier in this chapter, cost is simply one of the many factors for organizations to consider when choosing an SI. This next section discusses the questions that organizations and SIs should ask each other *before* signing contracts.

Client Questions

Ideally, organizations perform comprehensive due diligence throughout the selection and implementation of new systems. Senior management should look at everything: the organization itself, potential project team members, and the vendor and its software. Investigating and interviewing potential SIs and their individual consultants should simply represent a continuation of this process.

> **NOTE**
>
> After the organization identifies suitable SIs, it should seek to fully under-
> stand each candidate's consulting philosophies and previous outcomes.
> Check references and perform due diligence. The client's objective should
> not be to find the most malleable partner that will accede to each one of
> its demands.

The latter scenario is a recipe for failure, as several case studies in the book will demonstrate. Disagreement between client and SI is inevitable and even natural throughout a project. Organizations would be wise not to simply find a partner that they can "bully" into agreeing with poor decisions.

Aside from this general tip, some of the fundamental questions that an organization needs to ask potential SIs include

- Are the long-term benefits from working with this SI worth the costs?
- Does our potential partner have a history of satisfied clients?
- Will our potential partner challenge us if we start to go down the wrong path?
- Is our potential partner equipped with sufficient resources to handle this project?

Questions for the SI

Taking steps to ensure a healthy, productive relationship with proposed part-
ners is *not* the exclusive domain of the client. In a similar vein, SIs should also ask potential clients certain questions prior to accepting a new client, including these:

- Are the long-term benefits from working with this organization during this project worth the risks and costs?
- Is this potential client hell-bent on a setup that cannot be successful?
- Will this potential client let us do our jobs?
- Does the client have sufficient internal resources devoted to this project?
- Will the client provide the requisite sign-off at key points?

Foolish is the consulting firm that attempts to win business at any cost. SIs risk their reputations with each project. Although no consulting firm can guarantee a successful implementation, experienced salespeople and consul-
tants know red flags when they see them. By carefully screening prospective clients before signing contracts, the best SIs consistently minimize the chance of a highly publicized meltdown and maximize the chance of a productive, healthy, mutually beneficial relationship for all concerned.

Q&A WITH MARK HAYES OF JAT CONSULTING

Few professionals have a more complete point of view on implementing new systems than my friend Mark Hayes. Mark is a seasoned consultant and project manager involved in technical, functional, and project management aspects of large implementations. Mark is also typically involved in the sales cycle for his company, JAT Consulting, a boutique firm specializing in Lawson and Kronos, for which he is a vice president. I interviewed Mark about the many facets of the system selection process.

PS: What are the two or three main reasons that clients decide to implement new systems?

MH: There are a number of reasons. First, clients are compelled to change systems because they are changing hardware platforms, moving off a mainframe platform, or changing between UNIX and a Windows-based platform. Running multiple platforms is costly for clients because they need technical experience in each one. Consolidating platforms can represent significant savings for an organization.

Second, they are consolidating to an ERP package that can meet the needs of multiple areas within the organization. Companies running separate financial, HR, and supply chain packages from different vendors will look to consolidate. Ideally, they can support just one new complete package able to meet the needs of multiple areas within the organization. Cost savings will typically drive this decision. The technology base will be the same, support contracts will cost less, and internal support can be consolidated.

Third, acquisitions will typically require an organization to migrate to the system and platform of the parent company.

PS: What would you say are the three most important criteria that clients should use in choosing an SI?

MH: First, internal experience with the vendor is crucial. New management or key employees with a positive experience with a particular vendor hold a great deal of water.

Second, functionality is critical at the higher end of the market but less so with the smaller clients. At the higher end of the market, more users and more business requirements mean that new systems need to essentially work out of the box (read: without extensive customizations). Smaller organizations have a willingness to work around product deficiencies to realize a cost savings. Excessive features are often even seen as a detriment in the sales cycle due to the perception that the system will be more operationally complex.

The third factor is business relationships and comfort with the vendor during the sales cycle. It is critical to make prospective clients feel comfortable. You have to be able to communicate that you understand the business requirements and have the necessary skills to provide the solution. The client needs to trust the vendor to deliver on promised services.

PS: How often does a deal come down to cost? Do you find that clients get what they pay for?

MH: The deal comes down to cost about 20 percent of the time. When I estimate a project, I make all attempts to accurately gauge the actual effort to perform the required services. I will not underestimate a project in an attempt to get business (with a change request plan to augment my low estimate). Therefore, when I lose a business to cost, one of the following has happened.

First, another vendor has intentionally bid low. While I may have lost this business this time, this is the type of client from which I probably will gain future business. That organization is likely to have a bad experience with its vendor.

Second, I overestimated the project. If I have done proper due diligence and have understood the prospect's business requirements, this should rarely happen.

Third, my rate is higher than that of my competition. While I will routinely make minor rate adjustments while negotiating in good faith with a client, I rarely attempt to match rates that are outside of my profit margin.

PS: Do clients get what they pay for?

MH: The answer is somewhat nebulous. The client always gets what I propose. In rare instances where my consultant is not performing up to par, the problem is almost always addressed to the client's satisfaction.

Sometimes a consultant is put into a position where delivering services is hindered by lack of client availability, slow decision making, poor system design, or incomplete prerequisites. In these instances, it is important for me to bring these factors to the client's attention immediately.

PS: Talk to me about the importance of client references during the sales cycle.

MH: Clients universally want references. In fact, clients frequently ask for references that are within their same vertical, company size, state, platform, and release level. I sometimes think that clients miss the mark on this. By asking for such detailed prior experience, they may be eliminating some of the best consultants from consideration. A great consultant with no health care experience will do a better job implementing a system at a health care client than an average consultant with health care experience.

PS: How often are you able to successfully talk clients out of bad setup or design decisions?

MH: If the desired design is truly bad and decision makers have their minds made up, I will not pursue the business. I have recommended that clients not move forward on a project on which I was about to bid because the project did not make good business sense. Bad business decisions typically result in failed and over-budget projects and, ultimately, bad references.

PS: Let's talk about bad business. What are some examples of red flags?

MH: I occasionally run into a prospective piece of business that is not worth the risk of pursuing. An ineffectual project manager is one of those flags. Lack of consensus among the project team in regard to system direction is another.

PS: Can you comment on some of the root causes of some less-than-successful projects?

MH: Budgetary and calendar goals are one and the same: If you don't hit the implementation date, the budget will increase. So, this is really about hitting the date. I recognize that there are instances in which increasing the number of consultants on a project can result in meeting the date while, at the same time, result in budget overruns.

One of the biggest causes for project failure is the process that organizations use to determine the go-live date. Many clients start the process by picking the live date and backing into the effort that must take place to meet that go-live date. Organizations should first determine a reasonable start date and calculate the end date based upon effort and dependencies.

Poorly defined client business requirements often drive cost overruns. If a client discovers that it needs 20 interfaces and reports to go live rather than the 10 originally estimated, the project will go over budget. Clients not understanding their own current business processes happen far too often. Many of these items can be caught up front by a business-savvy consultant. If a client RFP omits a routine implementation task, the consultant should bring it to the attention of the client.

Scope control is another major reason for project failure. Scope overruns are largely a failure of the project manager. In order for a project to be successful, it must have a defined scope that cannot change mid-project. Critical scope items not included result from poorly defined business requirements. Increases in project scope—especially noncritical items—reflect the inability of the project manager to say "no" to the client.

Summary

SIs run the gamut in terms of size, philosophies, quality, and cost. Some relatively inexpensive consultants bring tremendous knowledge and tools to the table. Unfortunately, other consultants do not give clients the same bang for their buck. Although no consultant should have *carte blanche*, clients would do well to listen carefully to the consultants' recommendations. Organizations that doubt the expertise of their partners should probably not have hired them in the first place.

PART III

The System Implementation

This Part delves extensively into the inner workings and the key players within an organization during a typical system implementation. The objective is to analyze the root cause of the problems endemic to these projects. Along with a discussion of the different implementation strategies, phases, and issues, case studies are used extensively to illustrate how, why, when, and where projects derail.

Chapter 9

Implementation Strategies and Phases

> There's a difference between knowing
> the path and walking the path.
> —*Lawrence Fishburne as Morpheus*, The Matrix

- Implementation Strategies
- Implementation Phases
- Costanza Medical Case Study: A Flexible Client and a True Consulting Partner

This chapter focuses on the key decisions organizations make that will, to be blunt, make or break their projects. The right implementation strategy is like accurate driving directions: although a driver could still hit traffic or suffer an accident on the way to a destination, wrong directions virtually guarantee that he will not arrive on time and will waste quite a bit of gas. In the worst-case scenario, the organization that picks an unsuitable strategy has virtually no chance of meeting its time and budgetary objectives. We begin with a discussion about high-level strategies and then turn to the specific phases of an implementation.

Implementation Strategies

Arguably, the fundamental decision that an organization needs to make prior to beginning the project involves strategy. Particularly at large, multisite clients, senior management needs to determine the order in which modules are going to be implemented at each entity. Organizations have multiple options, ranging from pursuing little victories to going for the whole kit and caboodle.

Consider the fictitious example of Byrne Health Care. The organization consists of five relatively autonomous individual hospitals. Each runs its own enterprise system. Fed up with excessive maintenance costs and an inability to run simple, enterprise-wide reports, Byrne management purchases an enterprise resource planning (ERP) and intends to implement it throughout the organization. The next sections discuss Byrne's different options.

The Full-Blown Implementation

Byrne can implement all modules at all hospitals concurrently. This "full-blown" approach is depicted in Table 9.1.

TABLE 9.1 Full-Blown Implementation for a Multisite Organization

Hospital	HR	Payroll	Financials	Procurement
Victoria	Phase I	Phase I	Phase I	Phase I
Winfield	Phase I	Phase I	Phase I	Phase I
Mattingly	Phase I	Phase I	Phase I	Phase I
Gamble	Phase I	Phase I	Phase I	Phase I
Jackson	Phase I	Phase I	Phase I	Phase I

Advantages of this approach include

- Byrne does not have to build interfaces from the new systems to hospitals targeted for Phase II.
- Byrne does not have to continue paying maintenance on existing legacy systems.

Disadvantages of this approach include

- Implementation lessons cannot be applied to other hospitals in Phase II.
- In the short term, the project is more expensive and consultant intensive than a gradual implementation.
- A project of this scope has more room for failure; "problem" hospitals can cause the whole project to suffer, resulting in the entire organization missing key dates.

The Staggered or Phased Implementation

Another approach is typically called the staggered or phased implementation. This approach has two variations, best illustrated by an example.

Phased Approach, Version 1

In Version 1, all of Byrne's sites implement the system in the same modules in the same phases, as shown in Table 9.2.

TABLE 9.2 Phased Approach for a Multisite Organization, Version 1

Hospital	HR	Payroll	General Ledger	Procurement
Victoria	Phase I	Phase I	Phase II	Phase III
Winfield	Phase I	Phase I	Phase II	Phase III
Mattingly	Phase I	Phase I	Phase II	Phase III
Gamble	Phase I	Phase I	Phase II	Phase III
Jackson	Phase I	Phase I	Phase II	Phase III

Advantages of this approach include

- In the short term, the gradual approach is less consultant intensive than a full-blown implementation.
- HR and payroll are "out of the way." All HR and payroll headaches are dealt with at one point.

- Internal resources may be able to implement Phase II and IIII hospitals with less involvement from external consultants—if sufficient knowledge transfer has taken place.

- A project of this scope has less room for failure than the full-blown implementation; "problem" areas in an organization will not cause the whole project to immediately suffer.

Disadvantages of this approach include

- Relatively little learning can be applied across hospitals because Byrne implements HR and payroll concurrently throughout the organization.

- Byrne has to build temporary interfaces from the new payroll and HR system to individual hospitals' general ledger systems. It has to maintain those interfaces until it activates its new general ledger system in Phase II.

- Byrne has to continue to pay maintenance on existing legacy systems until all hospitals are live.

Phased Approach, Version 2

In Version 2, different sites at Byrne implement the system in different phases, as shown in Table 9.3.

TABLE 9.3 Phased Approach for a Multisite Organization, Version 2

Hospital	HR	Payroll	General Ledger	Procurement
Victoria	Phase I	Phase I	Phase I	Phase I
Winfield	Phase II	Phase II	Phase II	Phase II
Mattingly	Phase II	Phase II	Phase II	Phase II
Gamble	Phase III	Phase III	Phase III	Phase III
Jackson	Phase III	Phase III	Phase III	Phase III

Advantages of this approach include

- In the short term, the gradual approach costs less than a full-blown implementation.

- Lessons can be applied from other implementations at other hospitals. For example, the Winfield implementation should go smoother than the Victoria one. These lessons can potentially reduce project-wide costs over the long term.

- A project of this scope has less room for failure than the full-blown implementation. "Problem" hospitals *cannot* cause the whole project to suffer.

Disadvantages of this approach include

- Byrne has to continue to pay maintenance on existing legacy systems until all hospitals are live.

- Byrne has to build interfaces from the new payroll and HR system to individual hospitals' general ledger systems. Byrne has to maintain those interfaces until it activates the new general ledger system throughout the enterprise.

Phased Approach, Version 2a

Note that an organization need not have entities at multiple sites to go the staggered route. Although logistically a single-site employee does not face the same challenges as its multisite counterpart, a perfectly valid model for such an organization is presented in Table 9.4.

TABLE 9.4 Phased Approach for a Single-Site Organization

Hospital	HR	Payroll	General Ledger	Procurement
Garnett, Inc.	Phase I	Phase I	Phase II	Phase III

An organization certainly does not have to implement all modules concurrently simply because it is comprised of one entity.

Which Strategy Is Best?

There is no one correct strategy for an organization with regard to a system implementation. Cost is certainly a factor in terms of external consultants, temporary interfaces, and legacy system maintenance. The size of the organization is another major consideration. For the single-site organization, it is tough to argue that only certain departments should have HR and payroll implemented while others should not. Organizations should certainly know and assess the risks associated with each alternative. If internal political or financial conditions do not permit a "full-blown" effort, the organization should go with a phased approach. It's probably better to win a series of small battles, building momentum in the process, than to risk losing one spectacular war.

Implementation Phases

After an organization has recognized the need to implement a new system and selected a partner for that very purpose, it is ready for the next step: starting the actual transition from legacy system to new system. The number and severity of potential pitfalls can corrupt even the most carefully conceived project plans.

Although system integrators (SIs) typically have slightly different methodologies, most follow these phases for implementing a new system:

- Project planning
- Application exploration
- System design
- System testing
- System activation

Understanding the objectives and constraints of each phase—by itself and in relation to the other phases—is imperative. The phases provide the framework for understanding the entire implementation; every task in an implementation has its natural place and phase. Moreover, the issues brought to light in each case study become clearer when viewed against this backdrop.

NOTE

It is virtually impossible to predict with any degree of precision how long each of the following phases will ultimately take. As we will see throughout this book, an ostensibly logical project plan may become moot over things such as poor data quality, internal resistance to change, and unforeseen system and integration issues. Thus, the process of allocating exact periods of time to each phase is much more art than science. One of my graduate school professors, Lee Dyer of Cornell University, referred to these estimations as "strategic, wild-ass guesses" or SWAGs. I always liked that term.[1]

Project Planning

When thinking of project planning, I am often reminded of a quote from *Thirteen Days*, an excellent movie about the Cuban Missile Crisis. When confronted with the knowledge that the Soviets had placed intercontinental ballistic missiles in Cuba, President Kennedy—played by Bruce Greenwood—says, "First we gotta figure out what we're gonna do before we figure out how we're gonna do it." Well said. Each project begins with some sort of planning.

---

1. SWAGs are closely related to the brilliantly recursive Hofstadter's Law: "It always takes longer than you expect, even when you take into account Hofstadter's Law." While typically used by software developers and programmers, it applies equally to the implementation of existing technologies.

Phase Objectives

Planning a project of the magnitude, duration, and cost of a new system implementation is no small endeavor. Internal and external resources need to be mapped both to overall goals and to the individual tasks needed to accomplish these goals. Aside from extensive resource coordination, plans need to encompass dates and task dependencies. Whether using Microsoft Project, Excel, or some other project management tool, the first objective of the planning phase is to produce a comprehensive and realistic project plan. This is the single, unifying document that aggregates each group, person, task, and goal. The plan should easily produce project status reports. Further, delays should allow for the deadlines of dependent tasks to be automatically adjusted.

Ideally, the creation of a project plan should involve quite a bit more than mechanically applying dates, tasks, and resources to a predefined template. Remember that no two implementations are identical in terms of system design, challenges, resources, data, and so on. Without accurate task, phase, and project end dates, the road map to go live is meaningless. Absent a good project plan, it is hard to imagine a multimillion dollar project having a remote chance of being successful.

Project plans should not remain untouched and unaltered throughout the implementation. On the contrary, they need to be living documents, reflecting issues discovered and subsequent changes required. The final version of a project plan often bears little resemblance to the initial one. Resources, tasks, and dates are added and changed, often on a weekly basis. However meticulous the planning, issues invariably come to light during a project, requiring modifications to the original plan.

How Long Should Project Planning Take?

Planning a six-month (or longer) project takes time. Even the experienced project manager (PM) who starts with a template has to spend a great deal of time customizing it to meet the client's needs, resources, and objectives. Initially, project planning should take at least a month for a decent prototype to be presented to senior management. Good prototypes include high-level milestones, discrete tasks, and the resources assigned to those tasks.

Application Exploration

In this phase, end users and consultants sit down in front of the computer and literally explore the application. (At this point, the system typically contains test data.) Application exploration (AE) typically takes place in a training data area in which end users can perform dummy setup and processing without fear of "breaking anything." Note that end users do not need to make final or even preliminary decisions with regard to setup, processing, and reporting, although this should be in the minds of all involved. The point of AE is for end users to become more familiar with the new system and the different options available to them. This knowledge, in turn, enables them to ask better questions and make better decisions for the next phase—system design.

Typically, external consultants guide clients through AE. After all, it is difficult for an end user with no experience in the new system to explore it effectively without extensive help or input, even if that person attended training. During AE, consultants should foster an atmosphere conducive to learning and building end-user confidence. Consultants should answer questions as needed and provide tips on items such as navigation and processing. Nothing frustrates client end users more than not being able to get around in a system, especially when they will routinely have to work with that system in the near future.

Phase Objectives

The specific objectives of AE are as follows:

- To begin the process of knowledge transfer between client and consultant
- To identify gaps between what the delivered application can do and the client's business requirements
- To explore the different configuration options available to the client and the pros and cons of each

Finally, foolish is the client or SI that minimizes the importance of AE. I once worked with a project manager who told a client that AE could be combined with system design—to make up for delays caused by her own negligence. This was not a wise course of action, and the client soon requested her removal from the project.

How Long Should AE Take?

AE can begin before project planning is complete; it is not necessary to have the project plan finalized for end users to play with the system in a test data area. Typically, after a month of AE, client end users (especially those who went to training) are experienced enough with the system that they can contribute in a meaningful manner and begin to think about decisions related to system design.

Note that AE should primarily focus on items included in Phase I of an implementation. If employee self-service, for example, is clearly out of scope for the first phase, client end users should not spend much time learning it. There will be time for that in later phases. Although AE should focus primarily on items targeted for the upcoming phase of the implementation, Phase II items should *not* be completely ignored. Configuring the system with the knowledge that it needs to be substantially changed after go-live is ill-advised. Here, consultants must lead the way.

System Design

Based on the results of AE, the organization and its end users should be ready to move on to system design. In this phase, end users configure the system to meet the organization's business needs. Specific examples include the setup of the following:

- Organizational structure
- General ledger accounts, accounting units, and other financial setup
- Benefit plans, payroll structure, employee status codes, and other HR-related setup
- Item master, vendors, and other procurement items
- System security

At this critical point, consultant input is invaluable. With respect to the new system, employees who have been exposed to the application for several months (at most) do not know what they do not know.

> **NOTE**
> End users insisting on a suboptimal or cumbersome setup are creating problems down the road that can adversely affect the entire project, as well as the whole organization. Consultants should guide system design. Ultimately, the system configuration should be in line with best practices, lest the client be left with a system that it cannot (easily) support.

Customizations

Organizations often find that the off-the-shelf application does not meet their needs and may be tempted to customize their systems at this point. Customizations are not to be taken lightly.

To be sure, not all customizations are created equal; there are degrees. A database administrator (DBA) may create a custom view of vendor and invoice data to facilitate historical reports. That's a far cry from changing that system's batch program to match invoices in a different way. Individuals who do not know what they are doing in those instances may well cause a problem that cannot easily be fixed or reversed.

Any system customization ought to be viewed skeptically. If the benefits of the customization do not outweigh the costs by a significant margin and the organization does not have the resources to support it, the organization would be wise to "stay vanilla." Remember that vendors sell form design tools allowing clients to pretty up screens without changing the underlying software code or data structure. Finally, the organization considering a customization should extensively test it in a different data area—that is, not in the production data area—aka PROD. Testing the customization should be coupled with testing programs *not* ostensibly affected. Sometimes changing one program or form leads to breaking another. Depending on the level of support purchased, the client may be on its own to fix an unintended consequence.

Cautionary Tales

During the 1990s and 2000s, many large organizations purchased and implemented some type of enterprise system, moving away from mainframes and homegrown applications. Many of these systems remain in some form today, even if they are old versions that have been greatly customized.

Organizations often understand the major benefits of customizing their new systems. Frequently, this is an unwillingness to change an existing business process. Unfortunately, they do not usually understand the drawbacks that these modifications present, as the following examples show.

I know of one large financial organization (Alpha) that customized its version of PeopleSoft 2.0 to such a great extent that it has essentially become stuck on it for the past 10 years, unable to upgrade to a more current version. In the late 1980s, Alpha purchased PeopleSoft but simultaneously felt that the vanilla application couldn't meet all its needs. In this sense, Alpha resembled the Lifeson case study in Chapter 11, "Setup Issues." Alpha got under the hood of PeopleSoft and significantly changed the application.

As the company formerly known as PeopleSoft[2] released future versions throughout the 1990s and beyond, Alpha never upgraded from version 2.0 for one simple reason: it would have lost all of its customizations. Even if a new CIO wanted to move Alpha to a more current version of the application, say PeopleSoft version 8.3 in 2006, she was out of luck: there is no

---

2. Oracle acquired PeopleSoft in 2005.

upgrade path from PeopleSoft 2.0 to 8.3. To move to version 8.3, Alpha would essentially have had to reimplement the application at considerable cost, losing its customizations in the process.

The following is another example of the perils of excessive customization. Aircraft parts manufacturer and repairer Hawker Pacific saw firsthand the perils of replicating its old business processes in its new system.

> In 2003, the aircraft parts manufacturer and repairer kicked off a project to replace 15-year-old back office technology systems, some based on Oracle financials software and some developed in-house.
>
> Hawker Pacific set a two-year deadline to introduce software developed by Swedish firm IFS World, but the project schedule and budget blew out as users demanded the new enterprise resource planning platform be heavily modified to have the same look and feel as the old system.
>
> The back and forth required to modify a range of processes caused the project to be three times over budget, and it took 4 1/2, rather than 2, years to deliver, according to Hawker Pacific CIO Graham Owen.[i]

> **NOTE**
>
> Organizations considering customizations should look carefully at their available options, ideally with the help of experienced business and technical consultants. It is imperative that they carefully consider the short- and long-term implications of these customizations, lest they be stuck with an unsustainable status quo and paint themselves into a corner.

Security Design

Security is a critical part of system design. It is quite typical for an organization to use a security matrix that details the rights, roles, and permissions assigned to each user upon logging in. This matrix typically comes in the form of a relatively simple Excel spreadsheet, representing the security setup in the new system.

When creating the initial security matrix, consultants usually start with a template from a previous assignment. It is generally unnecessary to start from scratch because, more than likely, another client's security matrix can serve as a useful starting point. To be sure, the matrix will need to be refined based on an organization's unique roles. However, it's unlikely that the head of AP will need to run payroll batch processing programs or the IT manager will need to pay vendors.

Specifically, the matrix outlines the following:

- The names of the different security roles or classes
- The specific reports and forms assigned to each security role or class
- The assignment of specific role(s) to each system end user
- Limitations assigned to each end user (for example, the head of HR can view information on all employees, but a "line" HR person can see data only on the people whom she supports)

An example of a simple security matrix is provided in Table 9.5.

TABLE 9.5 Sample Security Matrix

User	Job Title	Security Class/Role	Form(s) and Reports	Notes
Alex	Head of AP	AP super-user	All AP forms and general ledger setup forms	
Geddy	IT manager	Administrator	All	Should not be able to see payroll data
Neil	Payroll manager	Payroll	All payroll forms and reports	Should not be able to change employee data
Mike	Procurement analyst	Procurement admin	All procurement forms and reports	
Kayla	Payroll clerk	Payroll clerk	Time record entry	Can only enter payroll data; cannot run reports
Jordan	Benefits manager	Benefits admin	All benefit setup and reports	
Marlene	HR manager, Eastern Division	HR user sales	All HR-related forms and reports for the Eastern Division	Should be able to change employee data for Eastern employees
Selena	VP of HR	HR user read-only	All HR-related forms and reports for the entire company	Read-only access; should not be able to change employee data

Phase Objectives

The specific objectives of system design are as follows:

- To create an initial security matrix
- To establish the specific framework of the new system
- To continue the knowledge transfer started in AE
- To finalize and document the client's desired system configuration

How Long Should System Design Take?

If end users participate to the extent necessary during AE, system design should go relatively smoothly. AE and system design are critical phases that serve as the basis for successful testing. As a result, it is preferable for an implementation team to spend a little too much time designing the system—within reason—than too little time. Remember that system configuration errors should manifest themselves in the next phase—testing. Perfection is *not* required at this point. Additional codes and rules can be added as needed, and the team will certainly need to make some tweaks. However, at the completion of this phase, it is common for the SI to ask the client formally for sign-off on the system configuration.

Let's return to the recurring house analogy. After system design, the client has agreed to build a ranch. It may later decide on a different color of paint or to move the furniture. However, it realistically cannot, after testing, blow up the foundation and design a duplex, expecting to meet its go-live date and budget.

System Testing

Before delving too deeply into testing, consider the following definitions of the major types of testing:

- **Parallel testing.** End users test an entire process (for example, running a complete biweekly payroll or month-end general ledger closing) in an attempt to replicate the results of the current (or a previously closed) period in the legacy system
- **Stress testing.** End users "pound" the system to see if it can handle expected levels of network traffic; testing may include entire business processes, individual scenarios, and extensive report generation.
- **System integration testing (SIT).** End users test entire processes from soup to nuts, not merely specific scenarios.

- **Unit testing.** End users test specific scenarios, not entire business processes from soup to nuts.
- **User acceptance testing (UAT).**[3] End users attempt to enter individual transactions into the system by using scripts provided by consultants. Participants typically follow test scripts—essentially, comprehensive sets of directions designed to see if the system does what it is intended to do.

Although consultants may participate in testing to some extent, employees should drive the majority of testing. Doing so maximizes knowledge transfer and readies them for "real life" under the new system.

System testing is both a cause and an effect of implementation issues. On the "cause" side, end-users' lack of system knowledge may create issues, such as their inability to match invoices correctly. An incorrectly matched invoice, in turn, may cause general ledger balancing issues. On the "effect" side, poor setup decisions should come to light during the testing process. Consider the payroll manager who tries to report on hours paid and discovers that the current system configuration does not separate types of hours worked to her satisfaction. This will require changes and result in delays.

Phase Objectives

Regardless of the type or name of testing being conducted, the main objectives of system testing usually include the following:

- To discover any design, data, processing, or application issues
- To refine the system configuration as required
- To test any customizations and custom reports
- To continue the knowledge transfer process and make end users comfortable with their roles after the new system is activated
- To identify any resource issues that may occur in the future—for example, training needs or extra personnel
- To identify any business process issues that may occur in the future
- To refine the initial security matrix to reflect changes discovered or required by testing

How Long Should System Testing Take?

Relative to the other phases, the amount of time required to complete system testing is the hardest to quantify. The short answer is, "As long as is necessary." If the previous phases have been successful, testing should go *relatively* smoothly. This is rarely the case, however. Often, project delays stemming from the issues uncovered (or not uncovered) in previous phases significantly

---

3. UAT may also be called conference room pilot (CRP).

delay and complicate testing. Because of these issues, it is not uncommon for testing to take twice as long as initially anticipated.

System Activation/"Go-Live"

Assuming that the new system has been properly configured, tested, fixed, and approved by the necessary players, it is ready to be activated in a production environment. The organization's legacy system will no longer be its system of record. After a brief down period (typically called *cutover*), end users enter real-world transactions into the new system.

Phase Objectives

The main objectives of this system activation[4] are

- To activate the system
- To formally and permanently retire the legacy system

How Long Should System Activation Take?

This is typically the shortest —but most important—part of the project. If testing was successful in identifying all the issues, system activation should be a mere formality that can be safely accomplished over a weekend. As is often the case, however, system testing does not manifest all the issues—and the resolutions to some known issues are still pending. In such a case, activation may be a gut-wrenching process that takes twice as long as expected, endangering mission-critical items: everything from employee paychecks to financial reporting to company sales may hang in the balance.

Note that a legacy system may remain as a source of historical data within an organization after it activates its new system. For example, data conversion and extraction may not have provided the desired results, but the organization forged ahead and activated the new system anyway. On occasion, the legacy system may remain for years with one purpose: to view previous transactions and information.

Costanza Medical Case Study: A Flexible Client and a True Consulting Partner

Let's return to project planning for a moment. As discussed previously, project plans conceived at the start of an implementation change, often based on

---

4. For years, system activation was actually called execution. To the extent that the term *execution* conjured up images of someone being put to death, most SIs and software vendors now use the more palatable term *activation*.

issues discovered in AE and system design. The following case study illustrates the dynamic nature of project plans and the need for clients to listen to their consultants.

Background

Costanza Medical[5] was in the middle of an implementation of its new system with its partner, Van DeLay Consulting. Van DeLay judiciously gathered Costanza's business requirements before even bidding on the work and submitted a simple T&E bid. Working as a subcontractor for Van DeLay, I served as the *de facto* PM on the project.

From the get-go, I was impressed with senior management at Costanza because they seemed to be pragmatic. Costanza purchased the standard level of vendor support, covering basic software patches and access to the vendor's support site.

A Potential Showstopper

The implementation progressed reasonably well. End users and consultants began configuring the application after successful AE sessions. With respect to payroll, end users set up the pay codes in Table 9.6.

TABLE 9.6 Pay Codes at Costanza Medical

Pay Code	Description
REG	Regular pay
OT1	Overtime pay
HOL	Holiday pay
VAC	Vacation
FMLA	FMLA unpaid leave
BON	Employee Bonus

End users continued designing the system and began testing the phase. At this point, the implementation team discovered the following major issue:

Many nurses at Costanza are paid hourly. Consider Kramer, a registered nurse who makes $20 per hour. Out of the box, the payroll application calculates Kramer's rate of pay at $20 per hour. For overtime (time-and-a-half), the ERP correctly calculates the rate of pay at $30 per hour for all hours over 80 in a two-week period and all hours over 8 in a day. However, Costanza has overpaid its employees for years because its legacy system could not calculate overtime correctly.

---

5. I was getting tired of 70s rock references and decided to run with a *Seinfeld* motif.

Why not just let the new system calculate overtime correctly? Costanza management feared lawsuits and employee morale issues stemming from a perceived pay cut by a large group of employees. Costanza wanted to explore the merits of customizing the ERP's overtime calculation program such that it would pay employees in a manner consistent with the old way.

I reported the issue to senior management, knowing that this customization would not be a small endeavor. As an application expert, I knew that these kinds of customizations required much more than merely using the application's existing functionality to meet the client's business needs. A change in the software's code—specifically in this case, to its overtime calculation—is fundamentally different from adding pay codes to track types of employee pay not identified during either the vendor evaluation or system design.

I had created the project plan and knew that it contained neither the time nor the budget for a major system customization. In this case, the customization would have severely compromised Costanza's desired go-live date and, by extension, the project's budget. Still, the ultimate decision rested in the hands of Costanza management; I could only provide the issue's context and different options. I immediately met with the steering committee to discuss the issue. In the meeting, she pointed out the following:

- Tweaking software code may cause something else to break in the future.

- Customizations are risky moves rarely sanctioned by the vendor. Translation: Costanza's vendor support would not cover the customization.

- Upgrades and patches may well compromise or even reverse the customization in the future.

I advised Costanza management that it should proceed with the customization only if it possessed the internal resources to support it. Because it did not, Costanza would need to upgrade its vendor support agreement—at considerable cost—to cover customizations. Costanza management wanted to avoid these outcomes and asked me to provide alternatives. I presented the options in Table 9.7.

Costanza selected option 2, and the project remained on track. Within a day, I created and fully documented a custom process by which Costanza employees would extract payroll data from the system, run it through a custom Microsoft Access application, and import it back into the ERP with employee overtime already calculated. Costanza could circumvent running the system's overtime calculation altogether, without changing its business process or customizing the software's code.

TABLE 9.7 Gap Resolution Options at Costanza Medical

Option	Cost and Date Impacts	Change in Business Process
1. Proceed with the customization and revise the project's dates and budget accordingly.	High	None
2. Get creative, perhaps by exporting time records from the application, modifying them via a tool such as Microsoft Access, and importing them back into the system.	Low	None
3. Change the business process to conform to the ERP's delivered functionality.	Low	High

Outcomes and Lessons

In the words of American author and journalist Anna Quindlen, "A man who builds his own pedestal had better use strong cement." I knew that Costanza did not have the financial and internal means to successfully customize. I did not look at the customization as a means to extend the project; I remained committed to ensuring that Costanza met its date. I listed the options available to Costanza, detailing the pros and cons of each. I helped Costanza make the best decision for its business. Ultimately, Costanza went live on time and within its initial budget. Costanza now uses Van DeLay exclusively for consulting services and provides it with glowing references.

Summary

Much time and effort is spent from the early stages of a project (planning) until the end (system activation). In the middle are major objectives, deadlines, and often hundreds of individual tasks, any one of which may have a detrimental impact on the entire project. This chapter provided the objectives, timelines, and tasks required in each phase. Beyond implementation phases, the chapter analyzed the pros and cons of the different implementation strategies, from phased or partial implementations to full-blown ones.

With strategies and phases made clear, the next section will delve deeper, elaborating on the different roles and responsibilities during these phases.

Endnotes

i. http://www.australianit.news.com.au/story/0,24897,25878113-24169,00.html

Chapter 10

The Group Responsibility Matrix

The leader follows in front.

—*Spanish Proverb*

- A Guide, Not Gospel
- Communication
- Involvement, Collaboration, and Backup
- Potential Red Flags
- Clarifying Roles and Contract Language

Having described the phases of the system implementations, let's now turn to the individual roles within those phases. This short but important chapter emphasizes which resources are most involved at each stage of the project.

Table 10.1 shows the required levels of involvement by key players during each phase of a *typical* IT project.

TABLE 10.1 Simple Group Responsibility Matrix

| Person/Group | Phase | | | | |
	Project Planning	Application Exploration	System Design	System Testing	System Activation
Senior management	High	Low	Low	Low	High
Project manager(s)	High	Medium	Low	Low	High
Functional client resources	Medium/ Low	High	High	High	High
Technical client resources	Medium	Medium/ Low	Medium	High	High
Consultants[1]	Medium	High	High	High	High

Note that you can expand the group responsibility matrix (GRM) to include more than milestones. Although it should not resemble the project plan in terms of detail, including items such as end-user training and data validation only serves to increase clarity about which party is responsible for each task.

A Guide, Not Gospel

The GRM is a generic and high-level document, unlike a formal and detailed project plan consisting of many tasks and goals. Because all projects differ, they require different levels of participation at different points from different end users and groups. Reverting to Chapter 8, "Selecting Consultants," and Figure 8.1 specifically, a project that uses extensive external consultants will probably rely relatively less heavily on internal resources.

For each person or group in the GRM, daily or weekly involvement might vary at any given point. For example, a gap found during testing by the functional team between vanilla system functionality and a business process

---

1. Like many of these levels, the role of the consultant in project planning varies on the presence of a dedicated external project manager. An empowered project manager from a consulting firm should absolutely be involved from the get-go in the project, especially if the client has limited internal expertise or experience with projects of this scope.

may require the immediate intervention of senior management, as was the case in the Costanza case study discussed in the previous chapter.

Also note that not every person and group is included in Table 10.1. For example, clients typically purchase vendor support—discussed at length in Chapter 7, "Support for the New System"—at significant cost. Based on the types of issues found, clients may not need much vendor support during the implementation. Alternatively, clients may need extensive vendor support at critical points as software bugs are discovered. However, to the extent that mature software works relatively well out of the box, especially when configured and tested by seasoned consultants, true bugs are not common occurrences.

Communication

Senior management and project managers should communicate and emphasize the GRM to each person and group early and often. Organizations face many dangers if end users are not involved at critical points. In a similar vein, key individuals need to have the requisite time and knowledge at key points to make optimal contributions.

Consider a payroll manager, James, who works at LaBrie Industries. James does not participate in application exploration (AE) and has had virtually no input into the setup of the new payroll system. This is due to James's time constraints and poor project planning. James is too busy fighting fires with current payroll to be bothered about future payroll issues. As a result, he misses key opportunities to both learn the new system and contribute to its setup. The project manager fails to recognize the importance of this issue. Under the pressure of deadlines and lacking sufficient documentation on LaBrie's business processes, external consultants make critical assumptions about the required setup of the system. Two months later, in the middle of parallel testing, James finally has time to look at reports and test the system. James finds issues with the setup that require major rework and, potentially, some customizations to the ERP. The net result is that the project is delayed by six weeks.

Involvement, Collaboration, and Backup

Low participation does not mean zero participation in the GRM. For example, a dedicated project manager is probably not also a functional or technical expert in the new system. For example, she will not be the one deciding whether the client requires 10 benefit plans or 2. However, the project manager should certainly be aware of the outcomes of these decisions because of their effects upon upcoming phases and the overall system activation date.

Collaboration at all levels is imperative throughout the project. As previously discussed, system design is an extremely important phase. As such, it requires input from—and the approval of—senior leadership. It is tough to argue that the decision to spend hundreds of thousands of dollars (at a minimum) on the purchase and implementation of a new enterprise system should be made independent of senior management. Obviously, executives should ensure that their organizations make the best decisions by considering all available information.

The type of involvement is critical. Folks in corner offices should *not* mandate how to configure the system before consultants have even arrived onsite.

NOTE

A poor system setup can doom a project from the beginning. Unfortunately, sometimes executives make irreversible configuration decisions in a vacuum, not reaching out sufficiently to internal subject matter experts (SMEs) or external resources beforehand. Decisions of this importance need to be made in collaboration with both consultants and the end users who will have to live by these very decisions.

Organizations should also ensure that they have backup and contingency plans in the event of employee departures. Let's return to the LaBrie example. Kevin the IT manager has a scheduled two-week trip to Europe starting May 1. Management approved his trip at the beginning of the project. April arrives, and the project has been delayed six weeks because of setup changes mandated by testing. The project is off course, and stress testing, which Kevin needs to lead, now must begin on April 28, *not* on March 14 as originally planned. Kevin needs to know this as soon as possible so he can arrange for appropriate backup. Telling him on April 27 does not allow him ample time to make arrangements. Doing so will exacerbate project delays.

Potential Red Flags

The process of reviewing and approving the GRM allows organizations to *potentially* identify major red flags prior to beginning a project in earnest. For example, Collins Publishing intends to implement a new system with neither a full-time PM nor consultant from its partner, Thompson Consulting. Collins's management believes that it can complete the project almost exclusively on its own, with a Thompson consultant *occasionally* onsite every few weeks. This is the milestone approach discussed in Chapter 8. In a nutshell, Collins's management simply does not appreciate the gravity of the task confronting it.

By placing Collins's proposed resources in the GRM, Thompson should be able to easily illustrate to its client's head honchos that the project is not sufficiently staffed. As such, it has a low chance of success. The GRM should immediately manifest practical questions, including these:

- Who will oversee the work?

- Without a full-time functional consultant onsite, how can Collins's end users successfully learn the new system, much less participate in its configuration and testing?

- Given the fact that Collins's end users will be wearing two hats throughout the project, how can management realistically expect the project to meet its objectives and hit its dates?

Although Collins and Thompson may uncover the same staffing issues by creating a comprehensive project plan, the GRM is much simpler. Moreover, why even bother developing a 400-line project plan based on wholly insufficient resources?

Clarifying Roles and Contract Language

The GRM offers a benefit to organizations that bother to complete the exercise: delineating responsibilities with its system integrator (SI). Imagine the following scenario. Zappa Industries is in the middle of system testing when it hits a major snag. Zappa expects its partner—Reed Consulting—to validate the results of testing and provide end users with detailed analyses of financial, payroll, and inventory discrepancies. Reed's senior management did not believe that it was responsible for data validation and, as a result, did not staff the project or budget the hours for such an endeavor.

Reed and Zappa now find themselves squared against each other precisely when they need to be working together seamlessly. The dispute requires a few days or weeks to resolve. The following options are bandied about:

- Reed provides consultants at its own expense.
- Zappa provides resources at its own expense.
- Reed and Zappa share the expense of providing resources.
- Zappa contracts a third party to validate the data.

In any event, the consequences of this misunderstanding will result in delays, budget overruns, strained client-SI relations, or a combination of each.

Further, these outcomes could have been avoided if each party had the pre-science to read the contract and ask fundamental questions related to roles and responsibilities in advance. To the extent that project planning is more art than science, it is difficult to account for every conceivable contingency in a formal contract. Again, had the GRM contained data validation, the confusion and subsequent delays posed by this "whoops" moment would have been avoided.

Perhaps the main benefit of the GRM is that it prevents each party from having to constantly reference a legal document in times of uncertainty and conflict during a project. Constantly referring to the statement of work (SOW) is hardly conducive to the type of partnership required to implement enterprise systems in a timely and budget-conscious manner.

Summary

The GRM is a high-level representation of the project plan. Spending the time to develop it prior to formulating a detailed project plan pays off in spades. At a minimum, for the organization embarking on a major IT project, the GRM will manifest clear deficiencies with regard to resources and answer critical questions such as these:

- Who's responsible for each task?
- Do we have enough resources to do this by ourselves?
- What are the risks if we attempt to conduct this by ourselves?
- What are we missing?

The previous two chapters have outlined the implementation phases and the roles that team members are supposed to play. Looking ahead, the next several chapters will explain how plans go awry, poor decisions are made, issues are missed, tempers flare, fingers are pointed, and systems ultimately fail.

Issues are separated into the following categories:

- Setup
- Testing
- People
- Reporting and interface
- Documentation

Chapter 11

Setup Issues

> How does a project get to be a year late?
> One day at a time.
> —*Frederick P. Brooks*

- Portnoy Case Study: A Square Peg and a Round Hole
- Lifeson Case Study: Replicating the Old in the New
- Comparison of the Two Case Studies
- Death by Architecture

The intelligent configuration of a system is crucial to its overall success. For an IT project that relies heavily on external consultants, clients would do well to let consultants guide them through the process. This is not to say that consultants should march into an organization and force the wrong system configuration on clients. Organizational business practices may vary quite a bit from one client to another, even for those in the same industries. For example, hospitals may pay their nurses differently, although one would hope that all pay practices abide by relevant legislation.

Consultants should not merely take orders from clients. Rather, consultants should ask their clients questions about what they currently do and what they would like to do in the new system. Most of the time, a new system can handle each client business requirement with the right system configuration, processing, and error handling. A single customization to the new system is often not required. During application exploration (AE), consultants continue learning about their clients' business practices. At the same time, client end users should learn about the new application—with consultants leading the way. Team members should document and report to the project manager any and all gaps discovered between the system and a client's business needs. The ideal relationship between client and consultant is symbiotic: by working together extensively and effectively, they can create the right system configuration, setting the stage for successful testing and, ultimately, system activation.

Of course, this is not always the case. The two case studies in this chapter focus on poor design decisions that plagued two projects from the beginning. It is instructive to note that, in both cases, external consultants did not recommend each organization's system configuration. Executives made these decisions independent of the input from their application experts, hired allegedly for their expertise.

Portnoy Case Study: A Square Peg and a Round Hole

Let's turn to the next case study. Portnoy Health Care is a large, multisite health care organization. Portnoy wanted to integrate a number of new systems via interfaces into its already complex existing systems framework.

Portnoy is particularly instructive as a case study because its setup essentially guaranteed the failure of a new system from day one. Its executives demanded a complicated system configuration, approved long before the first consultant ever showed up onsite. Portnoy manifests a number of different challenges and issues that plague, to some extent, many new IT projects (such as knowledge transfer and data integrity). However, by and large, most of Portnoy's issues are atypical: rare is the organization these days that attempts to integrate a set of completely disparate systems. Most organizations aim for relative simplicity, transparency, and integration on new IT projects.

Although the focus of this case study is system configuration, Portnoy is also a prime example of the following:

- A system integrator (SI) not knowing the definition of "bad business"
- An organization believing that its business processes are unique and thus warrant a unique, complicated system setup
- An organization lacking the personnel to support the monster that it has chosen to create

Background

Portnoy Health Care consisted of 10 different hospitals. Over the course of a number of years, Portnoy acquired a number of individual hospitals without imposing strict system and data standards on these new acquisitions. As a result, each hospital maintained a great deal of autonomy vis-à-vis maintaining its own systems. What's more, some sites outsourced their payroll, and some ran payroll internally.

Rather than fully implement a unified system to meet its needs, Portnoy senior management decided to create a monster. It attempted to stitch together numerous disparate legacy systems via a third-party ETL[1] tool and keep them all in sync. The overall system—and related ETL tools   would allow for disparate rules at each hospital. Note that, in the long-term, Portnoy intended to eliminate its legacy systems.

Portnoy executives listened to proposals from different SIs expressing their desire for a unique setup because of its "unique business needs." Portnoy's fundamental question to potential partners was, "Can your firm stitch together these different systems and make them talk to each other?"[2] SIs should have responded not in the affirmative but with two questions of their own:

- Why does Portnoy need to do this?
- Does Portnoy have the internal resources and expertise to support what it wants to create?

---

1. ETL is a process by which data is extracted, transformed, and loaded into a data warehouse or database. ETL tools essentially move data from one system and load it into another. ETL tools allow for additional integration among disparate systems, essentially allowing systems to "talk" to each other.

2. I am reminded here of Warren Buffett's quote, "Never ask a barber if you need a haircut."

As discussed in Chapter 5, "The Sounds of Salesmen," during the sales cycle, the majority of salespeople at large SIs do not want to appear difficult and risk losing potential business. As a result, Portnoy faced little resistance when courting vendors. It found that most SIs didn't ask these kinds of questions, let alone emphasize their importance.

Lee Consulting ultimately won the business, largely because of its name recognition. (The actual names have been fictionalized.) During the sales cycle, Lee salespeople strongly emphasized that their company had the talent to build the amalgam of systems desired by Portnoy. Lee did not fully advise Portnoy of the many difficulties that it would face by undertaking such an endeavor. If it had, Lee may not have won the business.

Lee was a large consulting organization. Within it, the enterprise resource planning (ERP) group represented a small percentage of total company revenue. The salespeople at Lee saw a multimillion dollar carrot and opted to ignore the major risks associated with chasing it. Surely, Lee had overcome more formidable client challenges than the one posed by Portnoy. Note that it is likely that smaller boutique firms—such as the ones described in Chapter 8, "Selecting Consultants"—would have walked away from this deal upon learning about what Portnoy was determined to build.

Lee and Portnoy mapped out the specifics of the system architecture. In theory, the systems were supposed to look and work like this:

- **Interface 1.** Basic employee demographic, payroll, and benefit data are transmitted via an ETL tool from different client legacy payroll systems into an ERP.

- **Interface 2.** Benefit information is transmitted from the ERP to the third-party benefit application (TPBA).

- **Interface 3.** Data is transmitted from the TPBA to the ERP. In theory, this ensures that the information in both systems is in synch.

- **Interface 4.** Benefit elections are returned to the legacy payroll systems, thus ensuring that employee deductions are accurate and employees are covered under health, dental, and other plans.

Note that each interface was actually a group of interfaces. To load employee benefits from the legacy systems into the ERP, for example, each of the following types of information needed to be loaded separately: employee, employee dependent, employee benefit, and employee dependent benefit. What's more, one error would cascade through the chain. For example, if the system rejected an employee due to an invalid social security number, her benefits, dependents, and dependents' benefits would also kick out.

Portnoy management wanted to go live in October, coinciding with its annual process of enrolling employees in health and dental benefit plans for the following year—a process also known as open enrollment. Although the project began in January of that year, the convoluted configuration in Figure 11.1 immediately challenged the feasibility of that date. Any remotely intelligent IT professional could argue that the architecture of this new set of systems was not sound. Further, that same individual may ask why any rational organization would even attempt to do this.

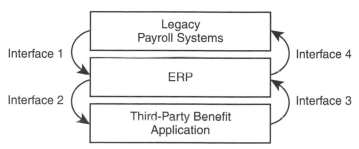

Figure 11.1 *Portnoy proposed system architecture.*

Implementation Issues

To be certain, many projects face last-minute, unexpected data issues and crises. A postmortem on such implementations can typically point to a few key points at which the project derailed. This project, on the other hand, had no viable chance of succeeding from the start; the system architecture virtually ensured that this project would never hit its financial and calendar objectives. Specific implementation problems included these:

- Each application (legacy systems, ERP, and TPBA) had its own business rules that, out of the box, did not mesh with other systems' business rules. All rules had to be created and maintained in external tables to interact with each other. These tables were technical in nature and, as such, were not available to functional users. Any change to the system would require IT involvement, thus making the system forever tied to IT for even the most basic of system edits.

- The ERP vendor had already released a relatively mature—and quite respectable—online benefit enrollment application. The application would have eliminated the need for Portnoy to continue using both the legacy systems as well as the TPBA. Although this Web app was certainly not "best of breed," using it would have simplified the project tremendously.

- The ERP did not conduct transactions; it simply housed transactions sent over via the first and third interfaces. In laymen's terms, the ERP just "got in the way."

- No one on the project team had ever worked with all of Portnoy's different systems, much less the ETL tool required to make these systems talk to each other.

- Portnoy's project manager's insistence on constant retesting magnified project delays.

- Integration issues aside, from a cost perspective, Portnoy had to pay license and support fees to each vendor.

As Table 11.1 demonstrates, Portnoy's system configuration led to nine categories of potential issues with this setup—three types of issues in each of three different systems.

TABLE 11.1 Types of Potential Issues During Portnoy Implementation

System	Setup	Data	Interface
Legacy Systems	×	×	×
ERP	×	×	×
TPBA	×	×	×

People Issues

The project lost momentum in early January, as Lee's sole functional ERP consultant, Bonnie, abruptly left the organization, leaving an enormous vacuum. Lee eventually filled the position five weeks later by bringing me in. Because Bonnie had not completed the ERP's setup before leaving, much of the interface development ceased during that period.

On the client side, issues abounded. Because the project was extremely technical in nature, most of the work required the sign-off of Portnoy's technical lead as well as the input of a few client-side functional end users who were, quite frankly, out of their element. Although they could appreciate the complexity of the different applications and interfaces, they did not have the skills to manage them independently once Lee's consultants were scheduled to leave. This situation fostered dependence on external consultants, making Portnoy's project manager justifiably weary. After all, how could the project be successful if it basically guaranteed that expensive consultants were required indefinitely? Also, what would happen if one of the consultants left? Consultant attrition is not exactly uncommon, as everyone saw back in January.

On the functional side, Portnoy also did not possess the necessary internal resources to address setup issues in the ERP. Remember that a benefit election from the TPBA had to pass through the ERP to make it all the way back to the individual payroll systems.

A perfect example of Portnoy's lack of internal expertise occurred when I moved on to another project. Despite my copious documentation and attempts at knowledge transfer to Portnoy personnel, interfaces failed because end users could not properly change codes within the ERP. A new or modified business rule could bring down the whole house of cards. Portnoy end users had to contact me to fix minor problems remotely. This was particularly scary given that the ERP passed so few types of data to and from the other systems via interfaces.

Beyond the core implementation team, the level of system expertise at Portnoy's local hospitals was wholly deficient. As a whole, these end users did not understand what was expected of them or, in fact, the point of the whole project. Most became frustrated and could not or would not follow test scripts, causing even more delays.

Tensions intensified throughout the project between employees from Portnoy and Lee. Testing revealed many errors stemming from the different and overlapping systems. From the perspective of Portnoy end users, their partner was one of the purported experts in the field. Portnoy, as an organization, was paying millions of dollars for this project to meet specific deadlines that were routinely not being met. Lee employees expressed frustration over their management's blind acceptance of Portnoy's complicated setup; the different systems and interfaces were *not* meant to work in the fashion that the client desired.

When Portnoy local personnel were summoned to corporate headquarters for integrated testing, additional people issues arose. Portnoy's employees resented being taken away from their day jobs. They had more pressing issues to address; they saw testing the new system as merely a distraction from their day jobs.

Finally, more problems stemmed from the presence of an internal auditor throughout the project. He would trust only reports that came from "the system." To the extent Portnoy was implementing three different systems, there was no one single standard report that could capture all the transactions sent up and down the chain. Although I created and ran such reports using Microsoft Access, the auditor chose not to trust them because they had the potential for human error. The auditor's questions about data integrity, however legitimate, served as a major bottleneck throughout the entire project.

Outcomes and Lessons

The project went live well after the initial date and well past the initial budget of $3.5M. Portnoy's project manager involuntarily left the organization well before system activation. Executives claimed that they did not know the extent to which the integration issues would prove problematic and wanted blood. Lee lost the Portnoy account and now has a less-than-stellar reputation in the ERP world. Portnoy brought in a new SI that essentially blew up the old configuration and recommended that the vanilla application be implemented at each hospital individually, with the legacy systems replaced altogether, not simply integrated into the rest of the systems.

Aside from a horribly conceived setup, Portnoy's disastrous system failure ultimately resulted from the inability of its senior management to enforce system or data standardization across the entire organization. End users at each hospital were used to having their own sandboxes; they were not accustomed to working and playing with other children. In the end, the executives who mandated this setup did not give the project a remote chance of being successful on any term.

CAUTION
Organizations cannot expect new systems to concurrently deliver the benefits of integration and decentralization. By definition, more of one means less of another. Decide in advance the acceptable trade-offs, and live by those decisions. Foolish is the organization that believes it can have its cake and eat it, too.

Portnoy can be rated on the failure scale as an Unmitigated Disaster.

Lifeson Case Study: Replicating the Old in the New

The following case study shows what happens when an organization rips out the guts of a new system to have it mimic its predecessor. It proves that nothing good can come from such an endeavor.

Background

With more than 50,000 employees across the globe, Lifeson is a large manufacturer that lacked a central repository of information on its employees. Simple questions such as, "How many employees work here?" took weeks to answer. By the time the number was calculated, it was doubtless incorrect. Also, relatively straightforward administrative processes, such as awarding employee bonuses and stock options, took nearly six months, thus crippling any attempt by the HR department to function as a truly strategic partner.

How could it? It was too tied up in basic administration and did not have meaningful employee data, much less the means to analyze it.

From a systems perspective, Lifeson was a mess. For years, management created disparate "band-aid" systems for specific purposes. The following facts put its internal systems architecture into context:

- Lifeson maintained more than 15 different homegrown HR and payroll applications.

- Even within the narrow area of employee compensation, data was widely dispersed. One system housed annual merit increases, whereas others contained bonuses and stock options. Foreign Service National and employee payroll data were stored in two completely disconnected systems.

- Many individual employees kept separate spreadsheets and stand-alone databases containing information on employee skills, training courses, and the like.

- Within the main legacy system, end users processed three out of every five HR and payroll transactions retroactively. Translation: Lifeson administrative personnel failed 60 percent of the time.

Reporting was less than ideal, as you can imagine. With so much data stored in so many different systems, most report requests were routed to IT. Also, as you would expect, end users often would have to submit report requests multiple times because the reports contained data that did not match their initial requests. Even when the IT folks got it right, the data was at best inconsistent and, at worst, it was incomplete and inaccurate.

In the late 1990s, Lifeson finally decided to implement a Tier 1 ERP, using a phased approach. At least Lifeson didn't attempt to do it all at once, which would have been a massive undertaking. Lifeson selected a boutique firm with both technical and functional expertise: Jordan Consultants.

Implementation Issues

The implementation started internationally. Lifeson wanted to activate domestic sites after other parts of the globe were already live. In retrospect, this approach allowed many of Lifeson's key domestic players—against the project from the get-go—to delay making important decisions and face the reality of the new system. Many of them hoped that the project would never gain traction internationally and the project would just go away.

A Campaign of Misinformation Leads to Successful Internal Sabotage

Through a campaign of misinformation, opponents of the new system were able, at least partially, to sabotage the project from the start. Rather than change business processes and retire systems that had well outlived their usefulness, Lifeson management had Jordan consultants dramatically customize the ERP, making it basically another system in the company's labyrinth. Jordan inserted additional code, screens, and batch jobs specifically to retrieve data from—and send data to—Lifeson's existing array of systems. The ERP would house certain data but would not actually create or alter it; it would simply be one big storage facility that would typically be out of synch with Lifeson's other systems. That's not exactly the best way to guarantee a positive return on investment (ROI)!

Aside from failing to deal with obstinate managers, Lifeson's top brass made a number of other critical errors in the planning phase of the project. Lifeson failed to create a central authority or committee within the company with the requisite "teeth" for holding the regions accountable to some type of data standard. For the most part, each region of the globe marched to the beat of its own drummer. This gave additional ammunition to those vehemently opposed to the new system. As they saw it, if things were already spiraling out of control internationally, why should Lifeson extend the project to the United States?

To say that everyone was "on board" with the new system at Lifeson could not have been further from the truth. A few heavy hitters saw the new ERP as a means to "blow up" the eye chart of internal systems that had evolved over the years. These people were few and far between; internal resistance to the project could not be understated. Specifically, two key directors at Lifeson, Dennis and Steve, fought tooth and nail to kill the project. The new system threatened their very existence at Lifeson. Many opponents were sacred cows under the status quo, rich with institutional knowledge on how the company's proprietary systems worked. In their eyes, the new system threatened their livelihoods.

At key meetings, Dennis and Steve routinely misrepresented the functionality of the ERP. For example, Dennis once claimed the new ERP could not update multiple salaries concurrently, unlike his system. Never mind the fact that he was flat-out wrong; the other executives in the room were hardly ERP super users and could not comment on the veracity of his claim. I happened to mention that the ERP could, in fact, perform this task quite easily. My protestations, lamentably, fell on deaf ears.

The amount of disinformation surrounding the system was astounding. In a different meeting, Steve openly expressed his anger over spending more than 3 million dollars "on a system that can't run a fucking report." He actually believed that a system that many other large, multinational organizations successfully ran could not provide basic information and that Lifeson's internal systems were vastly superior.

That the implementation was occurring in three regions concurrently—but not in the United States—posed its own set of problems. Jordan consultants were too geographically dispersed to alter the general direction of the project or any specific decisions, not that they had the power to do either. For Jordan, the Lifeson account was a huge win. Given the aforementioned obstinacy of folks like Dennis and Steve, the Jordan project manager treaded carefully around Lifeson, knowing full well that the company could pull the plug at any point and find more obedient consultants at a moment's notice.

When the implementation finally did turn to the United States, the project had a less-than-stellar reputation internally. Along with budgetary issues, Lifeson decided not to implement the ERP's core modules. Rather, in lieu of buying a new training system, executives made the unwise decision to implement the ERP's training module *without having core employee information in that very system*. This is analogous to having a branch of a tree without the trunk. The system would store some employee classes and certifications but would not store essential employee data such as job codes, departments, addresses, salaries, and key employment dates. Thus, a simple question such as, "Have all salespeople received product training?" could not be answered.

Outcomes and Lessons

After spending more than $5M, Lifeson eventually scrapped the system altogether and killed the project. Steve and Dennis won; the hodgepodge of internal systems, band-aids, and broken processes remained in place. A few years later, Steve and Dennis were shown the door, and Lifeson opted to implement a completely different ERP. As of this writing, that project is still ongoing after years of struggles.

Much like the Portnoy case study, Lifeson shows that systems initially meant to simplify processing can easily be corrupted by internal politics, executives with an agenda, and an organization's honest—but erroneous—belief that its business needs are fundamentally different from those of other organizations. This belief is almost always unfounded, but try telling that to a senior director who has never worked anywhere else and is five years removed from his pension. A project of this scope needs many things to be successful. First and foremost, however, senior leadership needs, in the words of the U.S. Marines, to "lead, follow, or get out of the way."

Attempting to re-create all the legacy system's functionality in the new system is almost always an enormous waste of time, money, and resources. Put simply, systems are different. Although basic outputs of two different systems may be fundamentally similar, the means to arrive at those outputs often vary by a considerable margin. Organizations that ignore this fact almost always shoot themselves in the foot.

Like Portnoy, Lifeson can be rated on the failure scale as an Unmitigated Disaster.

Comparison of the Two Case Studies

Table 11.2 illustrates the similarities between the organizations examined in the two previous case studies.

TABLE 11.2 Comparison of Portnoy and Lifeson Implementation Issues

Issue	Portnoy	Lifeson
Unsustainable setup	×	×
Excessive integration	×	×
Excessively customized ERP		×
Unnecessary maintenance of legacy systems	×	×
Phased approach	×	×
Failure to clean up and standardize data	×	×
Failure to standardize business practices	×	×

Both organizations attempted to integrate new systems into their spaghetti architectures—a term that I absolutely love. "A spaghetti architecture is one in which interapplication interactions are complex, numerous, and tightly coupled. This can result from bad planning and design either at the application or architecture level, or (more commonly) as an inevitable result of normal long-term incremental maintenance. Frequently such a situation is accepted by IT because "that's the way things are designed," "things work," and because it is perceived that there is no business value in rearchitecting. Unfortunately, in some cases, architecting can also be viewed as threatening by those staff responsible for maintaining the existing systems (whether IT owners or business sponsors)." [i]

What's more, both organizations were brownfield sites. End users were accustomed to doing things in a certain way. Rather than use the new system as a way to improve business processes and access to—and quality of—information, each organization erred on the side of excessive customizations. In each case, the organization would have been better served by changing business processes more than the systems and technologies purchased.

The majority of the problems associated with each implementation and, ultimately, system failure, can be traced directly back to management and setup issues. Executives at each organization believed that their business needs were unique and, as such, required a complicated and costly setup. This assumption is almost always a big mistake.

Death by Architecture

Mike Rosen, director of the Enterprise Architecture Practice at The Cutter Consortium, has called situations like these "death by architecture." Rosen writes that "perhaps nothing is more drawn out and aggravating for an IT organization than what I call 'death by architecture.' The story goes like this: the high priests and architects depart for the ivory tower and return some months or years later with 'the revealed truth,' in the form of 1,000 pages of architecture documents. In the meantime, new applications have been developed, requirements have changed, and the architecture is out of date on delivery. Other reasons may also contribute to its being DOA: it may be irrelevant to the development organization or might not have enough buy-in to be accepted. It may be hard to understand its value or how it achieves business goals, or dozens of other reasons."[ii]

Rosen rightly contends there are certainly absolutes with respect to system architectures. Even a moderately complex setup is bound to fail if the organization does not have sufficient human bandwidth to support it.

I know of one organization (call it Beta) that has extensively customized its ERP. Like other organizations, Beta calls its vendor when end users report a problem. *Unlike any other organization, however, Beta then usually tells the support specialists which line of code to change for future patches!*

How can Beta do this? The company employs 10 full-time IT employees supporting the application, in addition to its business end users. Obviously, Beta is fundamentally different from organizations with small IT staffs supporting a "vanilla" version of an enterprise system.

TIP
Although no organization should build an albatross, that which is "simple and easily maintained" to one may be unwieldy to another.

Summary

A poorly designed system has virtually no chance of succeeding in either the short term or the long term, as evinced by the Portnoy and Lifeson case studies. Excessive interfaces and creative system configurations may reflect the fundamental unwillingness of the organization to embrace the future. Perhaps they reflect the mistaken belief of senior management that their organizations and business needs are unique. Regardless of why, this is a recipe for failure.

The next chapter focuses on testing and will show that even a system configured in a straightforward and reasonable manner can run into formidable challenges.

Endnotes

i. http://www.ccpace.com/Resources/documents/Spaghetti_Architecture.pdf

ii. http://blog.cutter.com/2009/03/19/death-by-architecture/#comment-2825

Chapter 12

Testing Issues

> On two occasions I have been asked, "Pray, Mr. Babbage, if you put into the machine wrong figures, will the right answers come out?" I am not able rightly to comprehend the kind of confusion of ideas that could provoke such a question.
>
> —*Charles Babbage*

- Data Issues: Snakes in the Woodwork
- Security Issues
- Software Issues

> **NOTE**
>
> C-level executives might want to skim or skip this chapter, as the content is right from the trenches, and they are unlikely to be involved in such issues. This is not to say, however, that this chapter is not important. On the contrary, if minimized or overlooked, these testing issues can kill a project.

After an implementation team has designed the system, it moves on to the testing phase. The objectives here are to flush out any issues, to continue knowledge transfer, and to simulate real life for end users once the system is activated. Assuming that the application has been set up correctly (or at least in a manner that seems acceptable at first), testing the configuration should identify any issues with respect to data, security, and software.

Data Issues: Snakes in the Woodwork

Mr. Babbage's quote at the beginning of this chapter can be restated as garbage in, garbage out (GIGO). To be sure, enterprise systems have advanced to the point at which they can import data extracted from legacy systems. However, implementation teams typically understate the enormity of this task. Vendors often state that it's quite simple to load all sorts of data into their products. In practice, however, there are three main challenges involved in this process.

Getting at the Legacy Data

Often, a company's legacy data is difficult to retrieve from a "back-end" perspective. Older databases were not designed to facilitate data extraction. As a result, powerful and commonly used tools such as SQL[1] queries may not do the trick. The relational databases of today allow for the easy extraction of any and all data from SQL Server, Oracle, and the like. The same cannot always be said for 30-year old mainframes. The short answer to the question regarding the ease of data extraction is, "It depends."

Frequently, IT staff members or technical consultants can easily extract the data required to load into the new system. Getting at the data is only half the battle, however. Lest a client think that it is home free, it should carefully consider the format of that data. Is the data gobbledygook or is it in a usable

---

1. In his excellent book *SQL Fundamentals,* John Patrick defines SQL as "a computer language designed to get information from data that is stored in a relational database." SQL is relatively simple and powerful—both of which explain why it has been around for more than 35 years.

format? By usable format, everything does not need to be properly aligned or even remotely pretty. Whether comma-delimited, tab-delimited, or fixed-width, technical consultants and end users can convert data consistently formatted into a "conversion-friendly" format on a regular basis.

In any event, before an implementation team can even think about using vendor-supplied conversion programs to get legacy data into its new system, it needs to profoundly understand its data before testing commences. After all, true parallel tests should contain converted legacy data. Shortchanging this aspect significantly increases a project's risk of delays and budget issues.

An example will illustrate this point. The IT director at Montclair Bank, Neil, was able to parse weekly payroll data from its legacy system through a complex set of Microsoft Access-based routines. Using more than 60 individual steps, he was able to produce incredibly accurate results. Neil made those files available for the payroll end users to validate.

Montclair's resource constraints and the sheer number of conversion files made it likely that end users would miss many issues. Payroll end users validated a fair number of employees but, as expected, missed a major issue: employees at the bottom of a page of extracted data had hours totaled not just for themselves but for their entire departments. For example, an employee was converted into the new system with 500 hours worked for that week. As it turned out, Neil was able to easily fix this issue, but someone had to spot it first. Lamentably, Montclair end users did not discover this problem until the company was in the middle of going live with the new system. Obviously, this was a less-than-optimal time.

Readers resistant to new systems may claim one little victory. How good can a system be if it lets something like that happen? Those less technically savvy and new to conversion programs may be asking two questions:

- Why would a presumably superior application have no system edit against this field?
- Why is there no edit in the vendor's conversion program that would limit to 168 (or some other number) the number of hours that an employee can work in a week?

There are valid reasons for a lack of what may appear to be commonsense edits in many systems and, more specifically, conversion programs. For one, not every organization decides to load detail-level information; it's not uncommon for an organization to load summary historical information (quarterly or annual totals). In terms of the data being loaded, the number of hours in a "week" may be 500 because that week coincided with the end of a quarter. Remember, data conversion specialists use generic conversion programs, not something specifically written for their organizations and related business rules. If they attempt to load bad data, the conversion programs will not always kick out questionable values.

Clients should not lose faith in conversion programs. They have many edits that minimize the chance of bad data being loaded. Remember, many of these systems and their attendant conversion programs have been around for many years. They catch quite a few things, such as the following:

- Debits must equal credits for general ledger transactions.

- Employee checks with net pay not equal to gross pay minus employee deductions.

- An employee benefit cannot be added before the plan went into effect.

The bottom line is that vendor conversion programs cannot catch every conceivable type of data-oriented error. Although consultants can certainly provide tools, the onus is on client end users to validate the data.

Assessing the Quality of the Legacy Data

Let's say that IT has been able to extract, manipulate, and present to functional end users the data from the legacy system *en masse*. Let's also concede that the data extracted is perfect and that every field from the legacy system has been accurately captured. Marlene, the benefit manager, looks at employee benefit contribution amounts in a spreadsheet (shown in Table 12.1) and is baffled.

TABLE 12.1 Employee Deduction Amounts in Legacy System

Employee	Enroll Date	Benefit Plan Code	Coverage Option	Deduction Amount
123	1/1/2010	HEALTH1	Single	40
456	1/1/2010	HEALTH1	Single	40
789	1/1/2010	HEALTH1	Single	120

If the per-pay-period deduction for the health plan is $40 for single coverage, why is employee 789 having $120 deducted? IT tells Marlene that employee contributions were derived from the amount that employees most recently had deducted from their paychecks. Marlene looks at payroll history and zeros in on the true issue.

In the legacy system, Marlene finds that employee 789, Amy, took an unpaid leave of absence with her benefits continuing. Upon returning, Amy had the deduction taken out three times in the same pay period; she was paying the company back. Marlene goes back to IT and tells it to modify the conversion routine to ensure that employees enrolled in the same plan with the same coverage option should have the same amount deducted *for future paychecks.*

In the example in Table 12.1, the fix was relatively straightforward. Any decent technical resource can write a rule to set employee deduction equal to $40 if the coverage option is single. In this case, IT understands the issue and makes the requisite changes. Let's consider another, more complicated example.

A payroll clerk entered an employee's deduction incorrectly. Rather than attempt to correct this with one-time deductions, the clerk changed the amount of the deduction several times over a number of weeks to try to "make the employee whole." As a result, the deduction amounts stored in the legacy system are inconsistent.

After extracting the information, IT provides Marlene with the deduction history for this employee but cannot make this call. IT is not responsible for determining the employee's level of coverage and deduction amount; it can only assist functional end users in making these determinations. Table 12.2 presents the data for employee 678.

TABLE 12.2 Employee 678 Historical Deduction Amounts

Employee	Check Date	Deduction Code	Benefit Plan Code	Coverage Option	Deduction Amount
678	1/1/10	ABC	HEALTH1	Single	40
678	1/8/10	ABC	HEALTH1	Single	20
678	1/15/10	ABC	HEALTH1	Single	20
678	1/22/10	DEF	HEALTH2	Single	80
678	1/29/10	DEF	HEALTH2	Single	80
678	2/5/10	ABC	HEALTH1	Single	40

The obvious question is, "What should the employee's level of coverage and deduction amounts be?" Short of asking the employee, this can be a difficult question to answer. Because of the inconsistent data, the issue may take some time to resolve. Typically, these issues tend to be isolated but not unique. A 20,000-employee organization needs a considerable amount of data cleanup to load correct data into the new system.

Mapping the Legacy Data: Bridging Old to New

Data may well need to be mapped or translated from old values to new values. Typical names for these critical tables include translation ("XLAT") tables or crosswalks. A typical example might include the data in Table 12.3 for employee deductions.

TABLE 12.3 Tax Code Mapping Table

Company	Legacy Deduction Code	Description	New Deduction Code
100	1111	Federal Income Tax	T000
100	1112	Social Security—Employer	T001
100	1113	Social Security—Employer	T003

Table 12.3 indicates that employees who had federal income taxes taken by deduction code 1111 in the old system will now have the same taxes taken in the new system via deduction code T000. The new naming convention might facilitate grouping and reporting from the new system, because all taxes begin with the letter *T*.

Note that translation tables are not always required. In this example, the 1111 is absolutely a valid code in the new system; there is no technical requirement that new taxes start with the letter *T*. However, implementing a new system typically involves consultants who will bring along best practices, one of which may be smart-coding certain values like deduction codes, vendor groups, and the like.

Regardless of whether an organization decides to map its legacy data to new values, remember one thing: codes that are part of the index[2] of a particular table cannot easily be changed in the database. After going live, the payroll manager cannot decide that she wants the code to be another value, say T123. The description of the code "Federal Income Tax" can be changed because it is not part of the index. The short technical answer is that indexes—or fields within an individual index—often exist in multiple tables, often as part of the relationships to other tables. Imagine changing the foundation of a house: you cannot simply turn a colonial into a duplex. You would have to completely demolish the house, which would be no small task.

All data is not created equal. Critical fields of many systems include employee numbers, vendor numbers, the item master, and general ledger accounts. Client end users must agree upon these values—from a data-mapping perspective—as soon as possible, because they are prerequisites for setup, testing, conversions, and system activation.

---

2. Indexing fields in a database table offer a number of significant benefits. For one, indexes increase database performance. What's more, databases enforce referential integrity. A typical index might be an employee number. That way, an organization can employ 100 guys named Bruce Springsteen, but each would have a unique identifier. This is a very good thing.

Let's look at the example of Planet Appliances, an organization implementing a new Human Resource Information System (HRIS). Planet's implementation team mistakenly does not give much thought to the numbers that the new enterprise resource planning (ERP) will assign to employees. In the legacy system, employee numbers equaled their social security numbers. However, Planet initially activated its legacy system in 1984, long before the privacy concerns of HIPAA[3] carried the weight they do today.

Thus, the organization creates the crosswalk shown in Table 12.4.

TABLE 12.4 Simple Employee Number Mapping Table for Planet Appliances

Division	Old Employee Number	New Employee Number
100	123-45-789	1234
100	223-45-789	4567
100	333-45-789	7890

This is a straightforward approach. Planet will now assign employees an arbitrary but unique value that masks employees' social security numbers. Of course, Planet may have a hard time determining certain employees' real social security numbers. However, let's assume that end users can verify that information.

Already considerably delayed, Planet's implementation team discovers the following: not all pockets of the company used the same employee number conventions. As a result, there is no consistency, and the extracted data now looks like Table 12.5.

TABLE 12.5 Employee Number Mapping Table with Issue

Division	Department	Legacy Employee Number	Hire Date	New Employee Number
100	Admin	123-45-789	01/01/1999	1234
100	HR	223-45-789	1/11/1999	4567
100	Finance	333-45-789	1/21/1999	7890
100	Marketing	123-45-789	1/31/1999	1234
200	Marketing	7897	1/4/1998	7897
200	Marketing	333-45-789	1/14/1996	7890

---

3. The U.S. Congress passed the Health Insurance Portability and Accountability Act (HIPAA) in 1996 to protect the health insurance of displaced workers and to ensure the privacy of medical records.

Because of HIPAA, in 2006 the marketing department in Division 200 started entering employee numbers unrelated to their social security numbers. Although hardly an insurmountable technical challenge, discoveries like this concerning key fields can cause delays. What's more, they can cause key players to publicly—and loudly—question the accuracy of the basic data about to be converted into the new system. For projects to remain on track, influential opponents of the new system do not need additional fodder.

Let's look at another example of data mapping issues. King Motors is implementing an ERP throughout the organization. In preparing for the conversion, IT extracted data from its legacy system and revealed almost 50,000 job codes, many of which were unnecessary and ostensibly duplicates. Data for one job code is presented in Table 12.6.

TABLE 12.6 King Job Code Legacy Data

Company	Old Job Code	Legacy Job Title
100	S1111	Secretary
100	S1112	Administrative Assistant
100	S1113	Administrative Assistant
100	S1114	Administrative Assistant
100	S1115	Administrative Assistant 2
100	S11146	Administrative Assistant
100	S1115	Department Secretary
100	S1116	Secretary/Assistant

King has eight different job codes for what appears to be the same job. Obviously, King did not exactly have tight controls on which end users could add job codes. Many end users did not bother to look at existing values when entering a new employee or processing a transfer. What's more, the system allowed them to add as many codes as they liked.

To consolidate ostensibly duplicate job codes, most consultants use mapping tables such as the one displayed in Table 12.7.

Quite simply, the mapping table allows for the easy conversion of old values to new. The eight job codes from the legacy system become one (ADMIN1).[4]

---

4. Mapping tables or "translate" tables are quite common on new system implementations.

TABLE **12.7** King Job Code Mapping Table

Company	Old Job Code	Old Job Title	New Job Code	New Job Title
100	S1111	Secretary	ADMIN1	Administrative Assistant
100	S1112	Administrative Asst.	ADMIN1	Administrative Assistant
100	S1113	Administrative Assistant	ADMIN1	Administrative Assistant
100	S1114	Assistant	ADMIN1	Administrative Assistant
100	S1115	Administrative Assistant 2	ADMIN1	Administrative Assistant
100	S11146	Admin. Asst.	ADMIN1	Administrative Assistant
100	S1115	Department Secretary	ADMIN1	Administrative Assistant
100	S1116	Secretary/ Assistant	ADMIN1	Administrative Assistant

Here's where the human element muddies things, however. King's senior management argues ceaselessly about titles and job descriptions, not to mention the employees who may be recategorized. Elaine, the secretary in marketing, is about to be given the same title as Jerry, an assistant in HR. Elaine's manager, George, has a fundamental problem with that. (Yes, I am a big *Seinfeld* fan.) George knows of Elaine's work and believes that she adds more value to the organization than Jerry does. He's going to fight this reclassification tooth and nail.

Why does this matter? What are the reasons that a job code or title is important from a systems' perspective? In this example, the job code may drive government EEOC[5] reporting, wage analysis, and so on. Also, imagine King spending millions on a system and not being able to answer a simple question such as, "How many administrative assistants work here anyway?"

Now add the complexity of different countries, languages, and legal requirements. Is it even possible to have the same job title throughout King? ERPs typically have no practical limit on the number of codes that can be added, whether they are general ledger accounts, job codes, vendors, and so on.

---

5. The U.S. Equal Employment Opportunity Commission (EEOC) is a federal agency that fights discrimination against race, color, national origin, religion, sex, age, and disability in the workplace.

However, the following rule is typically a prudent one: set up as many codes as needed—no more, no fewer.

Even in the unlikely event that the extracted data is squeaky clean, King's implementation team must answer fundamental questions before the data can be loaded into the new system. For the examples mentioned previously, the questions include these:

- What are the values of the individual codes that will be set up in the new system?
- Can any codes be retired?
- Which new codes need to be created?
- Which unnecessary codes can be consolidated with other codes?

If all the legacy codes remain the same, no mapping needs to take place. This is never the case, however. Remember that no two systems are the same. Codes required for one system may well not be required for the other. Conversely, entirely new codes will be required. The mapping of old to new codes—and the defining of new codes—is imperative for conversion programs to work properly and completely.

To the extent that these codes are end-user driven, IT may ask functional resources to use applications such as Microsoft Access and to provide data maps or "translation tables." IT can then easily use them to convert legacy data into a format that the new system will accept.

Loading and Testing Legacy Data: The Inevitability of Errors

Many implementations stumble into issues related to loading data after it has been extracted, mapped, formatted, and represented in a format friendly to data conversion. Note that systems typically contain databases or other tools for advanced users that allow for the "cramming in" of data irrespective of the business rules. No respectable vendor will unilaterally recommend this approach, so this discussion will focus on mainstream data-loading methods.

Project managers, end users, and executives would do well to remember two things with regard to data conversion errors. First, to quote software guru James F. Cooper, "Systems are to be appreciated by their general effects, and not by particular exceptions." Translation: If a conversion program accurately loads 99 percent of its records, focusing on why 1 percent failed misses the point. Unfortunately, some end users—particularly those going through their first major system implementation—foolishly believe that they will not encounter any major data problems. They are misguided and naïve, at best.

Second, errors are actually helpful the majority of the time. They are essentially communicating information. In this instance, the value that the conversion program attempted to load did not mesh with the system's current configuration and rules. The data or rule needed to be fixed. End users should not want their new systems to blindly accept data that does not meet the business rules.

Going back to the earlier examples, let's assume that IT would not attempt a trial conversion until all end users had formally approved all the organization's pay codes, employee numbers, general ledger accounts, and so on. This is a crucial lapse in judgment that can significantly affect the timeline and budget of an implementation.

> **CAUTION**
>
> It is imperative that organizations "kick the tires" on conversion programs as soon as possible, even if all data values have not been finalized.

From earlier in this chapter, the IT director at Montclair Bank, Neil, understood this point and routinely updated his data cleansing routines. Each revision improved the accuracy of the legacy data about to be loaded, as well as the format the new system required. Thus, when Montclair's end users changed business rules or entered bad data into its legacy systems, Neil's routines—and the system's conversion programs—would isolate records with potential or actual errors. As a result, end users could focus on the root causes of the problem and not have to wade through hundreds of thousands of records in an attempt to find the problem records.

Conversion programs typically yield two types of errors:

- "Kick-outs" due to invalid data or business rule/data conflict
- Valid data accepted by the new system causing errors down the road

An example of the first type includes an invoice with a vendor number of "AAAA." Obviously, this is not a valid integer, and any conversion program will reject this value if the data type of the vendor number field is "number." Alternatively, consider a payroll history conversion program in which the system will not load a gross check for $1,000 with total deductions of $300 for a net check of $800. The math does not add up. These errors typically "spit out" in either a separate file or at the end of conversion program results, making it easier for them to be identified and ultimately fixed.

Errors of the second type are arguably more dangerous, because end users tend to uncover them during testing. Let's say that an organization loads employee payroll history, and the following basic equation holds for each employee payment:

Gross Pay – Total Deductions = Net Pay

End users evaluate the data and confirm that all payments have been successfully loaded. However, months after system activation, the payroll manager notices a problem. Specifically, employees are contributing to their 401(k) plans beyond the federally mandated limit. How could this be? The manager looks at an employee's deduction history and sees that payroll history was converted via one deduction code (H401), but the current employee contributions fall into a separate deduction code (401). During the setup, end users and consultants failed to notice that the two are not currently linked in the system, resulting in a significant number of employees contributing too much to the plan. What's worse, the company matches employee contributions.

Corrections in this scenario involve a number of methods. For one, on the payroll side, these employee deductions need to be given back. Also, the payroll manager must reverse the organization's matching contributions and modify general ledger history. Outside the payroll system, corrections may well have to be made with the third-party administrator (TPA) who manages the plan. Interfaces have sent out payroll information that needs to be fixed. If the data had been properly loaded, mapped, and tested, the new payroll system would have recognized the other deduction code and the entire problem would have been avoided.

Conversion programs may catch these types of errors. However, there simply is no conversion program in any system that can check every conceivable type of error. There are too many options and possibilities within the same organization, much less across a multitude of domestic or international organizations. The bottom line is that implementation teams need to test everything.

Manually Entering Legacy Data: The Final Option

Load programs have advanced quite a bit over the past 15 years. There are now more ways than ever to bring information into a new system without having to sit for hours at a keyboard. This is not to say, however, that all data can be loaded. Occasionally, the time spent reformatting data for the purposes of automatically loading it is much greater than the time required for end users to simply key it. End users must decide if the "squeeze is worth the juice."

The preceding examples illustrate two key points about systems and data:

- Different systems almost always represent data in different ways.
- The very process of converting data typically manifests significant data quality issues.

THE NINE CIRCLES OF DATA QUALITY HELL

In his popular and well-written blog "Obsessive-Compulsive Data Quality," Jim Harris writes about the nine major issues that organizations face with respect to data quality:

1. **Thinking data quality is an IT issue (or a business issue).** Data quality is not an IT issue. Data quality is also not a business issue. Data quality is everyone's issue. Successful data quality projects are driven by an executive management mandate for the business and IT to forge an ongoing and iterative collaboration throughout the entire project. The business usually owns the data and understands its meaning and use in the day-to-day operation of the enterprise and must partner with IT in defining the necessary data quality standards and processes.

2. **Waiting for poor data quality to affect you.** Data quality projects are often launched in the aftermath of an event when poor data quality negatively impacted decision-critical enterprise information. Some examples include a customer service nightmare, a regulatory compliance failure, or a financial reporting scandal. Whatever the triggering event, a common response is data quality suddenly becomes prioritized as a critical issue.

3. **Believing technology alone is the solution.** Although incredible advancements continue, technology alone cannot provide the solution. Data quality requires a holistic approach involving people, process, and technology. Your project can only be successful when people take on the challenge united by collaboration, guided by an effective methodology and, of course, implemented with amazing technology.

4. **Listening only to the expert.** An expert can be an invaluable member of the data quality project team. However, sometimes an expert can dominate the decision-making process. The expert's perspective needs to be combined with the diversity of the entire project team in order for success to be possible.

5. **Losing focus on the data.** The complexity of your data quality project can sometimes work against your best intentions. It is easy to get pulled into the mechanics of documenting the business requirements and functional specifications and then charging ahead with application development. Once the project achieves some momentum, it can take

---

on a life of its own and the focus becomes more and more about making progress against the tasks in the project plan, and less and less on the project's actual goal, which is to improve the quality of your data.

6. **Chasing perfection.** An obsessive-compulsive quest to find and fix every data quality problem is a laudable pursuit but ultimately a self-defeating cause. Data quality problems can be very insidious, and even the best data quality process will still produce exceptions. Although this is easy to accept in theory, it is notoriously difficult to accept in practice. Do not let the pursuit of perfection undermine your data quality project.

7. **Viewing your data quality assessment as a one-time event.** Your data quality project should begin with a data quality assessment to assist with aligning perception with reality and to get the project off to a good start by providing a clear direction and a working definition of success. However, the data quality assessment is not a one-time event that ends when development begins. You should perform iterative data quality assessments throughout the entire development life cycle.

8. **Forgetting about the people.** People, process, and technology. All three are necessary for success on your data quality project. However, I have found that the easiest one to forget about (and by far the most important of the three) is people.

9. **Assuming if you build it, data quality will come.** There are many important considerations when planning a data quality project. One of the most important is to realize that data quality problems cannot be permanently "fixed" by implementing a one-time "solution" that doesn't require ongoing improvements.[i]

Security Issues

The implementation team should extensively test the security matrix to determine that end users can do what they are supposed to do and see what they are supposed to see. The converse of this is equally important: end users should test to see that they cannot do what they are not supposed to do and cannot see what they are not supposed to see.

As issues related to security manifest themselves, the implementation team should address them and refine the security matrix. Issues may include the following (derived from Table 9.5):

- The payroll manager cannot access a key payroll report.
- A payroll clerk has read-only system access and cannot modify or enter new time records.

- A line HR manager discovers that she can actually view information about her colleagues in HR.

- Reports now required by Accounts Payable (AP) end users need to be added to their security roles.

Software Issues

During testing, a client might discover an issue not related to system configuration or data entry. The application may not be working as the client requires. Examples may include these:

- Employee taxes are not being taken from paychecks.

- Invoices are not matching.

- Employee life insurance is not being calculated correctly.

- A screen to which a user has access does not appear.

- A report "hangs" (that is, does not finish).

If researching the vendor's knowledge base proves fruitless, a consultant or client end user should open a case with vendor support. The vendor requires the following information to assist in resolving the issue:

- The specific version of the software that the client is running— for example, not just version 8, but version 8.1.1.1

- The software's operating system

- The version of the database, if necessary

- Detailed screen shots of the problem

- Additional screen shots related to system setup

- Other items, depending on the nature of the case

Under the typical level of support, the vendor will *not* help with items such as a customized program or screen, the writing of a custom report, or basic setup. Basic support only covers true "bugs"—that is, instances in which the application is not doing what the documentation clearly states that it will do.

Advice for Logging a Call to Support

Vendors employ product specialists to assist clients in resolving issues. These experts can resolve an issue much quicker when end users provide them with as much information as possible. For example, logging a ticket described as "benefit plan does not work" is not very descriptive. Rather, the description should detail the specific issue—for example, "employee 401(k) contribution is not permitted." Further, the ticket should contain as much backup documentation as possible.

Also, end users should demonstrate to support specialists that they have done their homework. To that end, they should provide the steps that they have already taken to resolve the issue—for example, verified that an employee is eligible to participate in the 401(k) plan, the plan start date is valid, and so on. Aside from eliminating futile options and saving time, such information shows the specialist that the end user is knowledgeable and cannot be dismissed with a facile explanation of the issue.

The Challenge of Replication

One of the most frustrating things that end users experience is an inability to replicate a problem. For vendor support to diagnose the issue effectively and find or create a potential solution, the support representative has to see the issue in action, typically in real time. To this end, the support representative may do the following:

- Try to replicate the problem independently on its own test area
- "Dial in" to a client's network to view the problem firsthand

Intermittent issues are the hardest for the vendor to spot and ultimately fix. End users encountering issues should take as many screen shots as possible to expedite the resolution of a problem.

Summary

As the great Woody Allen once said, "Eighty percent of success is showing up." The parallel for systems is that a properly designed application stands a much greater chance of withstanding the rigors of testing and the challenges of an implementation. "Creative designs," to be polite, increase the odds of encountering problems before, during, and after an implementation. The organization that wants to reinvent the wheel had better have enough bandwidth, documentation, and backup for when the brakes fail.

Endnotes

i. http://www.ocdqblog.com/home/the-nine-circles-of-data-quality-hell.html

Chapter 13

People Issues, Roles, and Responsibilities

> So much of what we call management consists
> in making it difficult for people to work.
> —*Peter Drucker*

- Project Managers
- External Consultants
- My Simple View of the World: Four Types of End Users
- Client Responsibilities
- Sufficient Human Capital
- Training
- Elton Case Study: The Stubborn Client
- The Practice Mentality

Implementation issues are not confined to the data and system realms. On the contrary, many of the problems encountered during a typical implementation stem from people, the roles they are required to play, political issues, and comfort zones.

Returning to the group responsibility matrix in Table 10.1, it is time to explore the main implementation roles in greater detail. This chapter focuses on the responsibilities of the following throughout the implementation:

- Project managers
- External consultants
- Client end users

Project Managers

Although all project managers steer the ship, the best ones rely heavily on their crew members. To continue with the metaphor, a project may be the equivalent of smooth sailing at the beginning. Everyone wants the same thing: a successful implementation under budget and on schedule.

Project managers should not focus on life at 30,000 feet. Although they should *not* micromanage and unnecessarily involve themselves in many of the day-to-day issues, project managers who focus exclusively on high-level objectives are remiss. Rather, project managers need to do the following throughout the project:

- Listen to consultants when they bring issues to light
- Proactively approach consultants to ensure that individual objectives are on track
- Broach issues and their impacts to senior management as needed

Let's look at an example of an issue on a project that requires action by the project manager, Tony. During the testing phase of an implementation, consultants discover that the integrity of a client's employee hire date (typically critical for HR and payroll systems) is suspect. The hire date drives items such as employee benefit eligibility, deductions, and vacation and sick time accrual rates. Until the date issue is resolved, the team cannot complete a key testing requirement: the employee data conversion.

Let's be clear about Tony's role here. He is *not* a Human Resource Information Systems (HRIS) expert and cannot be expected to know the impact of something as ostensibly trivial as employee hire date. What's more, it is not his responsibility to ask about each field on the conversion program. As will be discussed later, functional consultants must address these types of issues with Tony. He then must communicate this issue—and the potential solutions proposed by the team—to senior management as soon as possible. If he does not, it may result in further delays.

How does the project manager recognize such risks and determine what to do about them? Good project managers do not need to know answers to these questions much of the time. Rather, the best project managers solicit and rely upon consultants' expertise. After all, they are the subject matter experts (SMEs) in their respective fields. In so doing, project managers minimize project risk. The project manager is not, in all likelihood, a general ledger expert or a procurement guru. It is incumbent on project managers to rely on the people who are.

Is a Consultant Project Manager Truly Necessary?

On almost all projects, clients look for ways to minimize costs. They might question the need for a full-time consultant project manager. This is often a mistake. As a general rule, the need for a full-time external project manager is a direct function of the following:

- The size and scope of the project
- The number and expertise of the client's internal resources

At one extreme, a 50,000-person organization hires an external system integrator (SI) to implement a full enterprise resource planning (ERP), from soup to nuts. The SI brings 10 full-time functional and technical consultants because its client lacks internal expertise with the new system. As such, the client would be foolish *not* to employ a full-time project manager from the SI. Too much coordination exists among the different areas not to have someone with a global view. At the other extreme, a small 2,000-person hospital hires one consultant to implement a new module within its existing ERP. It probably can make do without a devoted project manager. In fact, the onsite consultant can often serve as the *de facto* project manager. In reality, most projects fall somewhere between these two extremes, making the presence of a full-time project manager a murkier matter.

Multiple Project Managers

On particularly large implementations, such as the one detailed in the upcoming Petrucci case study, it is not uncommon for a client project manager and consultant project manager to comanage the project. In this scenario, the client project manager is probably implementing the system for the first time. Perhaps the client project manager has managed a fairly large project or two before at the organization, but never one of this scope. After all, organizations tend to implement major enterprise systems only once.

As previously discussed, ERP implementations are expensive, highly visible projects in any organization. With items such as employee self-service, the new system may well touch each employee. Client project managers often stake much of their internal political capital and reputations on the success of these projects. As such, they may be reluctant to concede major points of contention. In their view, the vendor promised its organizations certain functionality prior to the beginning of the project. Come hell or high water, the organizations will have it.

This is a key point. Client project managers have to answer to senior management if projects exceed approved budgets, miss key deadlines, and do not deliver key functionality. As a result, they have a tendency to push both implementation team members and external consultants, often to their breaking points.

Unlike their client counterparts, the SI's project manager is rarely a first-timer. Ideally, she is a seasoned expert, having managed multiple implementations of the system before. More than expertise or a project management professional (PMP) certification, the consultant project manager must be willing to lay down the law. She must challenge the client project manager whose demands, timelines, and enhancement requests are unreasonable and will put the entire project at risk. During the course of a project, the level of alignment between the consultant and client project manager may diminish for good reason: the consultant project manager also has to "manage" the client project manager.

Problem Project Managers

Project managers play a key role in new system implementations, especially for large organizations with many moving parts.[1] Ideally, dedicated project managers act as a buffer between senior management, consultants, and client end users in the trenches. An experienced, qualified project manager is essential to the success of the large project for both the client and the consulting firm. The ideal project manager knows when to escalate an issue, when to call a meeting, and, just as important, when to let the implementation

---

1. On a smaller project, such as an upgrade or the introduction of new functionality, the lead consultant may serve as a *de facto* project manager. In this case, the same types of issues will usually not manifest themselves for one simple reason: the person charged with managing the project is almost always the same as the one actually doing most of the required tasks.

team work. The following six types of project managers should be avoided if at all possible:

- The yes-man
- The micromanager
- The procrastinator
- The know-it-all
- The Pollyanna
- The pessimist

The Yes-Man

Certain project managers fear conflict and agree to every demand that client end users or senior management make. These project managers may have a sales background and, as a result, are used to saying "yes." They typically mean well and certainly do not intentionally try to sabotage projects. Often, yes-men simply want their clients to be satisfied and provide future references. However, by failing to confront those with wildly different expectations, yes-men implicitly make promises and commitments that endanger entire projects.

The Micromanager

Much like yes-men, micromanagers mean well and merely want to understand each step in a process or the nature of a complex issue. However, on a project, the project manager is *not* supposed to be the product or application expert. During a project's crunch time, consultants often cannot explain each facet of a complex issue to anyone, much less an application newbie, regardless of benevolent intentions. Micromanagers need to let experienced consultants do their jobs. Depending on the timing, a project manager may have to live with a high-level explanation of an issue. Should the micromanager need more detail, he should bring consultants to steering committee meetings or have them write status reports providing the requisite level of detail.

On most projects, project managers convene many meetings. Although project and team communication is important, project managers need to let consultants breathe—that is, get the actual work done. No consultant can be effective if she spends most of her time briefing her project manager on the status of each issue. Project managers need to minimize the number of status meetings, especially as a project reaches critical points.

The Procrastinator

Project managers who routinely fail to deliver cause organizations to miss project deadlines. Procrastinators put consultants in the untenable position of having to defend the indefensible in front of clients. Speaking from personal experience, it's a no-win situation for the consultant having to deal with issues caused by procrastinators to a justifiably angry client. The procrastinator often ducks clients and does not deliver promised results, such as a project plan, documentation, and status updates. In such a case, clients are likely to lose faith in the SI and its individual consultants, whether the latter are contributing to the delays or not.

The Know-It-All

No project manager or consultant can know everything about an application. Some project managers have graduated from the ranks of application or technical consultants and might have the ability to answer questions about some system-related issues. Although being able to speak intelligently about issues is hardly a liability, project managers who do not engage their teams at key points do a number of inimical things. For one, these project managers can alienate their consulting teams and make client end users less likely to broach issues with them in the future. Second, by routinely not involving the experts, know-it-alls effectively minimize the contribution of those consultants, possibly causing clients to question the need for those consultants in the first place. Unless the consultant was specifically hired in a hybrid role of consultant/project manager, that individual should routinely involve the implementation team throughout the project.

The Pollyanna

Some project managers new to projects of this scope are ecstatic when the project makes any progress at all. Pollyannas tend to take a "glass is 10 percent full" approach to project management. Rather than realistically assess—and deal with—a project suffering from delays and budget overruns, Pollyannas focus on trying to make everyone feel good. In this sense, they are like yes-men. Project managers need to be able to call a spade a spade and not worry about sugarcoating dire situations. Part of being a project manager entails making tough decisions.

The Pessimist

The pessimist is the antithesis of the Pollyanna, failing to appreciate the gains that a team and its individuals have made in the face of considerable obstacles. Pessimists routinely overemphasize what still needs to be done—as opposed to what has been done.

Make no mistake here. Many projects can use healthy doses of skepticism and realism. However, both consultants and end users tend to put in long hours, especially during critical times. Few things anger a team more than unalloyed negativity from a project manager not burning the midnight oil. Project managers who constantly criticize a team for that which it has not accomplished (as opposed to celebrating a significant milestone) are likely to irritate their colleagues.

To summarize this section, the best project managers know when to use each tool in their kits. Sometimes they need to play the role of good cop, bad cop, shrink, confidant, and devil's advocate. Other times, they'll need to stroke the egos of key people or use project manager techniques to move the project forward.

External Consultants

Consultants should play an absolutely essential role in the typical implementation of a new system from day one until they leave. A point made earlier bears repeating:

> For an IT project to be successful, consultants must be able to immediately challenge potentially questionable client decisions that could have a substantial impact on the project.

A few examples will help illustrate this point. First, consider an organization that wants to utilize a complex general ledger configuration. This setup would require an enormous amount of customization of the system and, in the process, obviate the possibility of using a great deal of system functionality and a number of standard reports. The general ledger setup, for example, would mean that the "canned" P&L statement would not accurately break out expenses and revenue in a remotely accurate manner. Of course, the client does not know this; the CFO simply wants to replicate the old general ledger in the new system.

Second, consider Amy, a payroll manager who wants to change the default method of how the new system calculates employee local taxes. She just does not trust the functionality of the new system to correctly assign employee taxes. As a result, she wants to manually assign all federal, state, and local taxes to employees. She knows that the new system can technically support this process without modifications, and her management supports her decision.

The best consultants are the ones who, after listening to the business needs in each of the following cases, advise clients of the resultant problems if they proceed.

In the first example, the cumbersome general ledger setup means the following:

- The normal P&L statement won't work.
- The organization will either have to create a new P&L or modify the standard one.

In the second example, Amy is clearly unaware of the amount of work involved in manually enabling and disabling taxes when employees work in different states, change residences, and the like.

Remiss is the consultant who is afraid of conflict, even with client management. Again, the time, place, and tone of the disagreement are important to ensure buy-in, avoid personal rivalries, and ensure a productive, long-term relationship. The consultant's ultimate objective should not be to be right, although that might be the outcome. Rather, the consultant should make all attempts to ensure that the client is making the best decision to utilize the new system as efficiently as possible given the business needs, level of IT/end-user support, and so on.

This last point is critical: the consultant can only make the client aware of the work involved and the consequences of her decisions. If client management has budgeted the time and resources for suboptimal decisions, the consultant has truly done all that she can do. In the previous example, the CFO who will pay a Crystal developer to create a custom P&L report is well within her rights to do so. Also, if Amy has a dedicated and knowledgeable staff devoted to getting taxes right, her organization can absolutely manage taxes manually. Having made the point, the consultant should alert the project manager and then move on, whether she agrees with the decision or not.

Aside from exercising "freedom of speech," consultants need to do the following throughout an implementation:

- Transfer knowledge to clients
- Make themselves expendable
- Listen to client issues and broach them as needed to project managers, team members, and senior management

Although sometimes needing to work in isolation, consultants have an obligation to transfer knowledge to end users on a routine basis. Certainly, there will be times that a consultant is swamped with resolving a complicated issue requiring complete concentration. As a result, he cannot walk an end user through that issue's resolution at that particular moment. However, as a general rule, consultants should find the time to explain setup, processing, and error resolution techniques to clients in a timely manner.

Only by transferring knowledge can consultants make themselves expendable. Consultants do not transfer knowledge simply by fixing problems and providing answers. Clients can learn a great deal by observing the methods by which consultants resolve different issues. Testing will manifest issues, and end users will benefit from seeing how the new system created an error in, for example, a purchase order or an employee paycheck.

On any given issue, consultants may need to research a problem; no one knows all the answers. Rather, the best consultants know which questions to ask and how to answer them. To this end, consultants should freely share newsgroups, end-user documentation, application tips, and other "clubs in the bag" with the aim of making end users self-sufficient.

The type of knowledge transferred depends on the type of consultant as well as the type of client end user. For example, consider a consultant proficient in Crystal Reports as well as the financial suite of an ERP. He can extract and present the information in just about any fashion. As he works with IT and functional end users, he shows them tricks on how to write efficient reports. However, when working with the less-technical head of accounts payable, he tables his Crystal knowledge and demonstrates how to set up a vendor and pay an invoice.

Finally, consultants must report issues not only on a routine basis but also as situations warrant. Aside from reporting issues to the project manager, consultants should assess their impacts and propose solutions. The flip side to being left alone by the project manager is the implicit assumption that consultants will keep them in the loop. At first, consultants should keep issues at a high level for project managers because they are not application experts.

My Simple View of the World: Four Types of End Users

Before discussing clients' responsibilities throughout an implementation, it is instructive to break clients into the four categories into which they typically fall (regardless of job title and specific role in an implementation):

- Willing and able
- Willing but not able
- Able but not willing
- Neither willing nor able

Note that this book does not put consultants through the same "willing and able" ringer as client end users. *We consultants should be both!* If not, it's time to get new ones.[2]

Willing and Able (WAA)

At the risk of simplifying, certain people are much better than others in terms of configuring, learning, and testing new systems. Some people enjoy the challenges and complexities of new systems much more than others. Willing and ables (WAAs) view the new system as an opportunity to enhance their skill sets and embrace a new technology. WAAs quickly assimilate new information, make logical jumps, and ask pointed questions, thinking about the implications of the answers. I wish that everyone was as enthusiastic as these valuable resources! From a consultant's perspective, it is simply a joy to work with these people.

Close to the pure technology enthusiasts, some may not love learning new systems but recognize the reality of their situations: their organizations have made the decision to implement a new system, and they have to get on board. These individuals are realists and do what is necessary for the project to be successful.

From a project management perspective, WAAs do not need a kick in the pants. They tend not only to accomplish their tasks ahead of schedule but to identify potential issues missed by others. I once had the pleasure of working with a finance manager at a small hospital in the northeastern United States. For this project, I led the upgrade and implementation of the Lawson Absence Management application for her organization. Her job did not require her to be directly involved in the project. Despite this, she attended application training, participated in design sessions as much as her schedule would allow, and broached real and potential issues.

Now, let's move down the ease-of-use ladder.

Willing but Not Able (WBNA)

Not for lack of trying or desire, willing but not ables (WBNAs) very much want to learn the new system. They can grasp simple and moderately complex system concepts but do not appreciate every consequence of their

---

2. This is a far cry from implying that consultants should know everything. That's impossible. Consultants invariably have their areas of expertise and will occasionally have to look up answers to questions to which they do not know the answer. For example, an end user expecting a SAP procurement expert to also know everything about SAP's payroll product is in for a rude awakening. However, that SAP procurement consultant should know that particular application inside and out.

actions and inactions. In testing, they may become confused and panic, sending e-mails or making calls to others in a frenzied attempt to help. However noble their intentions, they can cause more harm than good, particularly when working with the able but not willing and neither willing nor able groups described later in this chapter.

WBNAs can certainly graduate to the WAA group, but they require time, training, and experience. If they possess the desire and have the bandwidth, they may very well make that jump.

I once worked with an HR manager and created a custom reporting tool for him. I documented the tool extensively and showed him repeatedly how it worked. He was able to follow my direction at a high level but was not able to maintain it independently. He certainly tried to keep up, but his technical skills were a bit lacking.

WBNAs attempt to meet their objectives on a project plan and quickly ask for help if they need it. To this end, it is also a pleasure to work with them. They attempt to learn as they go; they know that consultants will not be onsite forever, and the clock is ticking.

Able but Not Willing (ABNW)

Working with able but not willings (ABNWs) can be exceedingly frustrating for everyone on the project. ABNWs have the requisite skills to be vital contributors to implementations if they would only get with the program. ABNWs typically have an axe to grind. Perhaps they are not happy with their roles on the team or are offended that senior management did not involve them in the system selection process. ABNWs are intelligent and, if turned around, can be a true asset on a project. If left unchecked, however, they use every opportunity to say "I told you so" upon the discovery of an issue. Many times, the ultimate objective of the ABNW is to delay or sabotage the project. When they interact with WBNAs, ABNWs can be absolute poison, attempting to "turn them to the dark side" every step of the way.

ABNWs actively blame consultants for a task not being completed or a project delayed. For consultants pressured to meet deadlines, it is usually difficult to work with ABNWs in a constructive manner.

Neither Willing Nor Able (NWNA)

Like the ABNWs, neither willing nor ables (NWNAs) tend to view new systems as too complicated compared to legacy systems. NWNAs may be close to retirement and do not want to devote the required time to learning a new system. Many NWNAs fear new technology and, unless retirement is imminent, may also fear that the new system will threaten their jobs.

NWNAs may claim to be on board with the new system but simply too busy to do the tasks required for a project. Truth be told, the typical NWNA repeatedly finds excuses not to learn the new system. Like ABNWs, when issues arise, NWNAs may also assign blame to consultants. Many times NWNAs don't want to be bothered with issues and want the new system to just go away. As a result of their actions and attitudes, it can be frustrating to work with NWNAs. In a sense, NWNAs are less dangerous than ABNWs because NWNAs do not possess the same level of system knowledge, a limitation that may decrease their credibility with others on the implementation team.

Client Responsibilities

End-user responsibilities hinge on a number of factors, including these:

- Specific role (for example, functional versus technical)
- Systems aptitude
- Availability

An end-user's specific role in an implementation is typically a function of a number of things, including his current role in the organization, future role, availability, and individual capabilities. A few examples will clarify this.

Consider Ted, the finance director at Frobisher, Inc. In his current role, he is responsible for setting up and maintaining accounts, running Frobisher's P&L report, and investigating and resolving general ledger–related errors in the legacy system. After Frobisher activates its new system, Ted's role will largely be unchanged. Thus, Frobisher needs Ted to play a key role in configuring the new system's general ledger. Ted should be familiar with all general ledger accounts, subaccounts, and so on; they will no doubt affect financial reporting. If he does not have the technical aptitude or time to devote to this project, he needs to alert his management immediately. If the external financial consultant, Gary, is having difficulty making time with Ted, Gary needs to broach this subject with his project manager. After training and application exploration (AE), if Ted does not possess the systems aptitude to participate in design discussions and ultimately sign off on the general ledger setup in the new system, Gary needs to make that known.

Now consider Gwen, Frobisher's payroll manager. In her current role, Gwen runs payroll but has made it clear that she is going to retire at the end of the year. In this case, Frobisher has hired Ellen to run payroll for the new system when it goes live. Ellen's sole job is learning the new system, setting it up, and testing it. Thus, Gwen's lack of participation in the project is not a major issue.

Sufficient Human Capital

Organizations often spend hundreds of thousands of dollars or more on a new system, entranced by vendors' slick PowerPoint presentations and demos. Yet, those same organizations many times do not take the requisite steps to ensure that the project can meet its objectives. Specifically, many organizations have the unfortunate tendency to do the following:

- Fail to provide timely training to key end users
- Tolerate end users with an axe to grind regarding the new system
- Provide inadequate resources during an implementation

These shortcomings may stem from senior management buying into "the myth of easy implementation" created by the vendor or the SI. Unfortunately, many organizations do not know what they do not know. Although vendors and SIs often contribute to system failures, clients often play a considerable part. Often, problem employees bear much of the responsibility for many project issues and delays.

Clients with foresight understand the need to hire employees with previous experience in the new system early in the process. A company implementing Lawson Financials, for example, would do well to hire employees who have experience with it already. Note that this will not apply if the organization contracts an independent software vendor (ISV) to build a new system from scratch.

Aside from skill sets, however, client end users need to maintain a positive outlook during the implementation. End users should not let implementation or testing issues discourage them from getting the most out of the new system. Usually, system functionality is not a binary; systems have *levels* of functionality. Features can be enabled at different points. If a module or significant feature of a system does not make the cut for Phase I because of delays, budgets, or lack of successful testing, the organization should revisit it in Phase II.

Project managers and senior managers need to have serious discussions with disruptive end users early on. NWNAs are simply cancers on these projects. Carping from a disgruntled employee is the last thing that an end user enthusiastic to learn the new system needs to hear. NWNAs can do a tremendous amount of damage during a project, causing delays in testing, morale problems, and the like. If these end users are not going to help make the new system successful, they need to find either a different role in the organization or a different organization altogether.

This is not to say that a healthy skepticism isn't warranted, especially during the sales cycle when vendor promises might seem—and often are—mile-high.

Although end users should insist on accurate setup, data, and testing results during the project, outright negativity and, in extreme cases, sabotage can only hinder a project and, ultimately, cause it to fail.

I am reminded of a certain client experience. I worked for a few months at a hospital running Lawson and became friendly with its HR manager, Pilar. She initially had a less-than-stellar opinion of the system. Working with her, I was able to show Pilar ways that Lawson could be used to extract and track many types of information—things that she had never known. After a few months, I met Pilar's boss, the VP of HR. Right after meeting me, she remarked, "Lawson isn't very good software." I realized then how Pilar came to dislike Lawson: it's hard to like a system if your manager does not exactly share your viewpoint and you have never seen what it can do.

Finally, on a much more positive note, even if key processes remain the same in the new system, end users would be wise to let go of the old mindset. They should actively look for ways to improve both their jobs and business processes through the new system. Change might be tough at first because the new system, in all likelihood, does work exactly like the old one. What's more, some of the vendor's lofty promises may fail to materialize. The new system probably has some significant benefits for end users who give it a chance.

Dealing with Problem Clients

If only every end user were willing and able, consultants would have much easier jobs. More projects would be under budget and ahead of schedule. Alas, this is almost never the case. Management typically has three major means to redress destructive employee behavior:

- Carrots
- Sticks
- Outright removal

Carrots

After understanding the nature of the problem employee's issue(s), management should list the benefits to getting on board. They typically include the following:

- The project will provide the employee with an opportunity to learn an exciting new technology.

- The project will provide the employee with an opportunity to be more strategic because the new system will decrease your administrative burden.

- The skills obtained will make that employee more marketable, both internally and externally (should the employee decide to look elsewhere in the future).

- If the increased workload and stress are the source of the employee's poor attitude or behavior, either a flexible work arrangement (to the extent possible) or bonus might be appropriate.

Sticks

Of course, the carrot does not always do the trick. Some end users resist new systems as part of their *raison d'être*. Typical "sticks" include the following:

- Using the usual management techniques, including verbal and written warnings

- Indicating that other employees on the project embracing the new system are increasing their stock within the organization

Outright Removal

To quote from one of my favorite movies, *Cool Hand Luke*: "Some men, you just can't reach." Depending on the phase of the implementation, it may be best to simply cut the cord with a problem employee, particularly early in a project and if that employee plays a key role. Although a replacement will have a learning curve, a positive attitude may more than offset the lack of institutional or system knowledge.

Training

Organizations are wise to hire or place employees with previous system experience into key roles. However, organizations are not going to completely replace their entire AP, purchasing, HR, and payroll staffs. To this end, it behooves organizations to train their existing end users properly. This training allows end users to maximize their contributions to the project. The properly trained end user is simply better equipped for configuring, testing, diagnosing, and ultimately using the new system.

Although the preceding statement may seem obvious, not every organization properly trains its employees on new systems. As is the case in the Wilson Retail case study in Chapter 18, "Mid-Implementation Corrective Mechanisms," some organizations still believe in "trial by fire" and rely exclusively on on-the-job (OTJ) training.

Types of Classes: Public Versus Private

Organizations have two choices for formal training: public and private classes. Public classes typically take place at vendors' offices or at vendor-approved locations. These classes cost in the neighborhood of $500 per day per student. Many organizations in different stages of an implementation send end users to public classes to learn how their systems work in a generic sense. For example, a payroll manager should not go to a public class intent on learning how to set up and process payroll at *her* company, although she should walk away with more than a few ideas from the class. Because payroll personnel from other organizations attend public courses, the instructor will discuss the payroll application in general terms.

For public classes, clients travel to vendor sites, sometimes incurring significant travel costs. To the extent that client end users are out of the office, they should be able to focus exclusively on the class and the applications being taught. From a technical perspective, vendors should have sufficient computer terminals and training data areas. Clients need no IT involvement to attend a public class, nor do they need to bring laptops.

Private classes are very different from public ones, both in terms of costs and content. For one, it's not uncommon for a vendor to charge upward of $3,000 or more per day for a customized class at the client's site. Vendors know that employees will not have to incur travel costs. As for content, instructors will typically customize agendas specifically for each client. In a private payroll class, for example, the payroll manager can ask many specific questions related to her company's payroll setup and processing.

In fact, it may be less expensive for clients to host private classes in which trainers come to them. However, understand that end users during private classes are in the office. Crises or emergencies can take them away from the class, reducing overall learning. Also, from a technical perspective, the trainer is not going to bring laptops configured with the software and training data areas. The degree of IT involvement is much greater for a private class than for a public class. The organization that brings in an instructor at $3,000 per day should ensure well before its trainer's arrival that its hardware and software are up to snuff. Nothing inhibits a class and frustrates all concerned more than "buggy" software and the lack of a proper training data area. The last thing that a client's management wants from a private class is a disaffected end-user base.

Purpose

Regardless of the type of instruction, training should be a positive experience for all involved. End users need to soak in the new application, ask practical processing and setup questions, and fully participate. Above all, it is critical for end users to pay attention and absorb information. As someone who has taught dozens of classes to hundreds of students, all too often end users use classroom time as an excuse to surf the Web, make personal phone calls, or deal with issues related to their day jobs. The result from these distractions is that end users may be unprepared for AE, system design, and testing.

Timing

Although most organizations recognize the importance and need for end-user training, less consensus exists on when training should take place. Truth be told, there is typically not a single best time. At one extreme, training can certainly occur too early. End users who attend classes six months before projects begin are unlikely to remember very much from those classes. By the same token, end users should not attend training in the middle of testing. End users' first exposure to a system should not occur during a parallel test that needs to be completed in two days.

> **NOTE**
> Generally speaking, functional end users should take courses immediately before AE, because that phase reinforces the material covered in class. Technical users need to attend training prior to that because their jobs mandate that they create data areas, set up security, and perform other essential tasks.

Specific Classes

Many times, the audience for each course is fairly obvious. The IT manager should know how to create data areas. The benefits manager should know how to set up benefit plans and enroll employees. However, remember that a new system presents new challenges as well as new opportunities. To this end, end users should not necessarily be pigeonholed. For example, Julie is a bright, willing, and able HR specialist who has expressed a desire to learn Crystal Reports. To the extent that the organization is going to require a number of custom reports, it should send Julie to a three-day Crystal course.

After all, why have all reports written by expensive consultants who, after the implementation finishes, will walk out the door? Perhaps Julie can write some of them.

Elton Case Study: The Stubborn Client

This case study involves a midsized, single-site health care organization, Elton Hospital, implementing a new enterprise system. The project took almost twice as long as anticipated primarily because of the reluctance of key end users to learn the new system.

Background

Founded more than 20 years ago, Elton Hospital employs about 3,500 full-time associates. Elton utilized an antiquated HR and payroll system. As a result, processes such as annually enrolling employees in benefit plans were manual and fraught with errors. Elton payroll was split between its legacy system and Automatic Data Processing (ADP), resulting in key information being scattered among many sources. What's more, staff maintained many separate spreadsheets and physical files. In 2002, Elton management decided to enter the twenty-first century and implement a new ERP.

Management had the right idea in mind with regard to setup and resources: it chose to blow away its legacy system—unlike the management in the Portnoy and Lifeson case studies. Management staffed the project appropriately, proposed a reasonable timeline, and hired a boutique SI with expertise in the application, particularly in the health care industry.

Implementation Challenges and a Largely Unwilling Staff

Team members were trained on the new system soon after the decision was made to purchase it. Management spent tens of thousands of dollars ensuring that employees had the exposure necessary to make intelligent setup decisions. After training, however, end users focused almost exclusively on their daily responsibilities (that typically involved their legacy system). The momentum created by training largely dissipated, along with much of the knowledge gained.

Elton management chose a full-blown implementation with only one consultant, Charles, who worked onsite four days per week with all functional areas.

However, Charles could do only so many things at once. He could not concurrently train end users, act as *de facto* project manager, test the system, and force Elton end users to make setup decisions. As a result, Elton routinely missed key deadlines.

This is not a slight on Charles, because he could only do so much. End users found excuses to skip testing and incessantly argued about policy decisions. After more than a year of sputtering, Elton brought on an additional resource, me, to assist with the project.

Soon after starting, I created data validation tools and custom reports to expedite the resolution of issues. Elton management stubbornly would not give me access to live data, citing security concerns. Undeterred, I labored on and automated the validation tools to the extent possible. I presented end users with reports displaying the accuracy of testing results, setup decisions, and data entry. I also spent a great deal of time creating an automated report distribution tool.

Many Elton end users continued to resist going live, claiming not to be comfortable with the system setup and requesting additional time. Both Charlie and I expressed frustration at the inertia. Aside from the consultants, Elton's payroll manager, Georgina, was exasperated. Issues that affected payroll during testing stemmed from other (read: nonpayroll) end-users' lack of system knowledge.

Outcomes and Lessons

In 2004, after more than two years of implementing its new system, Elton management decided that enough was enough. It could not continue to keep consultants around at a cost of more than $10,000 per week and decided on an imminent go-live date. Elton activated its system with relatively few issues, although few end users ultimately took advantage of the new system's increased functionality.[3]

The project was initially slated for one year but took more than twice that, with related budget consequences. Elton management chose not to use my report distribution tool because of alleged security concerns, opting instead to print hundreds of reports each week and physically mail them. *No one ever opened someone else's intraoffice mail envelope, right?*

Elton can be rated on the failure scale as a Big Failure.

---

3. Sadly, this is not uncommon. Many end users ignore many systems' advanced functionality. This becomes a vicious cycle in which new employees are hired and shown how to do things without being taught properly. Bad practices are solidified within an organization.

The Practice Mentality

The Elton case study epitomizes a problem that I call "The Practice Mentality." Fans of the ESPN show *SportsCenter* will no doubt remember Philadelphia 76ers' guard Allen Iverson's infamous "Practice" rant. Say what you will about "AI" or "The Answer," but it's a fascinating video to watch. Unfortunately, many people on IT projects follow the lead of "The Answer." Applied to new technologies and systems, I have worked with many over the years who simply don't take testing seriously, or at least seriously enough. To them, it's just "practice."

I have found over the years that "the practice mentality" is more prevalent than you would expect. Specifically, end users on IT projects often and perilously

- Lack a sense of urgency
- Pretend that tomorrow will never come
- Assume that others will bail them out
- Ignore warning signs

Lacking a Sense of Urgency

Many end users do not realize that implementing a new technology is analogous to building a house. You can't decide after you have added the roof that the ranch now needs to be a colonial. Consultants like me need to have clarity on major design decisions as soon as possible. At a certain point, an ostensibly minor change can cause major problems, delays, and budget overruns.

Clients should make major decisions as quickly as possible and hold decision makers accountable for them. When facing a considerable bottleneck, stopping the project altogether might be a drastic step but will certainly drive the point home.

Pretending That Tomorrow Will Never Come

This one baffles me the most. I'll admit that, say, one year out, a new system or application might be difficult for many people to conceptualize. But three weeks?

I'll never understand how people can be remotely comfortable not knowing how essential features, reports, and the like work when they will be responsible for them in one month's time.

Consultants should escalate potential end-user commitment issues before they become potential showstoppers.

Assuming That Others Will Bail Them Out

At some point, organizations have to cut the cord with consultants. We're too expensive to keep around forever. During IT projects, we often save the day, finding a creative solution to an unexpected bump in the road. Lamentably, this often breeds a sort of codependence on the part of client end users. Yeah, I'll say it: consultants can be like drugs, and I'm talking about the addictive kinds.

During the later stages of testing, management should encourage consultants to be hands-off, at least to the extent possible. Dry runs will help assess end users' ability to fend for themselves. If current internal staff cannot handle the new demands of their jobs, think seriously about replacing them.

Ignoring Warning Signs

Many projects invariably reach their points of no return. Legitimate concerns raised by rabble-rousers like me often go unnoticed. The organization has to make its date, come hell or high water. If end users don't know how to do their jobs, how is ignoring this fact going to make it go away?

> **TIP**
> Don't be afraid to move a date if key areas of the business are not ready for a new technology. The pain now will probably be inconsequential compared to the pain later.

Summary

Even perfectly planned projects can easily go by the wayside with difficult or inadequately skilled team members. Knowledgeable end users with axes to grind can derail projects from the beginning, especially if not admonished. Staffing a project with willing and able end users dramatically increases the chances of a successful implementation.

Chapter 14

Reports and Interfaces

> This report, by its very length, defends
> itself against the risk of being read.
> —*Winston Churchill*

- Reporting Challenges
- Entity Relationship Diagrams
- Interface Issues

> **NOTE**
> Much like Chapter 12, "Testing Issues," C-level executives might want to skim or skip this chapter. I don't meet too many people in corner offices who ask questions such as, "Does this report require an outer or inner join?"

Functional end users are typically familiar with reports and interfaces emanating from their legacy systems. I have met payroll managers who have been looking at the same payroll register or "positive pay" files for 20 years. This chapter details the specific interface and reporting challenges facing organizations implementing new systems.

Reporting Challenges

Organizations that purchase or rent systems will find at their disposal many standard reports within each application. For instance, Lawson contains hundreds of standard reports for benefits, HR, payroll, general ledger, inventory control, and so on. What's more, Lawson is hardly alone in this regard. Even Tier 3 and 4 applications provide many standard reports. I actually use Mind Your Own Business (MYOB) to run my company, a small application containing more than 150 reports for sales, accounts receivable, payroll, accounts payable, and inventory.

The fundamental reporting challenge for an organization implementing a new system is that some standard reports may not, for a variety of reasons, meet all of its needs. End users often require many custom reports but lack the time and resources required to create them. Specific reporting issues and their causes can be broken down into the following categories:

- Traditional organizational roles
- Different systems represent data in different ways
- Time constraints
- The functional-technical disconnect
- Insufficient, incomplete, or inaccurate reporting specifications
- Overreliance on custom reports
- Inefficient reports

Traditional Organizational Roles

Mainframe-based systems did not exactly enable the creation of custom reports. In many IT departments, only one or two end users historically pulled information from legacy systems to fulfill end users' reporting requests. Typically, functional end users submitted formal report requests to IT. A few days later, they received responses related to the feasibility of the report requests. Perhaps the information was attainable, perhaps not. Often, IT had some difficultly retrieving that information. After IT created rough drafts of the report, end users volleyed back and forth with different versions. Often, much was lost in translation, and final reports took weeks to generate.

NOTE

As a result of these historical roles, many functional end users are not comfortable writing reports. This is unfortunate because new systems are poles apart from their predecessors in terms of reporting ease.

You need not be a "coder" or "techie" to create powerful reports from a new system. IT no longer has to be the gatekeeper for custom reports. In this sense, enterprise resource plannings (ERPs) and their ilk are democratizing forces: End users can easily obtain information via standard and custom reports without the involvement of IT. Although vendors make many lofty claims, this one is unequivocally true.

Many end users do not believe that they have the time, skills, and experience to write even simple listings, much less more complicated reports. In many organizations, report writing still tends to be seen as an IT function. The forthcoming Wilson case study in Chapter 15, "Documentation Issues," is a perfect example of end users whose old-school view of reporting did *not* change during or after the activation of a new system.

Different Systems Represent Data in Different Ways

Another reporting challenge stems from the fact that old and new systems tend to store similar data in different ways. Let's look at the fictitious data in Table 14.1 from a legacy system's employee deduction table.

TABLE 14.1 Records in Simple Legacy Deduction Table

	Deduction Codes			
Employee	ABC	DEF	XYZ	Total
123	40	20		60
124	40		10	50
125	40			40

Employee data is stored in summary format. From a reporting point of view, deduction totals can be pulled quite simply; no calculations are required. Table 14.2 looks at the way in which identical data is likely to be stored in a contemporary system with transactional tables.

TABLE 14.2 Records in New System's Transactional Deduction Table

Employee	Check Date	Deduction Code	Deduction Amount
123	1/1/2008	ABC	40
123	1/1/2008	DEF	20
124	1/1/2008	XYZ	10
125	1/8/2008	ABC	40
126	1/8/2008	DEF	40
127	1/8/2008	XYZ	20
128	1/8/2008	ABC	10

Although this example may not seem that significant, the implications for reporting are enormous on a number of fronts. First, the number of records is much greater in the new system relative to the old. Second, Table 14.2 requires summaries to be derived; there is no Total ABC field or Total Deduction field.

Typically, standard reports offer different summary options, requiring no additional work for the client. What's more, in the event that these standard reports do not meet clients' needs, reporting applications such as Crystal Reports, Business Objects, Microsoft Access, and Cognos Impromptu can do much more than calculate simple totals and sort results. Using any one of these tools, end users can easily calculate totals, among other things. The important point is that, by default, the data is not stored in the same manner to which end users have become accustomed.

It's a fallacy to blame all reporting delays exclusively on data differences—that is, one system stores data "better" than another. There is a much more fundamental problem: people. Specifically, end users are typically too busy to devote the necessary time to custom reports, both in terms of learning reporting tools and providing proper specifications to report writers. Many end users merely expect developers to write these reports without their input or provide them with insufficient reporting specifications.[1]

---

1. This is an example of the old-school view of IT.

Time Constraints

Freddie is a payroll manager who runs a biweekly payroll for 3,000 employees. Beyond this, he has to deal with adjustments, quarter-end, year-end, W-2 processing, and other emergencies. During the implementation of a new system, he casually looks at the new system's payroll register. In doing so, however, he neglects to notice that it lacks a key piece of information, rendering the new register inadequate. Only during testing does he realize this, thus creating more work for developers.

Alternatively, perhaps Freddie requires a report that needs to be run only at the end of a quarter. Developers build this report based on quarterly tables in the ERP, because they contain only a fraction of the records found in the weekly or transactional tables. In terms of performance, there's no comparison between tables that have X records and tables that have 5X records. However, upon further review, Freddie changes his mind. Now the report needs to be run on demand—that is, not always at the end of the quarter. The developers have to junk the original report and start from scratch.

This last example brings to light a major issue with regard to reporting.

The Functional-Technical Disconnect

During most implementations, client end users are, by definition, functional. The AP clerk goes about her job, for example, by entering vendor and invoice data into the system. She may very well not know—or care to know —the specific fields and tables that she is updating.

Now let's turn to Newman, the typical report developer. Unlike his functional counterparts, Newman does not enter data into the system or even know how the applications work. He only wants to know the fields and tables required by the end user to build each custom report. Equipped with this knowledge, Newman can then do his job. This begs the question: is the report truly required? Most report developers do not know if the new system contains a standard report that will meet an end user's needs. How would they even know? First, they are not functional. Second, they are often just as unfamiliar with the new system as the end user asking the question. What to do?

Ideally, consultants would be able to step in and tell end users when a custom report is truly required and when it is not. Unfortunately, much like clients, consultants tend to be either functional or technical; rare is the consultant skilled in both. As a result, many times organizations spend money and resources creating unnecessary custom reports when standard ones will suffice. Also problematic is the creation of inefficient reports that join[2] unnecessary tables—that is, linking table A to table B to table C when it's more efficient to go simply from A to C.

Insufficient, Incomplete, or Inaccurate Reporting Specifications

Nothing frustrates a conscientious developer more than unclear or incomplete specifications. Presented with a vague reporting request, such a developer will have more questions than answers. For example, a benefit manager might want a report of all employees' enrollments in its 401(k) plan. Simple enough, right? The experienced developer would respectfully disagree and respond with such questions as the following:

- Because employees can change contribution percentages or cease to participate in the 401(k) plan, does the report need to list *all* benefit enrollments or only *current* employee enrollments?

- What other fields are required for the report? (Name, social security number, and so on)

- How should the information be grouped and sorted? By department? Employment status type?

- What (if any) subtotals are required? Employee counts?

The list could continue, but the general point is this: the better the specifications that end users provide, the faster and more accurately the developer can write the custom report. I use a questionnaire or specification template for each required report with the following questions:

- What is the report title? Description?

- What are the name(s) and role(s) of the person(s) who need the report?

- In which format(s) do the reports need to be seen? Spreadsheet? PDF? Text file? Other?

- How often does this report need to be run?

- Does this report need to be archived? When? Where?

- Are there any similar system reports to your knowledge? What are they?

- Does this report need to be scheduled to run, or does it need to be run in real time?

- How does this report need to be summarized? Grouped? Sorted?

- Does the recipient of this report have data or security restrictions?

---

2. SQL JOIN statements allow end users to retrieve data from multiple tables. There are different types of JOINs for different purposes. Suffice it to say, many complex reports and queries (and often some simple ones) require JOINs to pull data from different tables.

Although it's often a challenge, I try to have clients answer each question before I even start writing a custom report.

Overreliance on Custom Reports

Some end users are so accustomed to seeing data in a certain way that they insist that new reports present the data in a manner identical to legacy reports. This is a problem: no two systems represent data in the same manner.

A standard report missing a key field might have to be created for the sole purpose of including that field. Consider the following reporting examples:

- A vendor's standard accounts receivable aging report that does not list a key date on each invoice. That omission renders the canned report useless.

- A report calculates employee tenure based on hire date, but the organization needs that calculation based on the anniversary date. Expect this to be rewritten.

Although the earlier examples clearly required custom reports, reporting can quickly become cumbersome and time consuming during a project. Overly fussy end users sometimes focus on minutiae, mandating that new reports *exactly* match their legacy equivalents. This tends to frustrate IT, especially when those same end users show no initiative to learn how to create reports for themselves.

Inefficient Reports

The performance of a report may be suboptimal even when written correctly—that is, it returns the right data in the right order and is summarized correctly.

For example, a payroll manager requires a custom report that lists employee pay period, month-to-date (MTD), quarter-to-date (QTD), and year-to-date (YTD) deductions. The manager submits a detailed spec to IT, and a developer is assigned to write the report. The report ultimately takes more than four hours to run because the requisite table (listing all employee deductions by paycheck) is added four times: once for pay period totals, once for MTD totals, once for QTD totals, and once for YTD totals.

To be sure, waiting four hours for a report to finish is not entirely unprecedented. Complicated reports with multiple joins on very large transactional tables may result in a long processing time. In this example, however, using a tool such as Crystal Reports, the same report can be written with a single instance of that table, significantly reducing the time needed for the report to finish.

One last note: systems in the same tier often have similar types of tables. For example, Tier 1 applications such as Oracle, SAP, and PeopleSoft tend to store data in very similar transactional and summary tables. However, the names of these tables and fields are typically different, as are the relationships among each system's related tables.

Managing End-User Expectations

Change management and scope creep are other important considerations with respect to custom reporting. I like to use the 80/20 rule. Let's say that a standard report from the new system is 80 percent similar to the equivalent report from the previous system. If this is the case, is it absolutely essential for a custom report to be created? Alternatively, can end users live with the difference? These answers may depend on the importance of the report, its audience, and other factors.

An organization should adopt a general rule of using the new system's standard reports. If possible, clients should limit the number of required custom reports, especially during initial implementations. Exceptions to this general rule include the following:

- There is a compelling business need to create a batch of reports.
- Canned reports do not exist in the new system.
- The organization is willing to devote dedicated and significant resources to reports—*i.e.*, a reporting specialist will be able to focus exclusively on creating custom reports.

This general philosophy helps keep projects on track.

Entity Relationship Diagrams

Warning: this brief section is a little on the technical side but, I promise, it is short.

On many projects, I create custom reports. Almost invariably, one of my clients will ask me, "How do you know how to get the data that you want out of the system?" Aside from years of ingrained knowledge of different applications that I couldn't forget if I tried, I share with them a little secret: the entity relationship diagram (ERD). An ERD is essentially a visual representation of the objects (typically, tables) in a relational database. It shows how the system's tables are joined, facilitating the selection of fields from different tables to appear on custom reports.

In fact, ERDs are no secret to developers and hard-core coders. However, for functional end users now able to write reports against the different tables in their new system for the first time, ERDs are tantamount to a treasure map. Let's look at a hypothetical ERD in Figure 14.1 for a simple customer relationship management (CRM) system.

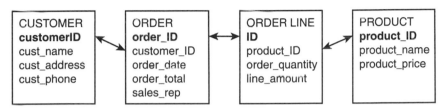

Figure 14.1 *Sample entity relationship diagram.*

In English, Figure 14.1 is saying that the system's data is housed in four separate tables: CUSTOMER, ORDER, ORDERLINE, and PRODUCT. To write reports against these tables, you have to join them properly. For instance, if my report only required the customerID and productID fields, I could not link the CUSTOMER and PRODUCT tables directly; I would still have to use the ORDER and ORDERLINE tables *in the proper order* for the data to appear correctly on the final report. I would not have known this without an ERD.[3]

Also, note the different "arrows" or joins on Figure 14.1. There is a one-to-many relationship between the ORDER and ORDERLINE tables because a customer could place one order that has multiple quantities, products, and amounts. Imagine the irritation of a customer who had to give her information 10 times to place an order for 10 different products!

Note that ERDs can be amazingly large and complicated. However, the alternative (looking at pure code) is much, much worse.

---

3. Of course, there's also sheer intuition and trial and error. Trust me, as a general rule, it's best to be sure about how to join tables *before* you run a report. Improperly joined tables on reports can cause a host of problems, not the least of which is irritating your IT department.

Q&A WITH JOHN HENLEY

I can think of no better person to provide additional insights into reporting than my friend John Henley. John has more than 20 years of consulting experience spanning multiple industries, including health care, nonprofits, public sector, and professional services. John runs Decision Analytics, a consulting firm located in Arlington, Virginia, providing software development support services to a number of diverse organizations. Decision Analytics focuses on technical projects and specializes in reporting, system customization, data conversion, and integration.

PS: How often are you asked to rewrite a report that existed in a client's legacy system but does not come delivered in an ERP?

JH: That happens quite often, which I think points to a larger issue beyond reporting. One of the prevailing themes underlying an ERP implementation is that of the organization modeling its new system to look just like the legacy system being replaced. While there are sometimes valid reasons for doing so—perhaps to retain a key core competency—it's often done to avoid confronting change and alienating end users who are comfortable with their current operating processes and reports. An ERP implementation is a unique opportunity in the organizational life cycle for reinvention. Frankly, I think that many organizations fail to embrace that idea.

PS: Generally speaking, what are some of the most common reporting requests that clients give you?

JH: What I see most often in smaller organizations using Lawson is that the finance people are either content with Excel exporting tools or the well-established financial ad hoc reporting tool, or they're much larger and they use some other reporting system or application like Hyperion or Microsoft FRx to generate their financials. The ones in between are the ones who usually contact me for developing financial reports. Procurement and materials end users tend to be more technical and database savvy and are able to generate their own reports using SQL or Crystal Reports. For HR and benefits, the HRIS administrator is usually good at satisfying the easier requirements, but not with more complicated reports like staffing plans and turnover.

PS: How often do clients change their minds once they see reports they have asked you to create?

JH: Report development is an iterative and collaborative process. It's a lot like a remodeling or building project. Sometimes a homeowner sees how a concept translates into a reality and then asks the builder to move the stairs or change the windows. It's the same with building a report. You try to accommodate the changes as best you can, and—unlike with most building projects—you sometimes do start over when the client decides what they were asking for wasn't really what they wanted. And just like those remodeling jobs, reports often do end up costing more than the estimate!

PS: What drives most of your clients to you? Do they lack time or experience?

JH: I would say it's generally both. Take a new customer who's just purchased Lawson applications or Lawson business intelligence (LBI). Lawson has about 2,000 tables. That's pretty intimidating to even a veteran developer. By leveraging my experience and understanding of the Lawson data structures and concepts like primary keys, complex joins, using Lawson's subset indexes, database-specific "null dates," and syntax, a new client can get a pretty good jump-start on delivering efficient high-quality reports to their users. But even still, most of my business is from repeat customers. I have some customers who go back 8 or 10 years, and even for them it's still a mix. Some of them just don't have the resources to create the report or aren't interested in making an investment in training their developers in the idiosyncrasies of how Lawson stores data. If you're only developing a handful of reports every now and then, it's probably not a good investment to have a high-caliber reporting person on your staff; it's more cost-effective to outsource it to someone [you] trust.

PS: What are some of the reporting tips that you would give an organization implementing a new system?

JH: Organize the report development project into a mentoring process. Bring in some outside help to guide you through the development of some of the more difficult reports. Catalog and prioritize your requirements. You can't create all the reports at once. Another piece of advice is to take some of the techniques used in software development and apply them to report development. Have peer reviews or use the pair-programming methodology. We can all learn from each other—I know I do—when we don't work in isolation. And it's usually a lot more fun! Design patterns, which have been used successfully in software development, can also be applied to report development.

PS: In your experience, are clients satisfied with the standard reports that they receive from ERPs? What about their satisfaction with system-delivered ad hoc tools?

JH: Well, I can only really speak from the Lawson perspective, but for the most part it depends on the audience. A number of the standard reports end up being "good enough," and there are some tools that ship with Lawson that can be used to augment the standard reports. For instance, HR users who take the time to learn Lawson's HR report writer seem to be happy enough with it. As for ad hoc tools, I think a lot of clients who purchase the LBI suite end up never really using it. It's just too wide open. It's really a big set of tools, and it's hard for them to get started. And they end up never using very much of it, if any.

PS: How often are you asked to rewrite a report that an end user has attempted? Are you typically able to make the report more efficient?

JH: I tend to work with developers probably more often than with end users, as sort of a mentoring "super-developer." I can demonstrate various techniques to the developers based on my experience and understanding of the Lawson data structures; they can leverage my experience to create more efficient reports. I have a good friend who worked at a client who once gave me the advice that if a report doesn't produce results within 90 seconds, it needs to go back through an efficiency analysis. I constantly use that as a guideline.

Interface Issues

Now let's move on to the related but separate topic of interfaces. Any time an organization retires its legacy system, it must rewrite its inbound and outbound interfaces. This is no small chore. Interfaces to other vendors, banks, and financial institutions are imperative for a successful system activation. Examples of common inbound and outbound interfaces include these:

- Direct deposit and "positive pay" interfaces
- Third-party benefit provider interfaces such as 401(k) contributions or health plan enrollments
- Supplemental employee data interfaces to external vendors, such as employment verification services
- Interfaces to any additional internal systems

Interface Tools for Clients

Clients have a head start writing interfaces to and from the new system. Vendors almost always provide detailed specifications on both the type and format of the data required. These specifications are extremely granular and specify the field length, starting point of a field, and so on. For example, the interface developer will not have to guess where to store employee social security numbers. That field should start on position 10 of the interface and contain nine digits—for example, 123456789.

These vendors have many clients, some of which run the same system that the client is now implementing. End users at an organization implementing SAP HR, for example, can find colleagues at other organizations hardly new to SAP that have essentially written that same interface. User groups and Internet bulletin boards allow clients to network with others who face the same challenges.

Issues and Limitations

Clients are not completely out of the woods, however. Because third parties have many clients, they cannot devote extensive resources to any one organization's testing. Typically, coordination well ahead of time can address this issue. However, it is unreasonable for end users to expect a vendor's complete attention just because they are in the middle of testing. Remember, the vendor may have 100 or more other clients in production or in testing. End users should tell vendors well in advance that they will be remitting test files.

A client can only expect a vendor to unearth formatting errors. Vendor import programs typically have functionality that automatically rejects records due to improper format. For example, an employee social security number of 1234578 does not have the requisite nine digits. Also, a 1234567a record would be rejected because "a" is not an integer.

Many clients do not realize that the vendor's validation stops at a certain point. In all but the most exceptional of circumstances, the vendor will not validate the accuracy of incoming data. If Elaine's benefit election is "single coverage" in a test system, the vendor will accept this value if formatted and transmitted correctly. Now, if Elaine's value *should be* "Single+1," the vendor will *not* know this.

Unfortunately, neither vendors receiving test files nor clients sending them look at the results of interfaces during testing as closely as they would in a live, production environment. As a result, sometimes end users discover interface issues only at the tail end of an implementation, if at all.

Other interface issues may surface during testing, including questions about current legacy system interfaces not documented very well. What's more, an interface's original designer may no longer work for the organization. As a result, a client may not know exactly which data it currently sends to a vendor.

Summary

In most organizations, the writing of custom reports and complex interfaces is performed by a technical individual. However, new systems obviate the need for reports to be the exclusive purview of the IT department, especially when more technical folks have access to tools such as ERDs and proper training.

Regardless of who writes reports and interfaces, the absence or inadequacy of a formal design specification will result in, at best, inaccurate data being sent to a vendor or report recipient. Quite possibly, the vendor will reject the interface. An end user may make incorrect business decisions based on the inaccuracy of the information contained in a report. Implementation team members should *not* take testing and approving interfaces and reports lightly.

Organizations should understand that end users cannot start working on interfaces and reports until key design decisions have been made and a prototype system has been built. Moreover, although essentially any interface or report can be written, the back and forth among end users, developers, and vendors (in the case of interfaces) typically increases the time required to complete these tasks on a project plan. The organization or SI that either ignores them or devotes insufficient time to them is "entering a world of pain," to steal a phrase from *The Big Lebowski*.

Chapter 15

Documentation Issues

> I wish I had an answer to that because I'm
> tired of answering that question.
> — *Yogi Berra*

- Types of Required Documentation
- Wilson Case Study: Good Design but Lack of Resources
- Julian Case Study: Building Its Own System

One of the items that typically falls through the cracks during the implementation is documentation. Proper system documentation is imperative in the event that one or more of the following occurs:

- A key team member leaves the company or becomes ill.
- The organization expands and has to hire employees with key setup, data entry, or processing responsibilities.
- Particularly for an organization governed by Sarbanes-Oxley, auditors decide that the new system needs appropriate checks and balances.

Organizations that minimize the need for comprehensive documentation expose themselves to major risks and additional costs.

Types of Required Documentation

During an implementation, organizations should formally document reports, interfaces, system configuration, testing results, and so on. This is not merely a matter of "CYA"—consultant-speak for "cover your ass." Table 15.1 lists the common types of documentation required and when each *should* begin.

TABLE 15.1 Common Documentation Types

Type of Documentation	Ideal Beginning Phase	Notes
Business processes	Project planning	Client sign-off is typically necessary to move forward
Reporting requirements and design specs	Project planning	Tends to be deficient
System configuration	System design	With revisions throughout project as needed; client sign-off is typically necessary to move forward
Testing results	System testing	Typically needed for internal or external auditors
Issues	Ongoing	Should be documented as soon as discovered
End-user guides	System design	Should be revised and kept up to date as an organization changes or enhances an application
Training guides	System design	Should be revised and kept up to date as an organization changes or enhances an application

This begs the question: if there are so many types of documentation and they are so critical to an organization preparing to go live, why is documentation so deficient? There are two main reasons.

Delays from Previous Phases and the Need to Catch Up

When implementations fall behind schedule, project managers and executives look for ways to make up time. One of their favorite places to "trim the fat" is documentation. For example, a project manager pressured to get a project back on track may determine that the six weeks initially slated for creating proper training and procedure manuals and contingency plans can now be done in two. Obviously, this is almost always a poor decision.

Just Do It: Wishful Thinking and the Limitations of Multitasking

Clients and consultants typically face enormous pressure to hit key dates on implementations, given the best practice of going live at the beginning of a quarter or a year, financial pressures, and so on. As a result, team members tend to devote more time to fixing issues and testing a system than to documenting the error resolution process or new hire training manual for that system.

Even the best-intentioned client or consultant may intend to go back after system activation and properly document—via detailed steps and screen shots—how a business process should be conducted in the new system. However, issues in the production world need to be addressed immediately, and documentation is typically relegated to the back burner.

Many project managers erroneously believe that documentation can be done in a client's or a consultant's spare time. Although this is sometimes possible, most people produce their best documentation in dedicated blocks of time, not with 15 minutes here and an hour there. The latter scenario typically results in missing steps and an overall inferior product.

Wilson Case Study: Good Design but Lack of Resources

This case study looks at a large retail chain, Wilson Clothing, implementing a new system with a design recommended by its system integrators (SIs). Unlike the Portnoy and Lifeson case studies, Wilson's system configuration was straightforward and involved no major customizations. The implementation failed due to a number of factors, not the least of which was its lack of internal resources.

This dearth directly caused the following:

- Wilson's implementation to go significantly over budget and repeatedly miss deadlines
- Many daily problems for end users immediately after going live
- Wilson to miss a key opportunity to redefine a key business process

Wilson illustrates the difficulty of key players having two jobs during an implementation as well as the need for projects of this type to be appropriately staffed from the beginning.

Background

Wilson operates in 48 states and runs weekly payroll for approximately 10,000 employees. Most employees work in the stores, aka "in the field." Due to the nature of its business, many employees work only during the holiday season, and it is common for employees to be rehired several times over the course of their lifetimes. Many employees are teenagers wanting to be paid every week. Although it may seem foolish to have teenagers dictating business practice, retail turnover is high enough that weekly payroll is often an important consideration for seasonal workers—that is, those who work only during the holiday season.

The logistics of paying upward of 10,000 employees weekly in 48 states should not be understated. Retail margins are not high and, as a result, Wilson runs a pretty tight ship with respect to personnel. In addition, the degree of employee turnover, particularly in the field, poses significant challenges with respect to three issues:

- Accurately paying employees
- Providing timely and accurate government reporting
- Ensuring that employee benefit deductions and taxes are correct

Impetus for Change

Wilson's prior HR and payroll system contained limited reporting capability and lacked real-time data. The legacy system's limitations placed IT in the middle of all reporting requests. End users did not "own" the system. Wilson executives decided that a new system with superior reporting capability would democratize the data. No longer would IT need to play the role of reporting gatekeeper. Impressed with several vendor presentations, Wilson made the decision to purchase and implement Tier 2 enterprise resource planning (ERP). Such a system could meet Wilson's growing business needs, empower end users, and reduce administration costs. Wilson initially selected the vendor to also serve as the SI.

Aside from increased functionality, cost was another important factor in Wilson's decision to retire its legacy system. Wilson's new system would allow the company to save a great deal of money on its increasing legacy software licensing down the road.

It is important to note that Wilson did *not* use this opportunity to effect an important business process change—that is, to switch to a biweekly or semi-monthly payroll. This decision compromised the implementation from the beginning and set the stage for recurring problems after system activation.

Implementation Challenges

Wilson faced significant challenges throughout the project, some of which affected organizations in the previous case studies. Unlike many of Wilson's counterparts crossing the technological Rubicon, however, a core business process was the root of most of its problems. Specifically, Wilson's weekly payroll created a formidable set of issues that plagued the project from day one.

The reporting front was a mess. Resources assigned to produce custom reports had no knowledge of the new system's basic functionality, fields, tables, or database structure. Previous attempts to create reports were either flat-out incorrect or, at best, wholly inefficient. Wilson hired me to manage the reports toward the end of the implementation. I knew the system cold but had enormous difficulty obtaining anything remotely resembling a formal reporting specification from Wilson end users. My expertise allowed me to build many reports without this key information, but I am certainly not a mind reader. Legacy reports merely described as "transaction listing" left me scratching my head, especially after Wilson end users admitted to me that they did not know what certain "essential" reports actually did either.[1]

The majority of Wilson's functional end users were simply too busy to write detailed reporting specifications, much less learn how to create reports themselves. Their day jobs kept them so occupied that they simply had no time. They would tell me what they wanted and I would try to create their reports, publishing them on a dashboard for electronic distribution. The hours that Wilson's end users devoted to learning how to create reports were few and far between, hardly a successful recipe for transferring and retaining knowledge.

---

1. You have to love this paradox: we don't know what this does, but we absolutely have to have it.

Inadequate Staffing and Acceptance of the New System

First, the decision to implement the ERP did not mean that Wilson's normal world would stop turning. On the contrary, employees still had to perform their day jobs in the legacy system while (in theory) learning, configuring, and testing the new system. For a company that processes biweekly or bimonthly payroll, staff members typically have periods of relative downtime in which they can devote attention to the new system implementation. This was not the case at Wilson. Without much time to relax, Wilson staff members were left with small pockets of time to do critical things such as define custom reporting requirements, learn and test the new system, meet with external consultants, and participate in training. These are not items that are best accomplished in half-hour increments. End users must devote significant blocks of time to accomplish these mission-critical tasks.

Perhaps because of their workloads effectively doubling, Wilson end users were not very receptive to the new system from the beginning. They neither embraced nor owned the new system, nor did they spend the sufficient time on data validation. As a result of the end users' lack of time and interest in the new system, Wilson relied on consultants to make decisions that clients typically made.

Wilson eventually changed partners, citing a need for more experienced consultants. However, the new consultants faced similar challenges in getting "face time" with end users. It is difficult for even the best consultant to come in from outside an organization and effectively set up a system without much time spent with existing end users. The situation is exacerbated when end users lack sufficient documentation on current business practices.

The sheer amount of work involved in weekly payroll in a high transaction environment such as retail made formal training of team members nearly impossible. Initially, some employees participated in classroom training away from their desks. Unfortunately, this took place too early in the project, well before the system could be tested. During the second round of training held at their desks, end users were distracted: answering phone calls and e-mails and dealing with employees knocking on their doors.

By giving its employees too much work, Wilson was left doubly exposed to the risk of employee turnover. On the core team, if any one of four key employees left, the project would have come to a halt right then and there. Although just about every organization today is lean and faces this risk to some extent, the issue was particularly pronounced at Wilson. For instance, no one knew how to do the payroll manager's job and, as stated, existing documentation was sparse. Throw in weekly payroll, and not only could the project have ceased, but Wilson would have had a difficult time cutting employee checks from the legacy system. Wilson simply would not have been able find a suitable replacement and provide sufficient training in such a short period.

Data Challenges

Wilson's legacy system stored data in a fundamentally different way than the new system. Given the number of transactions and data quality issues, creating conversion files proved extremely vexing.

One particularly daunting challenge involved converting payroll history, an essential component for an organization activating a new system in the middle of a year due to government W-2 requirements. Payroll history was essential to going live. In the words of the IT director responsible for the conversion programs, "the biggest challenge was creating the payroll history load with data for nine months of weekly payrolls. A close second was the validation effort." Although a lot of work went into creating accurate conversions, the data was only as good as the source systems. Without a proper (independent) way to validate values, we were open to inaccuracies that only revealed themselves during go-live. Although performed extensively, parallel testing never really reflected reality. Managers dismissed many issues with statements such as, "We'll fix this after go live."

Beyond the unexpected challenges extracting and validating payroll history, Wilson did not anticipate about 80 percent of its issues. Wilson management staffed the project based on the assumption that it would find minimal errors. Nothing could have been further from the truth. Among the tsunami of errors discovered throughout the project, some of the most significant included tax setup errors created by Wilson's prior SI. Attempts to load data revealed significant setup issues. A compromised series of parallel payrolls resulted in end users not testing fixes and "workarounds" before Wilson's final conversion (that is, the one prior to going live).

An Unresponsive Senior Management

Again, Wilson did not staff the implementation team sufficiently. Key internal resources identified the inadequate resource level to senior management, both during the first weeks of the project and routinely during steering committee meetings. Had senior management increased the number of internal resources devoted to the project—specifically by hiring two functional experts with prior ERP experience—the team would have found and resolved key issues quicker. What's more, Wilson would have spent much less money on external consultants.

Two years into the project, management was close to pulling the plug altogether. By this point, the project was several hundred thousand dollars over budget. An influential team member suggested to senior management that the project was not going to be cost effective and that team members were not learning the new system. Management rejected this suggestion and, by sheer force, decided to plow through the issues.

An Overreliance on Consultants Due to Inadequate Internal Staffing

Wilson heavily relied upon external consultants throughout the project at a cost of hundreds of thousands of dollars outside the initial budget. Specific consultant responsibilities included everything from the purely functional (determining setup of items such as tax codes) to the purely technical (building conversion and interface programs and analyzing their results). Consultants set up the payroll, benefits, and HR rules and created almost all the required custom reports. External consultants performed nearly half of the implementation tasks, minimizing the knowledge transferred to Wilson's end users.

The Go-Live Decision

Lack of comprehensive validation and end-user knowledge throughout the implementation came to a head during system activation. Fortunately, on a particularly vital payroll issue, I provided the solution to a data-oriented showstopper not worthy of explaining here. Wilson printed its first checks in the wee hours of the morning and, a few days later, discovered a key interface issue for employee direct deposit that required manual intervention to pay employees.

Wilson's final decision to activate the system was predicated on risk and cost. Although known issues existed, Wilson management knew that failure to go live would have delayed the project an additional four months and cost another $500,000. The implementation team believed that the data was sufficiently accurate and the issues minor enough to make the decision to move forward.

Outcomes and Lessons

In the end, the project took more than three years and exceeded its budget by more than $2M. The organization learned the hard way that a new system implementation is much more difficult than just acquiring some software and learning how to use it on the fly. In retrospect, end users realized that they needed additional internal resources from the onset of the project. What's more, they should have attended application training throughout the project, not immediately before processing the first real or "production" payroll.

Wilson employees encountered additional issues immediately after going live, stemming from a core implementation problem: they did not become experts in the applications that they needed to support. For one, payroll needed to watch individual employee taxes, making adjustments manually before cutting checks. Reports that end users had formally approved needed to be changed or rewritten, indicating that they never really looked at them in any detail during testing. Employees did not have enough time to fix all issues in the first week and were still trying to triage them six weeks after going live. Much to senior management's dismay, several end users still needed to rely on the same costly external consultants to find and resolve issues.

After the project began, Wilson management estimated that the organization needed three years to realize a positive ROI on the new system. After system activation, management revised that number to just over eight years. On the positive side, six weeks after system activation, data flowed to the end users much more easily than before. Some began to perform analytics on data previously unavailable to them.

Phase I contained only the basic functionality of HR, benefits, and payroll. Phase II called for employee self-service and online open enrollment. However, based on the issues encountered during Phase I and the related budgetary debacle, it is unlikely that Wilson will be undertaking a major system initiative in the near future unless compelled.

Wilson can be rated on the failure scale as a Big Failure. Its IT director offers the following advice for organizations going through a new system implementation for the first time:

> Reject anyone on the core team who doesn't want formal training. This is really a primer for the rest of the project. Insist that they invest the week to get the basics and also to learn third-party add-on products. I also suggest that companies hire employees with at least three years of related knowledge and experience to be added to each functional area. They are the ones who will lead your existing staff on how the application works. Nothing beats experience. This comes from someone with 13 years of experience with the ERP and 21 years in the industry. I'm still learning every day.

Julian Case Study: Building Its Own System

The next case study is quite different from the rest on a number of levels: it focuses on a custom-built system for a small company. This case study shows how strikingly different companies and systems often face identical issues. It illustrates that large organizations are not the only ones that tend to fail when implementing off-the-shelf systems; even small companies that build custom packages exhibit many of the same characteristics as their larger brethren. Finally, it evinces the dangers of both using a completely malleable systems framework and poorly documenting that framework.

Background

Julian Marketing Partners is a small sales and marketing firm with approximately 150 full-time employees. The company grew at a rapid pace, increasing both employee headcount and sales as fast as it could. As is the case with many high-paced, intense startups, employee turnover was a major issue. Julian was constantly hiring and retraining new sales representatives, many of whom were in their early or mid-20s. Few new hires looked at Julian as a long-term employment option. To be sure, it was kind of strange being an "elder statesman" in my early 30s at an organization.

Julian operated in a niche market and did not see any current systems off the shelf that met its business needs. Using Microsoft's .NET framework, Julian's external consultants built its own system for tracking sales. To be certain, .NET is a flexible framework, and many organizations have been able to deploy similar applications with varying degrees of success.

Data and Business Process Issues

Julian's home-grown system could certainly track sales as the individual reps entered them. However, the fundamental business question was never addressed: what constitutes a sale?

- Does the sale take place when the customer asks for information?
- Does it take place when the customer verbally agrees to make the purchase?
- How about when the paperwork is formally sent out?
- Or does it occur when the signed paperwork arrives by mail?

Asking four different reps resulted in four different answers. Julian should have bought a quality off-the-shelf solution or configured its own system appropriately. Either solution would have prevented a sale from being logged seven times, as was the case with some sales by the most ambitious employees.

Without the business question being answered, Julian's system would allow just about any customer contact to count as a sale. As such, a signed application from a customer might have four "sales" attached to it. The implications for forecasting future sales, much less paying commissions to the "right" representative, were substantial. Employees who stayed longer than a few months quickly discovered that their commissions increased significantly if they entered as many sales as possible. Given the low base salaries, employees who logged only true sales received lower commissions than those who inflated their numbers.

Reporting Issues

Julian did not provide its IT end users with a robust reporting tool. Rather, IT had to rely upon basic SQL statements. Functional end users with legitimate needs to view and analyze data could not do so on their own; they were not programmers and could not code in SQL. They had to ask techies like me to write custom reports, and invariably something was ultimately lost in translation. What's more, an employee absence meant that a report often could not be run. Who knew who stored what where?

Along with a few of my colleagues, I brought these issues to the attention of Julian's senior management, only to be ignored. In management's view, addressing the issues and reconfiguring the system were subordinate to increasing sales. Management opted to focus on growth rather than shoring up its systems.

Lack of Documentation and Knowledge Transfer

Because its system was developed on the fly, Julian did not maintain a data dictionary, formal documentation, or entity relationship diagrams (ERDs).

All of these would have allowed newly hired IT personnel to fully understand Julian's business processes, data, and the systems. No consultant or end user at Julian really knew why or how its system did everything it did. When one of the external consultants accepted a job closer to his home, Julian management panicked. They offered to double his hourly rate and provide local housing. Although this was understandable in the short term, Julian had no long-term plan of bringing system expertise in-house.

Several IT personnel expressed a desire to learn more about .NET as a platform. However, Julian management would not send them to formal training. Although a public .NET class obviously would not have covered the specifics of Julian's system, it certainly would have provided attendees with extensive knowledge of that platform's building blocks. No one can realistically learn a platform as robust as .NET on lunch breaks.

Outcomes and Lessons

Julian spent tens of thousands of dollars on recruiting and training costs, attempting to replace skilled sales associates, many of whom left over inadequate commissions. Julian kept its external consultants indefinitely. It had no choice; it did not have the internal expertise or the documentation to maintain—much less fix or enhance—its systems independently. Because of its overreliance upon consultants and an inability to track basic sales, Julian can be rated on the failure scale as a Mild Failure.

Summary

Documentation is often inadequate on legacy systems, thus setting the stage for suboptimal documentation in the new system. Due to the importance of testing and resolving previously discovered issues, budget and time considerations, and the firmness of a go-live date, documentation often continues to suffer. The need to document existing and future business practices and processes should not be minimized. Any postponement of documentation should be addressed immediately after going live. Employee turnover, an organizational audit, or newly discovered issues may well bring this underemphasized need to the forefront.

PART IV

The Brave New World of Post-Production Life

Going live with a new system typically proves more challenging than organizations and their end users anticipate. To be sure, there are typically quite a few stressful moments during "cutover" and "go-live," to use the industry vernacular. During system activation, the sum total of all the planning, testing, work, and meetings comes to fruition. Ready or not, organizations often go live not knowing or being prepared for their forthcoming challenges, both system and operations related.

This Part focuses on the issues that organizations will face after activating new systems. Testing has ceased—at least for the time being—as the dream of a new system has hopefully not become a nightmare.

16 Ongoing System Maintenance
17 Operational Changes and Risks

Chapter 16

Ongoing System Maintenance

Insanity: doing the same thing over and over
again and expecting different results.
—Albert Einstein

- Reporting and Interface Issues Revisited
- Database Views
- Data Areas
- Upgrades
- Customizations Revisited
- Patches
- Backup and Disaster Recovery

E instein was a smart man. Although this book is intentionally light on absolutes, this is certainly one of them: organizations and their employees should learn a great deal throughout an implementation with respect to its new system, testing, reporting, and so on. What's more, this knowledge should *not* be confined merely to the functionality of the new application and, fortunately, can be applied immediately after going live. This is imperative, as end users must maintain the system and troubleshoot issues as they arise.

By the time that an organization goes live, most end users have long disabused themselves of the myth of perfect software, if it ever existed. Senior management and end users are hopefully more realistic than they were during system selection, especially if the implementation was their first. This chapter is devoted to exploring organizations' ongoing *system* challenges, while the next focuses on their *operational* challenges.

Reporting and Interface Issues Revisited

Prior to going live, most organizations spend many hours defining, writing, testing, and tweaking custom reports. In the whole scheme of things, however, reporting tends not to receive the required attention prior to system activation. In this sense, it is like documentation. There are several reasons for this lack of attention.

First of all, there are only so many hours in a day. Remember, most employees are doing two jobs concurrently: their "day" jobs with the legacy system and their "future" day jobs. In the latter, they are setting up general ledger accounts, looking at item masters, and testing payroll. It's understandable that many end users do not have enough time to properly review the reports created for them.

Second, end users tend to look at reports more closely that reflect real—that is, production—data. I have had to redesign many reports that a client had previously approved after the organization has gone live.

The same holds true for interfaces. Although carriers provide their clients with file formats, errors will appear if the client interfaces pass data that does not meet the vendors' specifications. Zed's hire date, for example, cannot be sent as "aa/00/2008." Many carriers spit out error reports based on nonsensical data, even if the data type and format are valid. For example, the employee hire date of 1/1/1753—SQL Server's default null value—is probably not accurate; the employee is not 255 years old. However, many values may sneak through the validation process. To continue with the example, an employee hire date of 1/1/1995 is in a perfectly valid format and date range. However, perhaps Zed's true hire date is 1/1/1999. His seniority date (stemming from his first tenure with the company) is 1/1/1995. Carriers are not responsible for the integrity of their clients' data. An incorrectly sent value can have potentially dangerous consequences, as the Tate case study discussed in Chapter 22, "Intelligent Expansion," will demonstrate.

Database Views

As discussed in Chapter 14, "Reports and Interfaces," many functional end users have difficulty writing custom reports. Because the system is new, they may not know where to find key information, although entity relationship diagrams (ERDs) are exceptionally helpful. As has been stated, legacy systems store data differently. They often have fewer tables than transaction-based systems. Data is stored in different places, and a novice report writer may not easily be able to extract the desired information in the proper format. Although not overly complicated, building custom reports typically requires a fair amount of knowledge of each of the following:

- The reporting tool
- The application itself
- The application's fields and tables and the relationships among them

Beyond the difficulty of building reports, end users may complain that they take progressively longer to run each time. This truism stems from the fact that, absent a data purge, there is simply more data in these tables than there was when the organization went live. Figure 16.1 shows an example of a report that needs fields from three separate tables.

Figure 16.1 *Example of three joined tables.*

The POSITION table contains information on the employee's specific job in the organization. Both the PAEMPLOYEE and EMPLOYEE tables contain different information related to the employee. A report stitching together these tables might take too long to finish. To eliminate the need to run this report against the three tables in Figure 16.1, IT may decide to create a database view. Database views essentially take data from multiple tables and present it in a simpler format than it would otherwise appear.

Combining data from three disparate tables into one consolidated view offers three major benefits:

- End users require less time to create a report from one view, as opposed to three tables.

- End users are less likely to make mistakes, slow down the system, and anger IT departments. In fact, because a single view requires no joins, these reports are often reduced to "dragging and dropping" the desired data.

- Under most circumstances, report performance will be superior, because fewer objects are involved in the final query/report.

An example of a view based on Figure 16.1 is displayed in Table 16.1.

TABLE 16.1 Consolidated Database View for Three Transactional Tables

Dept	Date Hired	Emp#	Full Name	Current Age	Position	Description
740	2-Apr-82	100123	Paulson, Henry	60	123	Registered nurse
682	15-Aug-90	100396	Spacey, Kevin	56	182	VP of marketing
704	17-Jun-00	100412	Hayek, Salma	42	403	Internist and actress
720	10-Jul-05	100479	Wilson, Steven	41	423	HR specialist
880	16-Dec-03	100792	Mercury, Freddie	42	180	Office manager and lead singer
702	17-Jun-09	100958	Cruz, Penelope	41	144	Nurse technician
751	2-Jan-01	101147	Cruise, Thomas	46	144	Nurse technician

The view consolidates all the desired information from the three separate tables into one single database entity.

Note that most systems do not provide database views out of the box. Kronos Workforce Central is one exception to this rule. The view in Table 16.1 is a single database entity, expediting report creation and execution. Although vendor support will not assist clients in creating or maintaining these views, databases such as SQL Server and Oracle provide relatively easy methods for knowledgeable IT professionals to create and refresh views. These views can be immeasurably helpful, particularly with historical tables holding millions of records that need to be summarized on a report.

Most complicated or large reports *do not* require database views. I have written hundreds of efficient reports against large transactional tables native to the application and database. However, reporting skill cannot overcome a massive quantity of data. For example, if a report requires summary information on three distinct multimillion record tables with complex joins, a view may be the only feasible way to go, especially if that report needs to be run in the middle of the day while many employees are accessing the system.

Data Areas

During the implementation, organizations and their end users *should* have learned about the importance of testing and training. These things remain critical after system activation. As such, once up and running with new systems, organizations should devote the required resources to maintaining different data areas.

The production data area—typically called PROD—stores all current data created by end users doing their day jobs. Everything stems from PROD: running payroll, tracking inventory, keying journal entries, and so on. However, foolish is the organization that maintains only one data area. (Believe it or not, these organizations still exist.) Where will new employees be trained? What about testing new system functionality or applying patches? The organization that attempts to do all these in PROD dramatically increases its chances of encountering issues of all sorts.

Because of these different needs, organizations need to have a minimum of three different data areas in addition to PROD:

- A training data area (TRAIN) in which to train new employees
- A development data area (DEV) in which to store current and future setup but no transactions
- A testing data area (TEST) in which to test upgrades, patches, new functionality, and reports

This may seem like overkill, but organizations are wise to devote the time and resources necessary for maintaining these different data areas. Each has an important and distinct purpose.

Upgrades

Upgrades are certainly not of the same scope as new system implementations. However, depending on the new modules under consideration, upgrades may be comparable to a new system in terms of human and financial resources required. As such, lack of planning, data validation, and testing represent potential obstacles.

Typically, a major release of a software version has a shelf life of about six to eight years, give or take. Examples include PeopleSoft version 8, Lawson version 8, and Oracle version 11i. These major releases do not include "cyclicals" such as PeopleSoft 8.1, Lawson 8.1, and Oracle 11.5. Cyclicals are *not* major releases. Rather, they represent some improvements or changes from the vendor's last major release, short of the next major one.

Vendors change and, one would hope, improve their software over time. An organization that purchases annual support from a vendor can expect a number of years of support for its current version. Eventually, however, vendors refuse to support older versions of their applications. For example, an organization running Oracle Applications version 9 is on a burning plank if Version 11i is the current "preferred" version and has been for a while. Oracle will eventually decommission version 9 at some point, and version 9 clients will have to do one of the following:

- Upgrade to a supported version
- Find alternative support mechanisms
- Continue using version 9 unsupported

Consider Gilmour, Inc., a company that runs Oracle financials, procurement, and HR. Gilmour is an Oracle "shop," as they say. Unlike the legacy systems that Gilmour had built and previously controlled, now it is somewhat at the mercy of Oracle with regard to upgrades and support. Gilmour implemented Oracle version 9 in 2000. Suppose that, in 2008, Oracle announced a decommission date of May 15, 2009, for version 9. Newer versions of Oracle (11i and above) will become the standard. To prepare for the upgrade, Gilmour loads version 11i applications into its TEST data area for extensive testing well before the May deadline. PROD remains the system of record—with application or "apps" version 9—until that time.

As previously discussed, most organizations will eventually opt for the upgrade for two reasons: the risks of being unsupported and the perceived benefits of the upgrade not justifying remaining on an unsupported version. Although virtually no upgrade is as costly and resource intensive as the initial implementation, this upgrade is a major endeavor requiring a great deal of planning and resources. What's more, issues identical to those of a new implementation may well present themselves.

Note that some upgrades are more complex than others. The aforementioned cyclical upgrades are small potatoes compared to major changes in an application's architecture. Consider for a moment the following application timeline for SAP, one of the first ERP companies.

1973—SAP launches its first product, R/1.

1979—SAP launches its successor to R/1, R/2.

1981—The SAP R/2 system attains the high level of stability of the previous generation of programs. Keeping in mind its multinational customers, SAP designs SAP R/2 to handle different languages and currencies.

1992—SAP moves from R/2 to R/3 in 1992, moving from mainframe computing to a client-server architecture.

Late 1990s to mid-2000s—SAP has moved its applications to the Web, introducing mysap.com. The product underwent major surgery after its initial release.[i]

SAP's changes in 1981, 1992, and the late 1990s represented major technological shifts. SAP's competitors also made similar jumps around the same times. As a general rule, most organizations waited until their vendors' new platforms were mature and stable before uprooting their own systems.

Customizations Revisited

As stated in Chapter 9, "Implementation Strategies and Phases," customizations are always tempting to organizations and end users unwilling to change their business practices to conform to the new system. Customizing the new system in a production environment is much more dangerous than doing so during system testing. During testing, customizations may have unintended consequences such as delays or breaking other parts of the system. However, at least the issues are confined to testing; they do not affect the real world. Organizations customizing the new system need to be extremely careful when playing for keeps. A botched customization may result in the following:

- Gross errors on financial statements
- Missing payroll
- Administrative nightmares
- Employee communication issues
- Overpaid vendors and mismatched invoices
- Inventory mishaps

These errors make testing delays look insignificant by comparison. Tread carefully.

Patches

Vendors and clients typically find issues in current versions of the software. In either case, in the event of a true bug, vendors will issue patches or service packs—basically a group of patches—that supported clients can download from the vendor's support site. Because it is not completely unprecedented for a patch to fix the problem but break something else, these fixes should first be applied in a TEST data area, as discussed earlier in this chapter.

Backup and Disaster Recovery

The system administrator's motto states, "If it wasn't backed up, it wasn't important." This chapter has emphasized the importance of maintaining different data areas for different purposes—TRAIN, DEV, PROD, and TEST. However, IT departments need to do more than merely create these data areas. As a part of routine system maintenance, organizations should make backups or snapshots of their data and move them to secured areas on a different server.

One of my favorite maxims is, "It's better to have it and not need it than to need it and not have it." To that end, a number of things may cause an organization to restore data from one of its backups:

- Complete or partial loss of key data caused by a security breach, a software bug, or an "orphaned" batch job
- Corruption of key data caused by a security breach, a software bug, or an "orphaned" batch job
- End-user massive error

An organization's need to restore data often comes unexpectedly. For example, Stevenson Hospital (again, this is not the real name) a few years ago experienced a major issue, the resolution of which would have been much less painful if it had maintained such a backup. Rich, the Human Resource Information Systems (HRIS) manager, felt that some of the payroll tables were too large for his reporting needs. He ran a purge program in PROD and eliminated millions of records that others in the organization—particularly finance—needed.[1] What's more, Rich did this during a major upgrade.

---

1. IT and finance departments did not know that Rich even had access to this purge program. This brings to mind the term "security by ignorance."

The system integrator (SI) running the upgrade essentially had to stop the project and manually re-create the data from related tables in the system. This process took a considerable amount of time because Stevenson did not have a recent backup of its data. Needless to say, Rich was not too popular with the IT and finance folks.

Summary

Once an organization has activated its system, it has entered the real world. This chapter has described the system-related challenges associated with maintaining new systems—that is, after testing has ceased. At some point, even a smooth system implementation and activation will face issues related to reports, interfaces, upgrades, and patches. Organizations and their end users should be sufficiently prepared for these challenges. The next chapter explains why this is often not the case.

Endnotes

i. http://www.sap.com/about/company/history/index.epx

Chapter 17

Operational Changes and Risks

> Life is a risk.
> —*Diane Von Furstenberg*

- Key Employee Movement
- Change in Major Business Process
- Enterprise Risk Management
- Acquisitions
- Decommissioned Applications
- Errors and the Dangers of Automation
- Merger and Acquisition Activity
- Vendor Divorce

Up to this point, this book has focused on organizations migrating from legacy systems to more contemporary ones. However, the world is not a static place; people, processes, and systems are dynamic. Organizations face challenges of all kinds *after* activating their new systems. To be sure, these challenges are typically not as significant as those associated with going live. Still, executives and end users should never assume that system activation means that everyone is home free. Systems are hardly self-sufficient, and issues always appear. This chapter focuses on the steps that organizations can take to minimize operational risks.

Consider an organization that has successfully activated its new system. Over the past two years, its employees have gone about their jobs without major incident, entering data and performing regular processing. It is inevitable that an organization fortunate enough to smoothly make the transition from legacy to new system will experience one or more of the following issues, ultimately threatening this utopian existence:

- Key employee movement
- Change in major business process
- Enterprise risk management
- Acquisition
- Decommissioned applications
- Errors and the dangers of automation
- M&A activity
- Vendor divorce

Key Employee Movement

Mason Footwear successfully implemented a new system five years ago. Since that time, Mason has avoided software bugs, major upgrades, and system disasters. This is no coincidence. Prior to beginning the project, Mason's senior management, hiring managers, and recruiters worked hard to ensure that its implementation team was staffed with skilled and dedicated individuals. Since activation, Mason has retained all its key employees—that is, those essential to successfully supporting the new system. However, this is about to change.

Mason's management knows that, from a systems perspective, not all employee movement is created equal. Different types pose different risks.

Although not a definitive list, the following factors determine the severity of the risk posed by an employee's departure:

- The employee's role
- Organizational bench strength
- The type of move (internal versus external to the organization)
- The amount of notice the employee gives

Table 17.1 shows the risks associated with each type of employee move.

TABLE 17.1 Employee Movement Risk Matrix

Destination	Notice		
	None	Short	Long
Internal	Medium	Medium to low	Low
External	High	High to medium	Medium

Note that, for the sake of simplicity, Table 17.1 holds constant the importance of employee roles and organizations' bench strength.

> **NOTE**
>
> Suffice it to say that critical roles without suitable replacements leave organizations most vulnerable to employee turnover.

Let's look at two examples. If Nicole, one of Mason's four AP clerks, becomes ill and takes a medical leave of absence, one of her colleagues can at least temporarily pick up the slack. In this case, the overall risk to Mason is low. On the other hand, consider Alexandra, Mason's IT manager. She is solely responsible for creating new user accounts, maintaining security, applying patches, and overseeing upgrades. No one else knows how to do these things. If Alexandra were to abruptly leave the organization or even give two weeks' notice, Mason would scramble to find a suitable replacement. Although Mason cannot guarantee that Alexandra will not win the lottery or prevent her from being hit by a bus, it should certainly have in place a succession plan for the IT manager position.

Internal Movement

Table 17.1 manifests the obvious: generally speaking, internal employee movement poses less risk to organizations than employee departures. Whether via promotion or lateral move, employees often take on new roles within the same organization. In either event, several factors mitigate organizational risk in these cases:

- Within reason, organizations can control when employees begin their new positions, maximizing both knowledge transfer and the time needed to find replacements from the external labor market if necessary.

- Organizations typically set aside time for incumbents to mentor their eventual replacements.

- If replacements still have questions after the mentoring period ends, they can call their predecessors as needed.

- The circumstances surrounding an incumbent's transfer or promotion tend to be reasonably pleasant, thus minimizing any tension between incumbent and predecessor.

External Movement

The era of unabashed employee loyalty ceased long ago and does not require rehashing in this book. Compared to 20 years ago, organizations today face a much greater risk of losing key employees to competitors, especially in concentrated geographic areas. What's more, by virtue of implementing a widely used system, an organization typically makes its end users much more marketable than they were *before* the project began. It's hardly an exaggeration to say that certain organizations are so lean that the sudden loss of a single key employee could cause their systems to fail.

Table 17.1 leads to the following natural conclusions surrounding employee exits:

- Organizations cannot always control when incumbent employees leave, potentially minimizing both knowledge transfer and the time needed to find replacements from the external labor market if necessary.

- Organizations may not be able to set aside sufficient time for departing incumbents to mentor their eventual replacements.

- New employees with unanswered questions after the mentoring period probably cannot call their predecessors.

- Incumbents departing under less than ideal circumstances may not be willing to impart their knowledge to their predecessors.

Of course, not all turnover is voluntary. Organizations sometimes terminate employees for gross misconduct, allowing *no* time for knowledge transfer or on-the-job training of a replacement. The following example is true, although the company name has been changed. About six years ago, a medium-sized company, Gumble, fired its payroll manager, Barney, because he was giving himself raises.

Barney figured that, even if caught, Gumble management would not do anything about it because he was the only one who knew how to run payroll. Although this is hardly an excuse for this type of conduct, Barney was absolutely correct in one regard: *he was the only one who knew how to run payroll.* Gumble had not documented any part of its payroll process. To cut employee checks, Gumble had to fly me in on short notice. Obviously, this is not an ideal situation.

External Labor Market

As it pertains to the successful maintenance of systems, the relative increase in voluntary employee turnover over the past 20 years has created both problems and opportunities. As discussed, key end users may be more apt to walk away, especially now that they have participated in the implementation of a commonly used system.

The possibility of losing key employees is particularly acute on adversarial projects, such as that of The Page and Plant Company in Chapter 1, "Introduction." Certain P&P employees *may* have endured the turbulence of the Bonham Software project specifically to make themselves more marketable to other companies either running Bonham or in the process of implementing it. For instance, if P&P's Human Resource Information Systems (HRIS) manager, Colin, decides that he is underpaid, rest assured that Bonham will appear prominently on his resume along with the role that he played on the project. Should a recruiter call with the promise of more money, he can hardly be blamed for listening to the sales pitch.

For P&P, however, that same problem represents an opportunity. The fact that many companies use Bonham means that, if Colin leaves, P&P should have an easier time finding a suitable replacement. The pool of available applicants is, in all likelihood, much larger than that for P&P's legacy system. Again, Bonham is a widely used application.

This is not to say that P&P should view its employees as replaceable cogs. They are not. Let's say that P&P is able to poach the HRIS manager, Zach, from The Mercury Group, a competitor that also runs Bonham. Mercury and P&P will each have different system configurations, interfaces, and reporting requirements. Zach's learning curve may not be terribly steep but, rest assured, it does exist. P&P should not make the mistake of assuming that Zach can hit the ground running, especially if P&P lacks comprehensive system documentation.

Change in Major Business Process

Much less frequent than key employee turnover, an organization sometimes decides to change a major internal process, prompting a "mini-implementation" within a live system. For example, Deacon Entertainment activates its new system and, three months later, decides to start paying its employees on a biweekly basis—rather than weekly. Although this may not seem like an enormous project (and it really should not be), Deacon should *not* minimize the degree of work involved. Deacon will have to change specific settings in its system for employee paychecks to be correct. Employee taxes that were taken every week will now need to be taken every two. End users will need to run update programs in the new system. IT will have to modify interfaces to send accurate amounts to carriers. Reports that audited data for anomalies will need to be tweaked, if not completely rewritten.

Larger process changes require more work than smaller changes. Consider an organization that fundamentally changes its accounting basis from cash to accrual. To think that this can be accomplished from a systems perspective with a mere click of the mouse is the acme of foolishness.

NOTE

A significant change in business process may require major system ramifications vis-à-vis setup, processing, interfaces, and reporting. To be certain, organizations should extensively test such changes before rolling them out. Those that do not devote the required time and resources to changes of this magnitude dramatically increase the risk of either immediate or forthcoming system issues.

Enterprise Risk Management

Organizations face increased risk for a variety of reasons, some of which include these:

- Development and introduction of new products
- Issuance of additional stocks
- Major financial transactions
- M&A activity
- Expansion into different markets
- Activation of new systems

With respect to activating new systems, organizational risk increases for many reasons. Perhaps the most fundamental is that end users now employ different methods and applications to perform their jobs. These new methods and applications are almost always less understood than those of the previous applications.

Frequent international lecturer and author Robert Charette has written extensively on enterprise risk management (ERM). In the following article written for the Cutter Consortium, Charette details many of the issues associated with ERM in relation to implementing new systems.

TAKING A WHOLE ENTERPRISE APPROACH TO THE MANAGEMENT OF RISK

Over the past decade, a large number of corporate IT departments have focused their attention on implementing enterprise resource planning (ERP) and customer relationship management (CRM) systems. Although different surveys provide different results, it seems that all surveys agree that a majority of corporations have expressed dissatisfaction or disappointment with their ERP or CRM implementations. The highly publicized problems at HP, Hershey, Nike, Avis, and several others serve as reminders of what happens when an ERP or CRM system implementation goes badly.

Furthermore, the literature on both ERP and CRM implementation difficulties points to almost identical problems, such as these:

- Lack of senior management support
- Unrealistic expectations
- Excessive internal organizational politics among IT department and business units
- Organizational resistance to change
- Automation of inappropriate business processes and procedures
- Undercapitalization of the project in terms of time, money, skill sets, and so on
- Poor functional requirements definition, including excessive data requirements
- Inadequate training of staff in systems use
- Poor project management

Of course, the solutions proposed to these problems are to get senior management commitment, create realistic expectations, reduce the corporate politics, and so on. However, exactly how are IT organizations supposed to implement these solutions?

To have a prayer in making ERP and CRM initiatives successful, the first thing that needs to be recognized by senior management is that these types of initiatives are nothing less than ERM initiatives. They are not—and should never be—labeled as IT CIO initiatives. ERM initiatives are by their nature strategic activities meant to reduce the overall level of risk that confronts an organization, as well as possibly create new sources of business opportunities.

Second, ERM initiatives involve a wide range of risks that cover the entire enterprise, as the preceding list illustrates. The types of enterprise risk ERM initiatives involved include these:

- Insurable risks (those hazards or threats to the corporation that insurance typically covers)
- Financial/treasury risks (those that are created by approaches to managing the corporation's finances)
- Operational risks (those that are created by a corporation's dependence on its systems, processes, and staff)
- Strategic risks (those that may cause a corporation to stagnate or collapse because of a failure to adapt to a changing operating environment)
- Governance risks (those that are created by noncompliance with rules, regulations, or laws)

These risks are beyond the management reach or responsibility of the CIO and involve the whole corporation.

Third, because of the types of risks involved, successful ERM initiatives, unless they are lucky, require an enterprise risk management and governance (ERM&G) approach either in name or in practice. In other words, some process must exist that can identify, assess, and manage the strategic, operational, financial, insurable, and governance risks as a whole.

Look at the list of implementation problems once again. Again, is it realistic to ask a CIO—or worse, an ERP or CRM program manager in the IT department—to solve these problems?

Ideally, corporations should not embark upon ERM initiatives without a robust ERM&G approach in place. Because most corporations don't have an ERM&G approach in place, using an ERM initiative like an ERP or CRM development would be a good time to create one. Corporations should consider an ERM initiative as a forcing function to identify the need for as well as the beginning of an implementation of an ERM approach. This is especially true for midsized (or small) corporations that have much more to lose if they embark on an ERP or CRM implementation that doesn't pan out.

With an ERM&G approach in place, the potential problems can be attacked in a systematic and systemic fashion. Without one, no one—especially senior executive management—should be surprised that their ERP, CRM, or future ERM initiatives turn out to be disappointments.

Finally, even if you are lucky enough to deliver one successfully, don't expect to get the full benefits from your ERP or CRM system without their being tied to an ERM and governance approach. Without a comprehensive process for using the information these systems produce to address corporate risks in a holistic fashion, you are limiting yourself to only half or less of the true value of an ERP or CRM system.[i]

Acquisitions

Organizations sometimes acquire or merge with others, typically resulting in challenges of many different fronts, including systems. For example, Woods Construction acquires Mickelson Plumbing. As a result of the merger, Woods' management decides to integrate Mickelson's setup and data into its current system. Rare is the acquisition in which both companies are using the same payroll, general ledger, and procurement systems. This is no exception. In this case, Woods uses SAP, whereas Mickleson never retired its legacy system. Even if both companies had used the same system (and version), Woods would still have to convert all of Mickelson's data into SAP to process all transactions in the combined entity from the same system.

Organizations involved in acquisitions have a number of different data and system options with respect to integration. Each option is presented in the order of expected difficulty. Note that the expected outputs of each option vary in direct relation to its expected inputs. To get more out, organizations have to put more in.

Complete Integration

As was the case earlier, Woods can fully migrate Mickelson's data to SAP. Although this is the costliest and most time consuming, complete integration eliminates the need for Woods to maintain Mickelson's legacy system—and pay for its support. It also facilitates standard business processing and reporting.

Partial Integration

Woods can migrate Mickelson's data to SAP but store that data in a separate SAP configuration. This solution represents a decent amount of work for Woods, but it will not have to pay support costs on Mickelson's legacy system. What's more, Woods will not have to maintain two separate systems; it will have a central repository of all data after the merger. Note that partial integration means that data from the two organizations will *not* be standardized, resulting in complicated reporting and increased processing time.

Zero Integration

Woods may choose to leave Mickelson's legacy system alone. This choice represents the least amount of work for Woods. However, it also means that Woods has to maintain two different systems, pay additional support costs, and lack a central data repository.

Decommissioned Applications

Software vendors typically decommission older applications after giving their clients at least two years' notice. This should be plenty of time for most organizations to make alternative arrangements. Organizations unable or unwilling to stop using decommissioned applications have a number of options:

- Attempt to negotiate with vendors some type of "sunset" support beyond that which the vendor has agreed to provide to the rest of its clients.
- Opt for independent support through a third party.
- Opt to continue using the application unsupported—a risky move to be sure, especially if the application experiences some issues.[1]

On rare occasions, however, organizations will try to fight the vendor's decision. An example occurred in early 2009, as Sisters of Charity of Leavenworth Health System sued Lawson Software for decommissioning two products.[ii]

Generally speaking, the legal option is a risky one. In this specific case, one of the applications decommissioned by Lawson (Time Accrual, a product designed to track sick and vacation balances) has been generally available for more than 15 years. What's more, Lawson announced the eventual retirement of Time Accrual years ago and even postponed it by 18 months. At some point, vendors have to retire older applications.

Errors and the Dangers of Automation

At a high level, end users make two types of errors in enterprise systems: errors of omission and errors of commission. Commission errors are more common as employees adapt to their new applications; even with extensive training and system testing, there's always a learning curve. Examples of errors of omission include

- A payroll clerk forgets to process a pay increase for an employee.
- An IT manager forgets to assign security to a new finance director, not allowing him to view key financial reports.

In both instances, the fix is fairly simple. The first employee will surely call the payroll department about her paycheck, and the pay change can be processed retroactively. The finance director will receive an error message upon attempting to view the reports and will quickly call the IT help desk.

---

1. For more on support options, see Chapter 7, "Support for the New System."

Errors of commission can be more dangerous and time consuming to fix. Consider the following similar examples:

- A payroll clerk processes an incorrect employee pay change for an employee, keying an increase of 11 percent instead of 1 percent.

- An IT manager assigns incorrect security to a new finance director, allowing him to view *and change* financial information throughout the organization.

In each instance, organizational risk increases. In each case, the affected employee may be less likely to come forward and report the error.

Moreover, the dangers of automation often exacerbate errors of all sorts. Batch programs can significantly exacerbate both errors of omission and commission, creating thousands of incorrect individual transactions for as long as the mistakes remain undetected.[2] We saw this in Chapter 1 as Oates Health Care incorrectly calculated overtime for years via its application's batch program. We saw a similar issue with Satriani Consulting Group in Chapter 8, "Selecting Consultants."

NOTE

Organizations should ensure that newly hired employees are immediately and properly trained in how to utilize new applications in the context of their jobs. Although the need for new-hire training may seem obvious, many times a new employee will unknowingly make a simple mistake that cascades throughout the system, resulting in data quality issues and a time-consuming and expensive data cleanup effort.

Merger and Acquisition Activity

Although certainly not a common occurrence, sometimes software vendors acquire one another. In the ERP world, perhaps the two most prominent examples in the past decade are PeopleSoft's acquisition of JD Edwards in July 2003 and Oracle's subsequent—and highly contentious—acquisition of PeopleSoft in January 2005. Merger and acquisition (M&A) activity often and justifiably gives pause to clients running the software of the acquired companies. For example, many PeopleSoft clients expressed concern over eventually having to move to Oracle applications upon completion of that merger. (In fact, one of my clients involved in system selection at the time

---

2. I am reminded here of Aristotle's quote from *Metaphysica*: "The whole is more than the sum of its parts."

actually avoided both PeopleSoft and Oracle because of the uncertainty regarding the merger.) Up to this point, that fear has not been realized; Oracle as of this writing fully supports PeopleSoft applications.[3] Of course, this could change at any point.

On a general level, a client happily running a vendor's applications *may* find itself in a precarious position at some point in the future as a result of M&A activity. All else being equal, smaller, publicly held vendors are much more likely to be acquired than larger, privately held organizations. The Oracle acquisition of PeopleSoft, however, proves that even very large companies can be gobbled up.

Vendor Divorce

Sometimes the new system can no longer meet an organization's business needs. The replacement system has essentially become another legacy system, not unlike the one that it had replaced. The decision to supplant a vendor's applications should *not* be taken lightly for several reasons. For one, as has been stated in this book, vendors of the same tier tend to be more similar than dissimilar. This applies to vendor policies, support agreements, annual support fees, and the like. Before hastily showing your vendor the door, remember the axiom, "Better the devil you know than the devil you don't know."

Second, the cost of a new license, support agreement, and consultants is likely to be substantial. Being a tad peeved over a specific support incident or a software glitch is typically not a justifiable reason for looking for an alternative system.

Third, in the event of a major dispute between a client and its vendor, there are alternatives short of terminating the relationship. Organizations such as The Center for Information Technology and Dispute Resolution and the American Mediation Association can assist organizations involved in a conflict with their software vendors.

With that disclaimer, sometimes a marriage is just not working out. A consistent pattern of mutual antagonism, unmet expectations, or poor customer service means that it is time for the client to sever the relationship.[4] Dan

---

3. According to its Web site, Oracle continues to support PeopleSoft product lines for current users. The company has not forced its clients to migrate from PeopleSoft to Oracle applications.

4. Note that sometimes the same can be said about the relationship between a client and its system integrator (SI).

Tynan of InfoWorld offers five valid reasons for moving on. Note here that "it" refers to an organization's current vendor.

1. **It can't provide the service you need.** When it takes three phone calls to get a response or three repairs to get something working right, it's time to get out, says the Uptime Group's Patty Laushman. "If you're paying the vendor, they should know what they're doing. You shouldn't have to call three times to fix the same problem."

2. **It can't scale.** If the vendors you started with can't keep up with your company's growth, it's time to move on. "When you're a small company, you want to deal with vendors that understand your needs," says USAS Technologies' Seth Hishmeh. "Once you've grown from, say, 20 to 100 employees, you may need a different kind of company."

3. **It can't meet your security requirements.** Developers don't always build robust security into their apps, says Bruce Eissner, CEO of Polar Cove, a consultancy that specializes in information security. "We sometimes find those applications don't provide the level of assurance our clients need," he says.

4. **It can't meet compliance standards.** If the vendor fails to meet Sarbanes Oxley, SAS70, Health Insurance Portability and Accountability Act (HIPAA), or other federally mandated guidelines, you'll still be held responsible, Eissner says. "You can't say, 'I asked them to do this and trusted what they told me.' Ignorance is no defense."

5. **It is in financial trouble.** The last thing you want is the vendor's disgruntled employees with their hands on your IT systems, which can happen if the vendor skips payrolls, says Technisource's Jon Piot. Ask your service provider for financials, check its Dunn & Bradstreet scores, and listen to what its own employees are saying, Piot advises, as "that will give you a pretty good idea of what's going on."[iii]

Summary

The only constant with any widely used system is change; no system exists in a vacuum. This chapter focused on the effects of operational decisions on organizations' systems. Changes in personnel, business practices, and organizational structure can take place at any point. Wise is the organization that anticipates such changes with succession planning, comprehensive system documentation, and end-user backups. Danger and risk are always lurking with new systems, just as they did with the old ones. Organizations need to be prepared.

Endnotes

i. http://www.cutter.com/content/risk/fulltext/advisor/2004/041124.html

ii. http://www.pcworld.com/article/159105/hospital_chain_sues_lawson_software_over_retiring_erp_apps.html

iii. http://www.infoworld.com/d/developer-world/dumping-your-technology-vendor-let-reason-prevail-072

PART V

Maximizing the Chance of Success

The final Part of this book focuses on the specific steps that organizations can take to limit their risk of system failure. At a minimum, organizations should attempt to avoid the pitfalls mentioned in previous sections and case studies. For example, organizations would be wise not to start off on the wrong foot by selecting a less-than-reputable system integrator (SI), designing their systems with excessive interfaces, insufficiently staffing their implementation teams, and expecting end users to effectively do two jobs concurrently for a year. These are obvious steps in the wrong direction—examples of what *not* to do.

Avoiding the obvious is not enough. Organizations can do many positive things to increase the odds that their new systems not only realize the benefits promised by the vendor during system selection, but do so in a timely, budget-conscious fashion.

Chapter 18

Mid-Implementation Corrective Mechanisms

The perfect is the enemy of the good.
—*Voltaire*

Introduction

As a general rule, implementations do not just spontaneously combust. Failures tend to stem from the aggregation of many issues. Although some issues may have been known since the early stages of the project (for example, the sales cycle or system design), implementation teams discover the majority of problems during the middle of the implementation, typically during some form of testing. This chapter focuses on the different midstream mechanisms available to organizations. Specific measures include these:

- Mid-implementation audits[1]
- Adding resources
- Replacing individual consultants
- Replacing the SI's project manager
- "Losing" the project manager altogether
- Changing SIs
- Sunk costs and avoiding the point of no return
- Moving noncritical items to Phase II
- Killing the project

Note that not all organizations realistically have each option available to them, depending on a number of factors. Invariably, some will have reached the point of no return—that is, pulling the plug on the project is no longer a viable option. As such, organizations may be unwilling to replace a project manager or change SIs because the delays will, in all likelihood, cause them to miss dates etched in stone. In these cases, organizations have to make do with resources unacceptable under "normal" circumstances.

Mid-Implementation Audits

I am a big believer in checking the pulse of a project to see if things are on track well before the organization has passed the point of no return. Unfortunately, many projects are already so far behind schedule that few people can make the case that an additional week or so should be "lost" performing a mid-implementation audit.

Ideally, the project manager tracks the project's progress from the beginning and communicates issues in meetings with the organization's steering committee or project management office (PMO). Status reports and other routine

---

1. Note that pre- and post-implementation audits are covered in the next chapter. This chapter focuses on steps that organizations can take midstream.

methods also provide mechanisms to keep key personnel informed of the implementation's status, obstacles, and overall progress. Audits often manifest the need to take additional measures.

The next chapter provides additional information about the types of audits available to organizations before, during, and after the system implementation. Audits are so important that they warrant a separate chapter.

Adding Resources

Many project managers and implementation teams do not anticipate the time and resources required during testing. Faced with delays from previous phases of the project, their stopgap solution is to throw more people into the fray. For example, a company has tasked its HR, payroll, and finance managers with data validation. However, those three people are not terribly skilled in tools such as Microsoft Excel or Access. To remedy the situation, the organization involves IT more than originally planned. IT must create an automated tool that performs the validation electronically. On the less technical end, employees not critical to the project might be asked to spot-check some transactions from the new system and see if they match the equivalent transactions from the legacy system.

Note that the simpler the task required, the quicker end users can perform them. It does not take a rocket scientist to look at two paper or electronic paychecks or purchase orders from two different systems and note any differences. Very little formal training should be required for tasks as simple as these. If shown how to do something or given a formal script, most employees should be good to go. However, for more involved tasks, it is unrealistic to show previously uninvolved and inexperienced end users how to perform them and expect quick turnarounds. In these cases, the adding of resources may actually be a net negative.

Let's consider the example of Atlanta Medical. Henry is the payroll manager on an implementation in the middle of testing. In trying to make up time, he involves Aaron, the payroll clerk who had previously been peripheral to the implementation. Aaron attended training six months ago but really has not touched the system since then. It may take so much time for Henry to show Aaron how to process payroll that the time spent explaining the tasks to him actually exceeds the time that it would take for Henry to simply do it himself. Even assuming that Aaron is a quick study, he no doubt will have questions about what to do if and when issues arise, thus taking Henry away from his original task.

> **NOTE**
> Adding more resources can have mixed results. If the right people are involved at the right time to perform tasks within their abilities, the benefits will outweigh the costs. However, adding more people will not always fix an issue and make up for lost time. There is no guarantee that these steps will put a project back on target.

What's more, an experienced project manager should know this. When unsure about whether this tactic will work, the project manager should ask his seasoned consultants about the expected outcomes *before* committing resources.

Replacing Individual Consultants

From the client's perspective, an individual consultant might need to be replaced for several reasons. The first and most important is an inability of that consultant to contribute at a level mandated by the client. As discussed in Chapter 8, "Selecting Consultants," the type of SI selected often drives the type of consultants placed on the project. The larger firm might send in a team of consultants, some of whom are more junior than the lead consultant. To be sure, not all consultants possess the same background, skills, and expertise in any system or with the individual applications within that system.

Client senior management typically removes a consultant from a project for two major reasons:

- The consultant lacks the ability to contribute at the required level.
- The consultant has a personality conflict with other team members.

This has happened to almost every seasoned consultant, including yours truly. Sometimes clients and consultants just get off on the wrong foot. For example, more technical consultants might come off as abrupt with "warm and fuzzy" end users, causing conflict.

Clients certainly have the right to remove a problematic consultant at any point during the project, because they are the ones paying the bills. However, the effectiveness of this strategy cannot be guaranteed for a number of reasons. The following general rules apply for replacing external consultants.

First, timing matters. Organizations in the latter stages of an implementation will have greater difficulty in finding a suitable replacement. What's more, organizations close to system activation should almost never replace a consultant—absent some sort of gross misconduct. It is difficult for an organization to expect an SI to quickly locate and deploy a suitable consultant who can hit the ground running at this critical stage.

Second, trying to address personality conflicts among existing team members is typically more effective than bringing in a new consultant. As the project progresses, the institutional, system, and business process knowledge of an external consultant may become irreplaceable. Also, it is important to understand the source of the conflict. Is the client upset that a delivered feature in the software being implemented does not work as advertised or as it does in the legacy system? If this is the case, the consultant is simply the bearer of bad news. Supplanting that consultant will not resolve the underlying problem. A new consultant may provide the answer using different words or in a different voice, but the overall message to the client is the same: the software does not work as the client wants it to work without some type of customization.

Third, the greater the depth and breadth of that consultant's skills, the less willing the client should be to replace that consultant. Replacing the seasoned consultant who diplomatically challenges poor client decisions with a more malleable but less knowledgeable, less skilled consultant may appease a client in the short term. In the long term, however, that switch will probably lead to setup, testing, or validation issues. Perhaps the original consultant knew the ultimate outcome of poor setup or processing decisions and was simply trying to avoid them, not merely being difficult.

If a consultant comes across as abrasive from day one, the best course of action for both the SI and the client is to attempt to address the issue immediately. Sometimes it's simply best to cut the cord right at the start. If a personality conflict exacerbates over time, the resolution is much less clear. Client perceptions matter, and no one should have to tolerate demeaning comments or actions from a consultant onsite at $200 per hour. However, employees should put up with an expert consultant who means well and simply wants the project to be successful, even if he is a little quirky. (Working on projects like these tends to make people a little eccentric. Trust me on this one.) After all, that consultant brings a great deal to the table and will not be around forever.

Replacing the SI's Project Manager

For several reasons, project managers not performing up to snuff are not replaced nearly as frequently as individual consultants. For one, project managers are coordinators more than they are "worker bees" and product experts. The latter can come across as condescending to apprehensive end users who may fear the unknown of a new system. By their very nature, most project managers bring people together, ensure that goals are met, and soothe conflicts as they arise. As such, they are less likely to provoke daily conflicts with end users.

On a second and equally important note, project managers are harder to replace because SIs employ fewer of them. This is particularly true for boutique firms. Generally speaking, SIs have more consultants than project managers. As a result, project managers tend not to be "on the bench" as much as individual consultants.

This is not to say that an organization should tolerate consistently deficient performance from a project manager, a subject addressed in Chapter 13, "People Issues, Roles, and Responsibilities." However, clients should understand the often considerable logistical difficulty of replacing a project manager from the same SI. To that end, organizations may want to consider two additional options for the project manager consistently not meeting expectations: "losing" the project manager (and keeping the SI) or changing SIs altogether.

"Losing" the Project Manager Altogether

Perhaps an organization values the contributions of the SI as a whole—and the individual consultants—but cannot live with the current project manager. Rather than find a new SI (a drastic step to be discussed next), the client requests a replacement from the firm's senior management. That firm has no short-term replacement available. The client opts to remove the project manager from the project and will either permanently or temporarily manage the project and the individual consultants using internal team members.

This approach is fraught with risks. For example, Lars is a full-time employee at DM Metal, a large organization implementing a new enterprise resource planning (ERP) system. DM's management was not happy with Robert, the project manager from its SI, RTL Consultants. As a result, DM appoints Lars as the *de facto* project manager of the project but keeps Kirk and James, the RTL consultants. From a practical standpoint, there are a few challenges. First, Lars has insufficient expertise in the new system. Second, Lars is going to lean more often and more heavily on Kirk and James for updates than did Robert. The net impact is that the consultants will have less time to do their day jobs, and the project may suffer as a result.

Changing SIs

On occasion, an organization is so dissatisfied with its partner that it opts to bring in a new one. The client finds its partner's promises of skilled consultants and an organized approach lacking. Rather than attempt one of the strategies previously discussed, the client opts to find a new consulting firm.

Before deciding on a new partner, senior management should understand the nature of the fractured relationship. True consulting or project manager incompetence from the beginning is certainly grounds to sever the relationship. However, rarely is the situation that obvious. Organizations should look in the mirror to determine the true source of the conflict and consider the following questions:

- Can the issues be easily fixed with different personnel from the same SI?
- Can the issues be easily fixed with different personnel from the client?
- Can the issues be fixed with a different strategy?
- Do the issues stem from the type of contract signed?
- Are the implementation issues a function of the SI or of the new system? Is the SI simply the messenger of client-based issues—for example, bad data, insufficiently skilled end users, and so on?
- Is the SI "working to rule?" Or is it perceived as "obstinate" because it is simply attempting to implement the system in a traditional manner—that is, one that is known to work?
- Is another SI going to be appreciably better?
- What is the overall impact of changing SIs on the project timeline and budget?

The answers to these questions will help guide an organization toward the right decision. To replace SIs, clients should remember the following:

- The net benefits should exceed the costs of keeping the existing SI by a considerable margin. For example, the organization spending $2M on an implementation should not oust its consultants two months before going live solely to save $50,000 in consulting fees; the risks do not justify the rewards.
- The closer to going live, the tougher it is for a client to replace individual consultants, much less the entire SI, and still make the desired go-live date.

> **NOTE**
>
> Many implementation issues stem from overly ambitious vendor promises, bad data, and reluctance on the part of employees to "get on board." Simply changing SIs will in no way guarantee that a project will turn around. New SIs may very well tell clients virtually the same thing as their predecessor, simply in a different voice.

When considering changing SIs, it's imperative for organizations to consider the timing of such a change in relation to the overall project and its intended go-live date. Consider Soze, Inc., a manufacturing firm implementing a new ERP system. It decides to replace Hockney Consulting with Keaton Integrators. Soze may have decided to oust Hockney for all sorts of reasons, including these:

- Dissatisfaction with Hockney's consultants
- Dissatisfaction with Hockney's management
- Better rates offered by Keaton
- Lower expenses stemming from Keaton's geographic proximity
- Keaton's perceived superior experience (better bang for the same buck)
- Some combination of these

In considering such a change, timing is everything. Consider the following three scenarios in the context of a baseball analogy:

- **Scenario A: The Early Innings.** Hockney completed 25 percent of the system's design and testing, but Soze had yet to go live.
- **Scenario B: Midgame.** Hockney completed 60 percent of the system's design and testing, but Soze had yet to go live.
- **Scenario C: The Home Stretch.** Hockney completed 90 percent of the system's design and testing. Soze was on the verge of going live when it made the call to replace Hockney.

In Scenario A, it's relatively easy for Soze to axe Hockney. Although it may already have spent tens of thousands of dollars, Soze has not passed the point of no return with Hockney. In fact, it may best be served by simply cutting ties if it has no confidence that things will turn around. In this case, the perceived costs of inaction exceed the costs of action for Soze.

Scenario B is a bit more complicated. Even though reputable SIs typically follow industry- and application-specific best practices, no two SIs follow precisely the same methodology and employ consultants with identical skill sets. Translation: if Soze decides to supplant Hockney with Keaton, it might have to first take a few steps back to take a big step forward. It's not inconceivable that Soze will have to start from scratch, forcing the company to write off a significant sum of money in the process.

Scenario C is the most difficult and really the least justifiable. In fact, I'd argue that Soze had no business letting its dissatisfaction with Hockney linger for so long. Client-consultant relationships rarely sour over a single isolated incident. Generally speaking, a pervasive pattern of the following often leads to a *gradual* deterioration of the union:

- Suboptimal consultant performance
- Interparty communication
- Poor overall coordination

By getting so close to the finish line, Soze has essentially missed its opportunity to replace Hockney without having to eat prohibitive costs. If Soze really wants to go with Keaton, it will almost invariably have to postpone its go-live date. It's unlikely that Keaton's management would sign up for "hitting the ground running" and viewing Hockney's work as gospel. That type of blind faith is rarely justified.

CAUTION

Changing SIs can be tricky. If an organization's relationship with its SI starts to fray, it's imperative for senior management to address the issues immediately. The longer that issues persist, the more difficult it is for the client to replace its SI while remaining on schedule and within budget. Hoping and waiting for a bad situation to improve significantly increases organizational risk. Ultimately, financial considerations may make such a change impossible.

Sunk Costs and Avoiding the Point of No Return

Most organizations hold meetings at the *end* of their implementations to determine if they should activate systems on which so many have been working for so long. Given the amount of time and money already spent on the project, organizations almost invariably decide to proceed with system activation, *irrespective of the number and severity of the issues facing them.* In the end, this "go/no go" meeting is almost always a mere formality.

On a well-run project, however, everyone is much more proactive than this. Rather than wait until the decision is essentially made for them, the intelligent organization holds a formal meeting after the project has launched but *before* it has reached the point of no return. The objective of this meeting is for senior management—along with critical input from its SI—to determine whether the implementation should continue. If the implementation is unlikely to result in a successful system activation, the organization needs to stop the project and make major project and budgetary adjustments. Executives must realize that their organizations cannot recoup sunk costs.[2]

Under these dire circumstances, organizations should fight the urge to throw good money after bad. Of course, executives have options short of completely pulling the plug on a problematic implementation, one of which is discussed next.

Moving Noncritical Items to Phase II

Many delayed implementations have not hit previously planned system activation dates. The levers mentioned earlier in this chapter—for example, adding consultants, replacing the project manager, and so on—may *not* have resolved the issues. However, although employee and consultant hours tend to increase as projects near their magic dates, efforts cannot simply be redoubled by wishful project managers or senior management. If an implementation is considerably behind schedule and over budget and the go-live date is etched in stone, the client and project manager should make hard decisions about which features will make the cut. Delaying system features from Phase I is a much less drastic step than removing the SI or pushing the go-live date. In fact, it may be better for all concerned.

Table 18.1 displays functionality on a fictitious implementation viewed under the "essential" microscope.

Many organizations mistakenly believe that every application of the new system is essential for Phase I. In Table 18.1, the Payroll module happens to be mission critical, as are General Ledger, Inventory Control, and Benefits. However, organizations can implement items such as position management—in which employees are tied to positions for budgeting purposes—at a later date without causing significant operational problems. The same applies to items such as Web-based reporting. If reports have to be generated locally—and not delivered via e-mail—until Phase II, the organization will survive.

---

2. In *Economics of the Public Sector (Second Edition)*, Joseph Stiglitz defines sunk costs as "costs that are not recoverable upon the exit of the firm." Think of a movie ticket as a sunk cost. Economists would argue that you should always leave a bad movie after paying because you can't get your money back. You can at least recover your time.

TABLE 18.1 List of System Modules for a Common System Implementation

Module	Essential
Payroll	Yes
Benefits	Yes
General Ledger	Yes
Position Management	No
Activity Management	No
Inventory Control	Yes
Web-Based Reporting	Yes

Alternatively, organizations using a phased approach may consider postponing entire parts of the organization to a later phase. Returning to the example of Byrne Health Care in Chapter 9, "Implementation Strategies and Phases," unexpected delays stemming from poor data and end-user resistance have left Byrne management two choices. First, it can carry on and risk major issues with all five hospitals in Phase I. Second, it can focus its resources on the three "easiest" implementations as shown in Table 18.2.

TABLE 18.2 Phased Approach for Byrne Medical, Revised

Hospital	HR	Payroll	General Ledger	Procurement
Victoria	Phase I	Phase I	Phase II	Phase III
Winfield	Phase I	Phase I	Phase II	Phase III
Mattingly	Phase I	Phase I	Phase II	Phase III
Gamble	Phase IA	Phase IA	Phase II	Phase III
Jackson	Phase IA	Phase IA	Phase II	Phase III

Because of issues discovered at Gamble and Jackson Hospitals, Byrne senior management postpones their implementations until Phase I has been completed. Internal resources and consultants will spend two months working exclusively with end users from these sites, thereby maximizing the chances that those hospitals will go live successfully. Although these may be viewed as individual failures, the Victoria, Winfield, and Mattingly sites will go live on the desired date. From an organization's perspective, two Mild Failures are preferable to one Unmitigated Disaster. Had Byrne pushed through, it would have run the risk of *all* hospitals missing their go-live dates—arguably an Unmitigated Disaster or, at the very least, a Big Failure.

In an ideal world, Byrne would activate each application at the same time at each hospital. However, as discussed, the entire project is in jeopardy of missing its go-live date. The intelligent project manager should have made senior management aware of this possibility as soon as this became realistic, not at the last minute.

Postponing features can, in many instances, allow projects to recoup valuable time. Clients should consider the following three questions when evaluating which features to trim from a large project:

- What type of project is it?
- Are executives' incentives aligned with those of the organization?
- What are the risks and rewards of keeping nonessential functionality?[3]

What Type of Project Is It?

Consider two types of projects:

- Waterfall or sequential projects that follow a rigid methodology and produce, at the end of the project, a "big bang" result
- Agile-based projects that utilize iterative versions of applications and programs

Organizations are typically reluctant to cut functionality from Waterfall-based projects for one simple reason: there's typically a "now or never" mentality. In other words, key stakeholders believe that if the software isn't present immediately, they'll never see it.

This may or may not be the case. Delays, budget cuts, internal politics, and key employee turnover often mean that the best intentions regarding future rollouts are derailed.

On Agile-based projects, internal players are a bit less draconian. They are more likely to sacrifice nice-to-have functionality if it's unlikely to be successful. Project teams, developers, and senior management know that the next version of the software (or the next phase of the project) can easily incorporate enhancements. There's no "burning plank" mentality here: there will be a next version, and typically soon.

TIP
Determine in advance which features are essential. If necessary, be prepared to drop nonessential features for the overall good of the project.

---

3. Note that there may be other practical considerations for removing features, such as lack of funds, internal disagreement over policy or process, or resource restrictions.

Are Executives' Incentives Aligned with Those of the Organization?

Executives sometimes go "all in" with a particular feature, refusing to acknowledge signs of peril. For example, a few years ago I worked on a project in danger of imploding. System testing and data validation were months behind schedule, affecting the entire organization's financial health, not to mention little things like payroll and financial reporting. Less important, the rollout of a manager self-service application also looked doubtful, although this affected a small percentage of employees in the organization.

Although the overall project suffered, VPs refused to cut self-service from the project plan. Why? Because their bonuses were tied to the introduction of self-service, whether it was successful or not. This is a classic example of senior managers letting their provincial self-interest override their responsibilities to the organization at large.

From day one, make sure that senior managers' incentives align with those of the organization.

What Are the Risks and Rewards of Keeping Nonessential Functionality?

Consider an ambitious customer relationship management (CRM) project. Although everyone would love to have sexy analytics from day one, does that functionality come at the risk of not being able to enter new customer sales? Those dashboards aren't worth a red cent if they don't contain accurate data.

> **TIP**
>
> Remember that, even on Waterfall projects, there's always tomorrow. Absent some compelling business need, ensure that critical functionality is rock solid before chasing next-generation functionality.

Killing the Project

Sometimes the best move is to simply stop all work on a project. Admittedly, this is the equivalent of political or financial suicide for the senior executive most closely associated with the project. However, if the project stands no chance of going live absent major issues, the organization's best move is to step back and reevaluate.

Despite several instances in which such drastic action was warranted, I have never seen this done. A few times, steering committees and senior VPs proceed with a project knowing full well that the new system will be activated with major issues. In a sense, these higher-ups were right: no activation is issue free. Depending on the severity of the issues likely to be faced, however, killing a project should not be completely eliminated from consideration. An organization unable to produce employee checks, fulfill inventory, or run accurate financial reports should think long and hard about ignoring the warning signs.

A friend of mine once told me about a CFO of a public company overseeing a large system implementation in the 1980s. He refused to go live with the new system until his team could guarantee more than 99 percent accuracy with regard to financial transactions of employee paychecks. The CFO's concern was a valid one: if the company could not pay its employees due to a system issue, Wall Street would not care. Investors would believe that the company did not have enough cash to make payroll, and the stock would tumble.

Petrucci Case Study: Trying to Boil the Ocean

The following case study illustrates a number of significant pitfalls on system implementations, including the following:

- An organization that tried to do too much too soon
- The danger of a client project manager gone wild
- The inability of the consultant project manager to control a client
- The danger of a client attempting to implement immature applications of a vendor's application

Background

Petrucci General is a large, single-site hospital with 4,000 employees. Petrucci management bought a Tier 1 ERP and wanted to do all the following *at the same time:*

- Implement a completely new HR/payroll system with employee and manager self-service, including relatively new modules that had yet to gain a footing in the larger user community.
- Implement a completely new finance/general ledger system with self-service.
- Implement a completely new procurement system with requisition self-service.

- Create and activate multiple interfaces to and from different third-party administrators, banks, and other organizations.

- Enhance the core application by using almost all the vendor's add-on tools to enhance the system's default functionality—for example, reporting and e-mail notification.

- Implement a completely new, largely untested security structure.

This project was simply enormous in scope and cost. Rather than opting for a phased approach (which is typically the norm), Petrucci management decided to go for broke—"all in," in the poker vernacular. Note that organizations are not compelled to immediately use each piece of a new system upon activation. Remember the Portnoy case study that dealt with an organization attempting to integrate a number of disparate systems. The Petrucci case study is fundamentally different; its management at least had the intelligence to retire its legacy system and implement a single, unified, and new one. To lead this endeavor, Petrucci selected The Lemmon Group, an experienced partner of the vendor. I worked on the project as a subcontractor for Lemmon.

Petrucci management completely bought into the vendor's promises about its applications. It would transform their business, reduce administration costs, empower employees via self-service, provide meaningful business analytics and e-mail alerts, and unlock the power of their information. Petrucci management made the new system the centerpiece of a large organizational change and communication effort.

As is the case with implementations of this size, internal politics played a significant role. A key employee, Nick, was determined not to go live any earlier than January 1 of the next year. Now, if the project was scheduled for completion in November, someone hemming and hawing for a few months would not have been that problematic. However, the system was initially scheduled and, more important, budgeted for a go-live date in June or, at the latest, July. To extend the project by almost half a year, Nick would have to manufacture six months of delays and issues, creating reasonable doubt every step of the way.

Implementation Issues

On projects of the type of scale mentioned earlier, priorities can become completely convoluted. Mission-critical items, such as being able to correctly pay vendors and employees, are certainly paramount to items such as the ability to electronically track expenditures tied to several governmental grants. In the whole scheme of things, Petrucci end users would survive if they had to wait six months to roll out this functionality. Compared to being able to pay employees accurately, submit government reports, and so on, grants are pretty small potatoes. Unfortunately, Petrucci's project manager (Dorothy) vehemently disagreed, and the project manager for the SI (Andy) would routinely refuse to confront her about issues like this.

Compounding matters further, Dorothy insisted on perfection in all phases of testing. Her stance violated a central tenet of testing and, specifically, the conversion programs discussed earlier: it is simply not possible to import hundreds of thousands of often suspect records from a legacy system into a new system without incident. From Dorothy's perspective, a single error in an employee hire date on a data conversion program caused her grave concern. Never having been responsible for a project of this scale before, Dorothy would panic, call for emergency meetings, and stop both consultants and Petrucci end users from working on more pressing matters.

Andy failed to manage Dorothy and assure her that errors were part of the conversion process. He would simply listen to her complaints, apologize, and make promises about new dates, additional work from existing consultants, and adding consultants. Andy made the critical mistake of routinely making these promises before consulting with his own team: the experts who then had to make good on these new, overly aggressive deadlines and expectations.

By focusing on the minutiae and holding superfluous meetings, Dorothy contributed heavily to the implementation running further and further behind. In an attempt to make up for lost time, Dorothy demanded that different phases of testing occur in different data areas simultaneously. Payroll testing in data area A would take place while related—but separate—testing took place in data area B. Forget the processing difficulties of trying to juggle two major tests at once; it was logistically difficult for all concerned to remember who did what to whom and when. Were errors the result of a design issue, timing, a missed step, bad data, a true software glitch, or something else? Although consultants investigated issues in data area A, they ignored issues in environment B, exacerbating the situation.

Dorothy's "double threading" was disastrous, giving fodder to Nick and his quest to postpone the system until January 1. When errors appeared in testing, Nick would say, "I told you so" or ask the rhetorical question, "How do I know that something else is not wrong?" Somehow, Dorothy and Nick put the onus on Lemmon consultants to prove that every check, deduction, and transaction was correct to the penny; Dorothy and Nick did not need to find issues or provide evidence of an error. This bastardization of the burden of proof added to the frustration of the Lemmon consultants. Had Andy been willing or able to manage Dorothy and Nick properly, the situation would never have reached a crisis.

A Vicious Cycle of Retesting and the Devil's Triangle

Delays compounded, and Andy had to constantly revise the project plan, devoting fewer and fewer days to critical tasks. What's more, the plans were overly aggressive; *there was no margin for error*. As soon as one major task would be theoretically completed, another equally important task was supposed to start—often that very day. Therefore, a delay to one phase would reverberate throughout the project plan. Andy's project plans were predicated on the notion that the team would complete tasks without incident. Despite never having completed a single major task on time throughout the project, Andy's revised project plans would routinely "back in" to Dorothy's desired go-live date, despite the objections of the consultants who knew that the dates were totally untenable.

On the software side, Petrucci management decided to concurrently implement some of the vendor's relatively new modules—for example, Grant Management, Mobile Supply Chain Management, the Business Intelligence (BI) application. As a result, many of the issues that Lemmon consultants and Petrucci end users discovered had never before been reported to the vendor. This meant that the vendor had to both replicate the issue and develop a new patch. At any point toward the end of the project, the implementation team had roughly 10 open cases pending with the vendor.

Of course, Dorothy considered the majority of these issues to be showstoppers. Andy again would not stand in her way. Dorothy pressured the vendor's support staff to *immediately* find solutions to reported issues. In these cases, the individual consultants could do nothing to move the issue forward; the issue rested solely in the hands of vendor support specialists. The vendor's patches often did not resolve the issues immediately, requiring redevelopment. On more than one occasion, a patch fixed one problem but caused another.

Respected blogger Michael Krigsman has referred to this relationship as the devil's triangle.[i] He explains that the triangle is composed of the following:

> Virtually all IT projects involve three parties: customer, technology provider, and integrator. Each of these groups has its own independent set of goals, which leads to a series of interlocking, overlapping, and sometimes mutually exclusive agendas. Customers want low prices and top-quality work; consultants seek high margins and large projects; and technology vendors often bow toward system integrators since consultants are a source of vendor deal flow. Understanding why IT projects fail requires analyzing relationships among these three groups.

Krigsman goes on to write that the successful alignment of the interests of these three groups is essential for an IT project to be successful. In the Petrucci case, this alignment was less than ideal. This resulted in additional delays and frustration throughout the project.

Systematic Chaos

A prime example of Nick's obstinacy occurred during system testing. Pete, a Lemmon consultant, electronically stitched together legacy data with test data from the ERP, kicking out differences on employee checks. For example, let's say that a nurse was paid $2,000 (gross) in the legacy system with a net amount of $1,200 for a two-week period. In testing, that same nurse was paid $1,950 with a net amount of $1,150. Pete produced spreadsheets showing only differences greater than a user-defined amount. An employee paid the same amount in both systems (both gross and net) would not have appeared on the report because the records were correct and did not warrant further validation or investigation. Pete's tool could potentially bring the project at least partially back on track.

Rather than use Pete's slick tool, Nick insisted that all checks from both systems for the same period be printed and compared *manually*. If Petrucci employed 50 employees, this process would not have taken very long. However, Petrucci was much larger than that; end users and consultants printed thousands of pages as the team stayed well into the night trying to identify discrepancies that Pete had already provided in a user-friendly spreadsheet.

Manual validation of a handful of records is common during implementations. To be sure, paper makes people feel good, and client end users benefit in simply seeing how data will appear on new standard reports, forms, checks, invoices, and the like.

> **NOTE**
> However, there is no remotely compelling or logical reason to refuse to take advantage of accurate electronic validation tools, especially when a project is grossly behind schedule.

Efficiency aside for the moment, Nick's scattershot approach may well have identified some issues but missed many more. Making matters worse, Nick insisted that the same process be repeated for the next round of testing. The term "systematic chaos" comes to mind.

Although Dorothy's and Nick's motives were different, their net effects were the same: the project became highly contentious. Both consultants and employees worked endlessly, routinely cancelling trips home for the weekends and skipping previously scheduled vacations.

Misplaced Concerns

Dorothy did not realize or even care that, with the sole exception of Nick, everyone on the implementation team wanted Petrucci to go live as quickly and accurately as possible. No one wanted hundreds of hospital vendors and employees paid incorrectly or late. Reports needed to work, and Petrucci's end users should have been able to conduct business as usual upon system activation. However, no one can rationally expect a project of this scope to go live without at least a few minor issues. Cutting checks with a 99 percent accuracy rate during the first payroll run, for example, is a home run. What's more, the ERP contained many well-tested error correction tools—for example, adjustments for payroll, reversing journal entries, and the like. Refusing to confront reality, Dorothy and Nick pressed on in their quest for perfection.

It is interesting to note that even though Petrucci decided to use technology in a much superior fashion to Portnoy, both projects suffered from similar issues:

* Deficient project management by the SI
* Refusal of client project managers to listen to consultants

Outcomes and Lessons

Petrucci ultimately went live with relatively few issues in late September of that year. The project missed major deadlines and came in hundreds of thousands of dollars over budget. Petrucci received significant financial concessions from Lemmon. In the end, this project derailed due in large part to the unwillingness of both the project managers to accept the basic premise that one cannot boil the ocean. In the end, Petrucci can be rated on the failure scale as a Big Failure.

Summary

The organization with a project gone awry has a number of tools in its arsenal. Many times, the organization's focus is outward bound; for example, the vendor made false promises, the consultants are not sufficiently skilled, and so on. Although these may be true to some extent, the intelligent client also looks inward. Rather than placing all the blame on the easiest targets, the sage organization assesses its own resources, data, and internal politics. Clients that simply replace Consultancy A with Consultancy B—and fail to address core issues—will in all likelihood find themselves soon looking for Consultancy C.

Endnotes

i. http://blogs.zdnet.com/projectfailures/?p=433

Chapter 19

Audits

> If you don't know where you are going,
> any road will get you there.
> —*Lewis Carroll*

- The Need for an Organizational Readiness Assessment
- Mid-Implementation
- The Postmortem: A Unique Opportunity to Learn
- Managing and Auditing Data

Put simply, IT projects result in one of two basic outcomes: the new system is activated or it is not. With respect to the first outcome, most organizations go live with an imperfect system. The real question is whether the implementation team identified the risks that could cause the new system to fail. The success of the new system hinges directly on the implementation team's ability to quickly identify and resolve system-related issues. For organizations that fail to go live, the finger-pointing begins, with vendors and consultants being the easiest and most visible targets.

This chapter focuses on pre- and post-implementation audits. Unfortunately, organizations do not utilize these tools nearly to the extent they should.

The Need for an Organizational Readiness Assessment

Many organizations begin a new system implementation without sufficient forethought or a formal readiness assessment.[1] On these projects, senior management somewhat arbitrarily picks a date, calculates a budget, submits requests for proposals (RFPs), selects its vendor and system integrator (SI), and jumps in feet first. Perhaps some executives at similar organizations compare notes prior to undertaking a project of this magnitude.

Consider Rudess Health Care, an organization about to implement a new system. Rudess' executives believe that a new system will cost $1M to purchase and another $1.5M to implement, with support costs running about $200K per annum. Albert, the IT director, decides to perform some due diligence. His friend Boris recently implemented a similar system at Roscoe Health Care. Albert asks Boris the same questions and receives the following answers:

- **Q:** How long did the implementation take?

  A: Two years

- **Q:** What functionality did Roscoe implement?

  A: Full HR/payroll, financials, and procurement

- **Q:** How many full-time consultants did Roscoe utilize?

  A: One functional expert in each (three total) and one technical consultant

---

1. Note that many organizations only conduct a readiness assessment immediately prior to going live—not before a project begins. This readiness assessment typically takes place during a single, tense meeting. The organization asks itself, "Are we ready to go live?" Given that these projects are typically over budget and past their initial deadlines, many employees are afraid to voice legitimate concerns over major issues.

- **Q:** How much did the project cost?

  A: $2.5M

Boris also provides Albert with a breakdown of the costs of the implementation at Roscoe, simplified as shown in Table 19.1.

TABLE 19.1 First-Year Costs of Implementation at Roscoe Health Care

Item	Number
FT consultants	4
Hourly consultant rate	$175
Weeks per consultant	60
Total money spent on consultants	$1,440,000
Software license plus first-year support	$600,000
Hardware upgrade cost	$820,000
Total cost	$2,500,000

To be sure, ballpark figures such as Boris's serve as useful guides for determining items such as expected budget, resources, and project timing. However, these answers should serve only as guides and approximations, not as gospel. Each organization has its own set of challenges that individually and collectively can have enormous impacts on just about every facet of the project.

Beyond comparing notes, the single best thing that Rudess can do prior to even purchasing a new system is to determine whether it is ready to go down this road in the first place. Management should perform this analysis well *before* it signs millions of dollars in contracts and commits months or years of employees' time.

But who will conduct this analysis? Rudess can appoint an internal team to conduct a study on the feasibility of this project. Alternatively, it can ask an SI to determine if it is ready for such a massive undertaking. For this, Rudess has in mind two firms:

- Burns Consultants, a delivery-based firm that clearly wants to win the system implementation
- The Wright Group, a management SI with no stake in the outcome of this vital assessment

For Rudess, choosing Burns would be a catastrophic mistake. Burns would be strongly tempted to suggest two things at the end of the feasibility study:

- Rudess is ready for the implementation.
- Rudess should choose Burns for this project, because it already possesses intimate organizational knowledge.

How can Rudess ensure that it receives a truly objective analysis? Rudess's management fears that an internal team may also be biased from the start. It ultimately and wisely chooses The Wright Group, because it offers the greatest objectivity. Wright has tremendous expertise in the field and is not affiliated with a vendor. Wright is onsite for a period of two months at a cost of $40,000. During that time, Wright delves deeply into the crux of the organization.

From a purely financial standpoint, Rudess is behooved to discover as soon as possible if it would face significant dangers by implementing a new system. Wright's analysis includes the following emphases:

- Data readiness
- Business practice variation within the organization
- People and organizational readiness
- System readiness
- Documentation
- Political obstacles

Data Readiness

Wright sees vast data inconsistencies across Rudess's hospitals. The cleanup effort alone should take about four months. Rudess does not currently possess the internal expertise required to clean up its data. As a result, it requires more consultants than expected.

Business Practice Variation Within the Organization

Beyond simply cleaning up the data, however, Rudess must decide on the extent to which it wants to standardize business practices and policies across the organization. Different parts of the organization currently employ different pay and accounting practices. Rudess's management cannot simply issue a decree consolidating them throughout the organization. If employee paychecks change, Rudess must conduct an employee and management communications blitz. Nor can Rudess' management standardize its general ledger throughout the organization without input from the staff in each area's finance department.

People and Organizational Readiness

Wright personnel meet with each hospital's staff to understand their jobs as well as to assess their individual capacities to potentially handle the new system. Wright also notes the level of work at each site, an important factor when considering resource allocation. Wright observes that employees at certain hospitals are so swamped with work that they would only have, on average, roughly four hours per week to devote to a new system implementation at current staffing levels.

Beyond the actual work involved, Rudess's employees have not had to learn new system functionality in more than 15 years. Few of these people have even heard of the new system, much less had experience with it. The training need is particularly acute in the payroll departments of several hospitals. In fact, a few of the people are close to retiring and may not have much desire to learn a new system—or much time to use that system after going live. Wright recommends that payroll managers continue to work on the legacy systems. However, Rudess should hire new staff for these hospitals who have previous experience with the new system.

A few years back, Rudess implemented new medical billing and operating room systems, resulting in some bumps. Fortunately, the company has addressed these issues, and the scars have healed. Further, Rudess has in place a solid IT structure and personnel. Wright determines that these other systems would pose minimal risk to Rudess's implementation of a new enterprise system. The internal staff members at Rudess who implemented—and currently support—the billing and operating room systems have those issues under control.

System Readiness

Wright's technical consultant discovers some hardware issues at Rudess. Specifically, the company's existing servers and databases do not have the capacity to handle the new system. Whatever the limitations of the legacy system, it is fast; current employees have come to expect a certain performance level. Without significant purchases of new hardware, Wright does not see how the new system can provide the same speed, a requirement in Rudess's high-transaction environment.

On the reporting front, Rudess may have to create many custom reports from the new system if end users insist on exact replicas from the legacy system. No system to Wright's knowledge comes with the array of custom reports ostensibly required by Rudess personnel. End users need to retire a significant number of reports and opt for the new system's standard alternatives. Wright's final report notes this red flag.

Documentation

Wright finds that certain hospitals have better documentation than others. External consultants certainly need to review all documentation to understand Rudess's functional and technical requirements. Rudess should get its ducks in a row with regard to documentation *before* deploying expensive consultants. Wright has often seen consultants arrive at a client site only to discover that this vital information is not available or simply does not exist.

Political Obstacles

By meeting with employees and senior management, Wright notices that certain executives and key personnel do not believe in the need for a new system. The "If it ain't broke don't fix it mentality" is more prevalent in certain pockets of the organization.

In its final analysis, Wright determines that Rudess faces significant risks if it immediately opts to commence the project. The net result is a roughly 40 percent chance that the project would suffer from considerable budgetary and timeline issues if started today. Wright proposes a number of specific recommendations, along with the costs associated with each one.

Armed with Wright's organization-specific analysis, not merely ballpark numbers from Roscoe, Rudess's management considers the anticipated costs of the implementation. These numbers are shown in Table 19.2.

TABLE 19.2 Comparison of First-Year Costs of Implementation

Item	Roscoe—Actual	Rudess—Expected	Difference (%)
FT consultants	4	4	0%
Hourly consultant rate	$175	$175	0%
Weeks per consultant	60	80	33%
Total money spent on consultants	$1,440,000	$2,240,000	56%
Software license plus first year of support	$600,000	$600,000	0%
Hardware upgrade cost	$820,000	$820,000	0%
Total cost	$2,500,000	$3,660,000	46%

Although this example is fictitious, it is instructive on a number of fronts. For one, Rudess's executives now know its risks *before* it commits itself to the project. What's more, via Wright's recommendations, it knows the steps it should take to address these risks. Finally and most important, Rudess's management can trust that Wright's findings are unbiased, because Wright is not in the systems delivery business.

Rudess spent a small fraction of the overall anticipated project costs ($40,000) for extremely valuable information on whether it should even undertake this project. Rudess's management can now

- Walk away from a possible train wreck at minimal cost
- Opt to delay the project for a number of months or years until it overcomes the aforementioned hurdles
- Proceed with the project knowing the risks well ahead of time

Regardless of its ultimate decision, Rudess is in a far superior position than before engaging Wright's consultants. Based on those findings, Rudess delays the implementation of a new system until its issues have been adequately addressed.

When Rudess begins its system implementation, it can expect to realize a number of significant benefits from Wright's work. For one, prior to system testing, internal staff will have addressed many of the issues. As a result, team members will not have to work 14-hour days. This will minimize the risk of employee turnover. What's more, Rudess's management will probably not have to make its go-live decision under duress.

On its implementation, Rudess will certainly have its challenges, expected and unexpected. In this sense, Rudess is no different from most of the organizations in the case studies in this book. Unlike their counterparts, however, Rudess can rationally assess the pros and cons of the project *before* beginning; senior management knows the risks well in advance.

Mid-Implementation

Larger SIs often deploy some type of "delivery excellence" team tasked with periodically assessing midstream project issues and impacts. Typically, these teams have no specific knowledge of the application specific to the project. This is not sold as a limitation; an "outsider" perspective is supposed to be an advantage. By focusing on different types of systems, these teams can look at projects from 30,000 feet and make observations ostensibly lost on both client end users and consultants heavily involved in the project's day-to-day activities.

The mid-implementation audit aims to identify technical, functional, and "people" issues that may cause the implementation to fail. The audit that brings important issues to the attention of senior management is certainly valuable. If the project manager previously broached these issues, the audit confirms what senior management already knows. If the project manager did not, manifesting them as early as possible can potentially right the ship.

On the downside, the audit requires time and resources from employees who are already juggling their day jobs with the additional responsibilities required by the implementation. Also, the auditors bring with them broad perspectives and may well not be able to appreciate some of the specific complexities that, although possibly appearing trivial, are actually driving the issues. Everything looks simple at 30,000 feet, and auditors often do not know the implications of their specific recommendations. They may not know what they do not know.

In the end, auditors may make completely impractical and facile recommendations that do more harm than good. I worked on one project in which an auditor proposed an additional parallel test late in the project. There was no time to conduct this test under the existing project plan, but this did not concern him. After all, he would not be personally involved in this additional round of testing, and client senior management could hardly argue with more testing on a problematic implementation.

The Postmortem: A Unique Opportunity to Learn

To paraphrase a Chinese proverb, in crisis there is opportunity. Consider an organization that has pulled the plug on its implementation, wasting millions of dollars in the process. The Portnoy case study in Chapter 11, "Setup Issues," was one such example. Immediately after killing the project, Portnoy management should have carefully analyzed what went wrong and why. Less extreme than Portnoy's cancelled project is an organization like Wilson that activated its systems with considerable issues because it had no other realistic alternative.

Regardless of a project's outcome, organizations have unique opportunities for self-assessment after their projects end. Organizations can learn a great deal about their employees, data, business processes, and politics from both a failed implementation and a relatively successful one. A postmortem can shed light on the specific issues that delayed or derailed a project.

Much like the pre-implementation audit, an unbiased and seasoned independent consultancy or individual should perform the postmortem. The objectivity of the third party is crucial here. For example, let's return to Lifeson, the subject of the third case study. Lifeson spent $5M and ended the project after repeated delays, budget overruns, and limited results. Remember that opposition from senior management played a key role in that project's demise. If those same senior managers drive the postmortem, they will surely minimize their own culpability, blaming the vendor or the SI (frequent targets of misplaced blame). Wilson needs to understand the core issues before it thinks about undertaking a project of this scope again. If senior management does not recognize and ultimately address those issues, the next system implementation will more than likely yield similarly unsatisfactory results.

A project need not be an Unmitigated Disaster to benefit from a postmortem. Remember that even a successful IT project is far from perfect. Management may have tabled issues, allowing the project to continue. Perhaps management is still unaware of existing issues. Returning to the Oates Health Care example from Chapter 1, "Introduction," if management had performed an audit immediately after going live, it might have identified the following:

- The problem with the payroll setup causing overtime issues
- The need to hire more technical employees and to provide additional training for current end users
- The need for a more robust reporting tool

> **NOTE**
>
> In the end, a postmortem can provide valuable insight into the organization's implementation, irrespective of the outcome of that project. Aside from identifying past problems, this type of analysis can list possible (if not likely) future issues and the methods to address them.

Managing and Auditing Data

The data cleanup and migration efforts in moving from a legacy system to a new one are typically quite significant. Because of previously discussed differences among the ways in which different systems store data, the very process of mapping old to new manifests inconsistencies and inaccuracies in any data set. As a general rule, larger and older data contains more problems than smaller, newer data.

To be sure, organizations will realize major outputs from these painful inputs: a new system represents a unique and opportune time for organizations to purge or correct historical inaccuracies that have long plagued end users and rendered reports less meaningful. Organizations should audit their data routinely to ensure the following:

- Incipient problems are nipped in the bud.
- End users are sufficiently trained in utilizing the system.
- Reports contain meaningful and accurate information.

As Chapter 22, "Intelligent Expansion," will show, hybrid employees are perfect for this type of work. They tend to understand the front end (the functionality of the system) as well as the back end (how the data is stored in fields and tables).

Summary

Pre-implementation, post-implementation, and ongoing data audits are invaluable tools for organizations. Used judiciously by knowledgeable and impartial resources, audits can detect, avoid, and minimize issues that can derail an implementation or cause a live system to fail. Rather than view them as superfluous expenses, organizations would be wise to conduct them at key points throughout the system's life cycle.

Chapter 20

Contingency Planning

Hope for the best but prepare for the worst.
—*Proverb*

- A Margin for Error
- A Contingency Fund
- Probabilities

> **NOTE**
> Feel free to skip this chapter if you never expect anything to go wrong.

As has been discussed at length, many projects suffer delays and do not have the requisite time and resources to overcome them. The result is that the project goes over budget, misses its deadline, loses key functionality, or some combination of the three. At this point, the myth of the delay-free system implementation should be shattered. Perfection on projects of this scope and cost—regardless of tier—is virtually nonexistent.

I fully understand the need for precision[1] and cost certainty. During the sales cycle, CIOs and CFOs are not going to write blank checks to vendors or SIs. What's more, the latter groups can appear weak if they constantly answer, "I don't know." At the same time, however, it never ceases to amaze me that organizations of all kinds believe that they can precisely determine the time and money required to undertake a massive project like implementing an enterprise system. This is the very definition of a strategic, wild ass guess (SWAG).

Many people have heard the classic consultant response to any client question: "It depends." To be fair, clients are often justifiably frustrated over not being able to get straight answers to ostensibly simple questions. However, the answers to many questions are sometimes anything but simple. Consider the following client question, posed to a system integrator (SI) during project planning: "How much time will it take to convert data from the old system into the new one?"

In reality, this question consists of many subquestions, including the following:

- Is the legacy data easily accessible?
- How clean is the legacy data?
- Who will extract and validate the data?
- At what point in the year will extraction and validation occur? (Note that end-of-month, -quarter, and -year activities heavily affect finance and payroll end users.)
- Are there tools to extract and validate the legacy data?
- How much time is required to validate the legacy data?

---

1. As an avid golfer (or hacker, depending on the day), I know that a few inches or even millimeters can mean the difference between success and failure.

No one can accurately answer the overriding question without knowing the answers to the subquestions—and many of those cannot be truthfully answered until those processes have been started. Pressed to give a simple answer, however, the SI might give "two months" as its SWAG. This number may or may not be accurate. Odds are that it's a conservative estimate that may well cause problems down the road.

This chapter covers two of the simplest things that organizations can do to avoid death marches: a margin for error and a contingency fund. These are remarkably obvious yet almost always overlooked.

A Margin for Error

Oddly, few SIs and clients build in a margin for error. Although no panacea, project plans with reasonable amounts of slack minimize the chance of an outright failure. Projects without such buffers undertake enormous risks.

For example, two companies, Lebowski and Sobchak[2], are implementing the same system at the same time using consultants of the same caliber. Let's assume that the two companies face identical challenges vis-à-vis data, testing, design changes, and personnel. The final stretches of the two organizations' project plans are represented in Table 20.1.

TABLE 20.1 Original Project Plans for Lebowski and Sobchak

Task	Lebowski		Sobchak	
	Start Date	End Date	Start Date	End Date
Conduct system testing	12/1/2009	12/15/2009	11/10/2009	11/24/2009
Final end-user training	12/16/2009	12/17/2009	12/3/2009	12/6/2009
Readiness assessment	12/18/2009	12/21/2009	12/11/2009	12/14/2009
Final preparation for production	12/22/2009	12/28/2009	12/18/2009	12/22/2009
System activation/ go-live	12/28/2009	12/30/2009	12/28/2009	12/30/2009
Post-implementation audit	1/11/2010	11/13/2010	1/11/2010	1/13/2010

---

2. *The Big Lebowski* by the Coen brothers may well be the funniest movie ever made.

Note how the tasks in Lebowski's project plan are sequential and have no room for error. As soon as one task ends, the next is immediately scheduled to begin. In other words, should a major task suffer a delay, all subsequent tasks will suffer. Now, should the same issue confront Sobchak, task dates can be tweaked—that is, the dates of other phases may *not* need to be moved. Most important, the requisite time required for each phase can be left intact.

In mid-November, both organizations discover a previously unreported bug with the vendor's software. The vendor has promised to make this a relatively high priority but, because both organizations are not yet live, will not assign it critical status. The estimated time of arrival of the software patch is one week.

Despite the similarities of their projects, the net impact of this delay on each company is dramatically different. Sobchak management was prescient enough to anticipate such problems. As a result, they built in a margin for error early in the project planning stage to be used if and when such a delay or issue presented itself. Lebowski did not and is in danger of missing its go-live date. Certainly, senior management at Lebowski will escalate the issue with the vendor, and perhaps a resolution can be expedited. Lebowski is left with the following ugly alternatives:

- Move its date and face increased consulting and support costs.
- Compress tasks to "back into" a date. In this case, it can attempt to per-form the testing in one week instead of the necessary two. To do so, Lebowski must push consultants and internal staff harder and effectively complete work originally set for two weeks in only one.

Faced with these delays, the revised project plans for Lebowski and Sobchak are shown in Table 20.2.

Lebowski management opts for the second alternative. In the process, it has considerably increased its risk of failure. Two weeks of system testing prob-ably cannot be accomplished in one, even if employees and consultants work 16 hours per day. Under that kind of pressure, it is also likely that employees and consultants will miss certain issues due to fatigue. Although Sobchak management cannot be happy about the software bug and its resultant effect on the project, its pain is not nearly as severe as that of Lebowski.

TABLE 20.2 Revised Project Plans for Lebowski and Sobchak

	Lebowski		Sobchak	
Task	Start Date	End Date	Start Date	End Date
Conduct system testing	12/8/2009	12/15/2009	11/17/2009	11/30/2009
Final end-user training	12/16/2009	12/17/2009	12/3/2009	12/6/2009
Readiness assessment	12/18/2009	12/21/2009	12/11/2009	12/14/2009
Final preparation for production	12/22/2009	12/28/2009	12/18/2009	12/22/2009
System activation/ go-live	12/28/2009	12/30/2009	12/28/2009	12/30/2009
Post-implementation audit	1/11/2010	11/13/2010	1/11/2010	1/13/2010

In this example, the major benefit of including a margin for error in a project plan is that a sudden, unexpected crisis does not necessarily imperil the go-live date. However, there are also many side benefits of using slack. First, employees and consultants can use the time to catch up on noncritical tasks that may have been delayed. Documentation and report writing come to mind. Second, organizations can use this period for supplemental training and knowledge transfer. Finally and often overlooked, the time can be used as a "down week" in which everyone can relax. Employee hours worked during implementations, especially as organizations prepare to go live, can be quite onerous. Well-rested employees and consultants are better prepared for the final, critical hurdle: going live.

Challenges, Realities, and Aligning Interests

Admittedly, the margin for error often does not exist in many project plans because its very notion faces an uphill battle. First, if an SI asks a prospective client to accept a margin for error in the project plan, it runs the risk of appearing weak and ostensibly less organized, as if it expects the project to fail. Translation: it may not win business in the first place.

For example, Manilow Entertainment has purchased Oracle applications and is soliciting bids for the implementation work. It receives two responses to its request for proposal (RFP). Maiden is a large firm with many lines of business. It promises to perform the work in 10 months sans delays and prices the project at $400,000 on a time and materials (T&M) basis. Judas is a boutique shop, specializing in Oracle. It commits to a full year with a potentially unnecessary margin for error at the price of $450,000, also on a T&M basis. All else being equal, Manilow may naively and immediately rule out Judas for cost reasons. However, the $400,000 submitted by Maiden may balloon to $500,000 or more with issues and delays.

Judas needs to position its bid as follows. Judas very much wants Manilow to implement Oracle successfully. In its experience, comparable organizations need about a year to do this. Rather than underprice its bid, Judas commits to a year, with a built-in margin for error. Judas assures Manilow management that it has every intention of implementing Oracle in a cost-efficient time frame. Specifically, if the project plan's margin for error is not necessary, Manilow and Judas will jointly accelerate individual tasks in a fashion conducive to their successful completion. Aside from potentially saving Manilow money, this approach sets a positive tone from the beginning, aligning consultant and client interests. Think about it. Oracle may actually go live ahead of schedule and under the proposed budget. Perish the thought!

NOTE

Of course, progressive SIs often make this argument in vain. Clients need to listen and not race to the bottom on consulting rates and total cost. Remember from Chapter 8, "Selecting Consultants," that sometimes SIs intentionally price bids on a time and expense (T&E) basis on the low side based on a strict list of client requirements. Organizations that deviate from this list must submit change requests for out-of-scope items. As a result, both the initial budget and timeline ultimately increase, often considerably.

The need for a margin for error will become particularly acute for a system activation scheduled at the end of the year. Forget for the moment that employees tend to take time off during the holidays. More than that, the realities of their day jobs often set in. Accounting folks have month-end, quarter-end, and year-end balancing. Payroll has to process W-2s. These are examples of nonnegotiable items that end users have to complete in a timely manner. Project plans should be sensitive to end-users' availability during such periods.

A Contingency Fund

The previous section addressed challenges with respect to time. However, time does not exist in a vacuum on IT projects. Time is inextricably linked with money. Organizations foolishly assuming that all tasks will occur in sequential order sans delays are often not allocating additional funds in the event that something goes awry.

Let's return to the Lebowski and Sobchak examples from before. At the beginning of its project, Sobchak management allocated $100,000 to be used in the event of an emergency. Lebowski did not.

Table 20.3 reflects each organization's budget. Note how Lebowski management was not prescient enough to allocate money in advance in the event of a major project issue.

TABLE 20.3 Budgets for Lebowski and Sobchak

	Lebowski	Sobchak
Initial budget	$1M	$1M
Contingency fund	$0	$.1M
Total approved funds	$1M	$1.1M

Again, let's assume that a showstopper threatened each organization's system activation date. This issue required the expertise of an additional technical consultant not covered in the budget and initial statement of work (SOW). Unlike Lebowski, Sobchak could immediately tap into its kitty and resolve the issue. To obtain more funds, Lebowski would have to go to its board and make this request—a process that also costs the company valuable time. Lebowski's board may not have the funds available and, as such, the project would suffer.

Each project's different outcomes can be expressed in Table 20.4.

TABLE 20.4 Final Numbers for Lebowski and Sobchak

	Lebowski	Sobchak
Initial budget	$1M	$1.1M
Showstopper	10% over	On budget
No showstopper	On budget	9% under

Depending on whether it encounters a showstopper, Sobchak either finishes the project on or under budget. On the other hand, Lebowski will either just squeak by or exceed its budget by 10 percent. The contingency fund is like an umbrella: it's better to have it and not need it than to need it and not have it.

Probabilities

The need for a hedge against delays can be further illustrated by a simple probability example. Assume that an organization is 90 percent confident that each of the following six steps will take place as planned:

- Its SI realistically planned the project.
- It has properly defined its requirements and provided its SI with comprehensive documentation.
- Its end users will effectively learn the new system without major issues.
- The project has been staffed adequately.
- Its data is clean enough to be converted in two months.
- There will be no last-minute software glitches approaching system activation.

To go live on time and within budget, each of these six events has to take place; any one that fails causes the whole project to miss its date and exceed its budget. Because each of the six events has a 90 percent chance of happening, the probability that *all* six will occur is only 53 percent (90 percent to the sixth power[3]). Imagine if 10 different events have to take place, each of which has only an 80 percent chance of happening. In this case, the related odds are only 10.7 percent. Given these statistics, is it really a surprise that so many projects fail?

Summary

Although hardly rocket science, organizations can utilize two obvious but overlooked tools that can help them avoid project failure. First, they can bake in margins for error at natural breaking points. As a result, they will be better able to withstand invariable last-minute delays. Second, contingency funds actually allow projects to finish within their initial budgets. Foolish is the SI or client that assumes that perfect execution is likely or even attainable.

---

3. According to probability theory, these events would be described as independent—that is, each event has no effect on the likelihood of other events occurring.

Chapter 21

Employee- and Consultant-Based Strategies

> Good management is the art of making problems
> so interesting and their solutions so constructive that
> everyone wants to get to work and deal with them.
> —*Paul Hawken*

- Finding and Retaining Hybrids
- Using Employee Retention Bonuses During an Implementation
- Preempting Key Employee Turnover
- Immediately Removing or Redeploying Difficult Employees
- Emergency Triage: Send in "The Wolf"

This chapter focuses on the most important part of any IT project: people. Very often, the talents of individual consultants and employees can make the difference between success and failure on an implementation and beyond. This is *not* to say that the most talented and dedicated employees and consultants can always or even often overcome poor system design, bad data, horrible project planning, or last-minute crises. They cannot. However, finding and retaining quality people is one of the best things that an organization can do on IT projects.

Specific employee- and consultant-based strategies include these:

- Finding and retaining consultant and employee hybrids
- Using employee retention bonuses during an implementation
- Immediately removing or redeploying difficult employees
- Bringing in a hired gun
- Preempting key employee turnover

Finding and Retaining Hybrids

As discussed, most project "worker bees" fall into one of two categories: technical or functional. The following section discusses why this is the case.

Consultants

System integrators (SIs) hire and train new consultants at considerable costs. It typically takes freshly hired consultants anywhere from three to six months to gain certification and become proficient enough with a product to guide clients effectively through an implementation, although some take quite a bit longer. After this period, SIs rightfully expect a return on their investment—that is, consultants need to start billing clients as soon as possible. After obtaining their certifications, consultants should *not* expect to attend additional training sessions. Down the road, ambitious consultants may have opportunities to expand their skill sets. However, in the short and near terms, it is not reasonable for SIs to produce "techno-functional" superusers.

Whereas SIs place a great deal of emphasis on billing, the individual consultant typically possesses a tremendous desire to maximize bonuses. Such bonuses are almost always tied to utilization. In tandem, these incentives tend to create consultants with a great deal of depth in an individual application but not nearly as much breadth. A financial consultant at a large firm, for example, may know invoice matching inside and out but know little about fixed asset management. Alternatively, many payroll consultants know a great deal about how the application processes paychecks but nothing about the fields and tables updated by each payroll program in the process.

Let's look at an example at one organization with a traditional, purely functional payroll consultant, Donna, interacting with the client's designated report developer, Sam:

1. The client's payroll manager, Anna, needs a custom report from the new system.

2. Donna creates the reporting specification for Anna, leaving out key technical pieces of information.

3. Sam attempts to create the report but cannot without additional information. He e-mails Donna.

4. Donna receives the e-mail but is fully engaged in system testing. She is unable to answer Sam's questions for three days.

5. Donna asks Anna to elaborate on the reporting requirements.

6. Donna finally provides the information to Sam, who then creates a template of the report and sends an example to Donna.

7. Donna reviews the report with Anna and makes some changes.

8. Frustrated, Sam receives the requested changes and has to re-create the report because it contains tables and joins that make the original version of the report useless.

9. After a month of back-and-forth, the report is ready for Anna to sign off.

This is hardly an ideal process, especially if the report is essential and the project is running behind schedule. Now let's look at the same process spearheaded by Pete, a highly skilled functional consultant with extensive experience in Crystal Reports:

1. Anna needs the same report.

2. Pete asks Anna specifically what is required, already thinking about the required tables and fields.

3. Pete knows that the number and size of the required tables will cause this report to take six hours to complete soon after the client goes live; he does not even attempt to build the report using the traditional tables because he knows that the effort is ultimately futile.

4. Pete quickly puts together a formal reporting specification and creates a custom view in the database that aggregates this information. He provides the code for this view to the IT department for sign-off.

5. Pete creates the report and provides Anna with a sample.

6. The report is spot-on and takes minutes to run. Anna signs off on it immediately.

Now, multiply this process by 50—a conservative estimate of the number of custom reports typically required by a client during an implementation. Isn't the hybrid consultant worth 20 percent more?

An organization's desire to keep *initially expected* consulting costs at a minimum often results in its staffing projects with consultants who wear only one hat. Remember the example of "Joe the Independent" in Chapter 8, "Selecting Consultants." His rate exceeded Rena's by a considerable margin, but he brought a great deal more to the table.

> **NOTE**
> Depending on the role required, hybrid consultants are almost always well worth their premiums. Organizations that utilize hybrids tend to reduce total consulting expenses.

Employees

On the client side, remember that legacy systems typically result in segregated responsibilities for many employees. Let's return to reporting, first discussed in Chapter 14, "Reports and Interfaces." In many organizations, legacy systems and traditional roles do not permit functional end users to easily write reports and extract system data. As a result, reporting has historically been viewed as an "IT function," and most functional end users do not have much experience in that vein.

Although an implementation may represent an ideal time for curious employees to learn new reporting applications, there are only so many hours in a day. Consider a benefits manager involved in an implementation. Her day job requires her to attend to current employee enrollment issues. In her spare time, she needs to set up and learn the new system's benefits application. She probably does not have a great deal of time to devote to learning how to create custom reports.

By staffing their projects with one dimensional end users, organizations tend to discover issues relatively late in the process—often well into testing. Consider the following examples:

- A payroll manager with a decent amount of general ledger experience can tell during system design that a decision will have a negative or unexpected general ledger impact.

- A Human Resource Information Systems (HRIS) manager adept at Crystal Reports knows that a poor setup decision will limit the organization's future ability to extract vital employee information.

- A database administrator (DBA) realizes that the organization's desired security setup will prevent the distribution of important reports.

Again, an isolated and minor issue uncovered relatively late in an implementation tends *not* to derail a project by itself. However, to the extent that projects scheduled to go live often already push their dates, even relatively minor issues increase the risk of a system failure. To this end, organizations are best served by employing experienced, *hybrid* end users.

Applicant Questions

Prior to beginning projects, organizations may determine that existing staff members do not have sufficient experience with the new systems. Consider Terrence Pet Supplies (TPS), a large company about to implement SAP with the help of its partner, Lumbergh Consulting.[1] Although TPS management believes that its employees can be trained on SAP, it simultaneously realizes that a team staffed exclusively with newly trained employees would benefit a great deal from the presence of at least one experienced superuser. Such an employee would also decrease the number of required external consultants.

TPS is in luck. Unlike its legacy system, the available pool of prospective employees familiar with SAP is quite large. Although there may be geographical and budgetary restrictions, TPS can find and hire individuals who already possess deep expertise in SAP. Its existing team would not need to start with a blank slate. TPS moves forward with filling the position.

TPS recruiters visit job search boards such as Monster.com and perform a keyword search on the term "SAP." Thousands of prospective candidates immediately appear. Before continuing, a note of caution is in order.

CAUTION

Different projects require individuals and implementation teams to play various roles. As a result, candidates may or may not have performed the tasks indicated on their resumes. Don't assume that all candidates did the same things, even if their roles and titles are identical.

---

1. Yes, these are not-so-subtle references to the classic 1999 movie *Office Space*. For those of you yet to see it, just buy it.

TPS finds Samir and Michael, two ostensibly ideal candidates who claim to have "extensive experience configuring and testing SAP." Here's the problem: they may actually have been light SAP users. To the extent that TPS and its end users have not yet implemented SAP, its hiring managers may not be able to assess each candidate's proficiency accurately. What should it do?

Although a formal examination may not be practical, TPS should engage its partner, Lumbergh, to interview Samir and Michael and ask many detailed questions related to SAP. TPS needs to ensure that it is hiring a true SAP expert, even though its management and end users are not in positions to make that call.

Lumbergh consultants should probe each candidate about their SAP experiences, either independently or in conjunction with TPS hiring managers. In the end, Lumbergh personnel should make a recommendation to its client about each candidate's SAP proficiency and suitability for the position.

I have seen job candidates exaggerate their roles on previous implementations more than once. An end user on one project who was only peripherally involved claimed on her resume to be a key member of the team after leaving the organization. Also, in the Portnoy case study, management hired an alleged superuser who grossly embellished her experience with the system.

Behavioral-Based Interviews

How can an organization guarantee that it is hiring a true system expert? In short, it cannot. There is no scientific way of determining expertise in an application. One method that *should* weed out "posers" is the behavioral interview. During a behavioral-based interview (BBI), the interviewer attempts to discover how an applicant has previously responded in specific situations.

The underlying premise of a BBI is that past performance predicts future performance. As such, BBIs do *not* consist of hypothetical questions, such as, "What would you do if you saw this kind of problem?" Rather, interviewers ask questions such as, "Tell me about a specific challenge that *you* faced on a project and what you did about it."

In BBIs, interviewers tell applicants to frame their responses in terms of three things:

- The background or situation establishing the issue
- The tasks or actions that *the individual* took to resolve that issue, *not* the team
- The outcome or results of those actions

A useful acronym for behavioral interviews is *STAR*: situation, task/action, and result. Returning to the TPS example, consider the two responses in Table 21.1 from Michael and Samir.

TABLE 21.1 Comparison of Applicant Responses in Behavioral Interview

	Michael	Samir
Situation	As we were about to go live with SAP, I discovered a data issue with a key financial conversion program.	We had problems with SAP as we were about to go live.
Task/action	I alerted senior management of the issue and researched the options. I wrote extensive queries isolating the suspect data and distributed it to end users, emphasizing the need for immediate action. I coordinated the validation of that data. Also, I found a patch on the support site and alerted the IT manager, who installed it in a TEST data area. I tested the patch and determined that it resolved the issue. I recommended that it should be applied to the PROD data area.	IT handled the issue. I kept people informed.
Result	The patch resolved the issue. We activated the system as scheduled.	The patch resolved the issue. We activated the system as scheduled.

Note how Michael can articulate the specific actions that he took to identify and resolve the problem. Samir can only speak in general terms about the problem and its resolution. As such, Samir appears to be an inferior candidate. At this point, TPS should ensure that Michael's references check out.

In behavioral interviews, the outcome of a situation is not nearly as important as the steps taken by each individual in response to that situation. The applicant who did everything possible to resolve an issue may not have been able to save the day through no fault of her own. Conversely, the individual who acted as though "things would work themselves out" may have been right. More than the outcome, the interviewer should look for what each applicant did and did not do in response to the problem.

Using Employee Retention Bonuses During an Implementation

Internal staff members are critical not only to an IT project and activation but to that project's ongoing performance. During an implementation, additional resources may well be hired, even beyond external consultants. The fact remains, however, that the workloads of key team members increase significantly throughout the project, often by considerable amounts. For the most part, these key members will not be freshly minted college graduates. Often in their mid-30s at least, these employees are likely to have families. An increased workload means a great deal of personal sacrifice on their parts.

To address such issues, intelligent organizations do more than merely acknowledge these personal sacrifices. Although a pat on the back is always nice, a financial incentive for key team members to remain with the organization during and after the project is often wise for at least two reasons. First, it tangibly rewards key contributors for the extra work and hours that they will devote to the project. Second, such a carrot decreases the likelihood of employee turnover, particularly at critical and stressful points of the project.

Obviously, both parties must keep these bonuses confidential. The last thing that a team member not receiving a bonus needs to hear is that her colleague is going to be compensated beyond her additional salary. As for amounts, there is no one magic formula. To quote my grad school compensation professor George Milkovich,[i] the amounts should amount to "meaningful hits." For example, a senior manager pulling 60-plus hours per week for six months may well view $1,000 as a slap in the face. After all, that employee probably did not sign up for two jobs when joining the company: a day job as well as additional responsibilities related to the implementation. However, $20,000 is probably excessive, especially if the team member is not entirely essential to the project.

This is Risk Mitigation 101. Organizations that understand the need to retain and reward key contributors, particularly on high-visibility projects such as system implementations, are simply protecting their assets. Used appropriately, the retention bonus can be an effective mechanism in counteracting the sometimes natural desire of a frustrated, burned-out employee to simply walk away at a critical point in the project.

Preempting Key Employee Turnover

Hybrids are rarely wanting for job offers, if they decide to look or not. The functional financial consultant who also knows how to run payroll or match invoices has quite a bag of tricks at her disposal. Remember that HR and payroll end users tend to be much less technical than financial and procurement folks. Rare is the functional HR person who can also build complicated Crystal Reports and Microsoft Access applications to address complex issues such as the one encountered by Oates Health Care in Chapter 1, "Introduction." Hybrids often eliminate the future need to bring in expensive external consultants to solve system and data problems. Aside from a retention bonus during an intense implementation, the smart organization should consider the following items mentioned to preempt valuable hybrids from jumping ship.

Formal Training

Hybrids like to learn and develop their skills as much as possible. Going back to Chapter 13, "People Issues, Roles, and Responsibilities," hybrids are the very definition of "willing and able." To be certain, much of this learning takes place on the job. Hybrids like to get their hands dirty and dive into issues; the unknown does not scare them. However, most applications and products are so robust that no one can effectively learn them one hour at a time on relatively slow days. Dedicated training is often required to learn an advanced product with the intent of applying that knowledge in the organization. Hybrids repeatedly denied chances to participate in formal training may become frustrated and more apt to listen when a recruiter calls.

Compensation

Hybrids do not fall easily into many traditional job descriptions. Although they often have a primary source of expertise, hybrids tend to do a little bit of everything. Often overlooked is the fact that many hybrids interface extremely well with everyone in an organization, from the purely functional to purely technical and everyone in between. Aside from their vast system knowledge, they often know how to speak both languages. Many know when to dial up or down more "technospeak" as the audience and situation warrant. This in turn expedites the resolution of all sorts of issues, minimizing the "back and forth" between disparate groups. Less is lost in translation when a fluent interpreter is present.

All these skills add up to considerable value for the organization. Management should recognize hybrids' contributions by paying them above-market salaries. After all, hybrids are exceptionally hard to find and replace.

Strategic Input

Money and training may go a long way, but hybrids often want something else: involvement in organizational decisions. As people who typically solve problems created or exacerbated by others, hybrids can typically provide keen business and technical insight into the ways in which systems can be effectively deployed—both now and in the future. The converse holds true as well: they are likely to have strong opinions about what should *not* be done and what will cause problems usually unanticipated by others. Although turning over the entire IT or finance department to a single hybrid employee may not be feasible, organizations should seek the input of hybrids for key systems-related decisions *before* they are made.

Immediately Removing or Redeploying Difficult Employees

As shown in Chapter 13, some employees on a project may not be willing and able to perform necessary tasks in the time allotted. Those with good intentions but without the requisite skills—willing but not able—may need help. As a result, the implementation team might have to augment or remove end users.

Now, consider able but not willings (ABNWs) and neither willing nor ables (NWNAs). Ideally, management would never have assigned them to the project in the first place. However, sometimes these characters hide their true colors until the project has started. Sometimes the organization is simply so lean that it has no other choice. It has to bite the bullet and assign potentially problematic employees to project teams.

Employees may pose problems for a variety of reasons. Some people may find the new system too complicated. In the words of Swiss computer scientist Niklaus Wirth, "A primary cause of complexity is that software vendors uncritically adopt almost any feature that users want." That is, legacy systems may have been easier to use because they simply did not do as much. Today, organizations buy, build, and rent systems that offer much more functionality than legacy systems. Patience and training may not quell employees' fears or help them assimilate to a new system. Faced with an uncertain future, they may kick and scream throughout the project.

If the carrots and sticks mentioned in Chapter 13 do not do the trick, it is best simply to remove or redeploy problem employees as soon as possible. The longer that organizations wait to remove internal obstacles, particularly those in key roles, the greater the risk to that project. Going back to the Petrucci General case study, had management reigned in Nick from the beginning, the project may not have failed to the extent that it did.

Emergency Triage: Send in "The Wolf"

One of my favorite movies is Miramax Films's *Pulp Fiction*, written and directed by Quentin Tarantino. Trust me. I am going somewhere with this. I particularly enjoy the scenes involving Harvey Keitel's character, Winston Wolfe, aka "The Wolf." Hit men Jules (Samuel L. Jackson) and Vincent (John Travolta) have accidentally shot a man in their car, the inside of which is now covered in blood. They arrive unexpectedly at the house of Jules's friend, Jimmy. Aside from needing to dispose of the body and clean themselves up, they must sanitize the car within an hour, as Jimmy's wife is due home from work soon. Panicked and unsure about how to handle the situation, Jules calls his boss, Marsellus, who is able to calm Jules down by telling him that he is sending in The Wolf.

The Wolf arrives at Jimmy's house less than 10 minutes after receiving the call from Marsellus. The Wolf quickly gathers information, assesses the situation, and starts telling Jules and Vincent what to do. Told abruptly to clean the car, Vincent snaps that "a 'please' would be nice," prompting the following exchange:

> **THE WOLF:** Get it straight, Buster. I'm not here to say "please." I'm here to tell you want to do. And if self-preservation is an instinct you possess, you'd better (expletive) do it and do it quick. I'm here to help. If my help's not appreciated, then lots of luck, gentlemen.
>
> **JULES:** No, Mr. Wolf, it ain't like that. Your help is definitely appreciated.
>
> **VINCENT:** I don't mean any disrespect. You know I respect you. I just don't like people barking orders at me.
>
> **THE WOLF:** If I'm curt with you, it's because time is a factor. I think fast, I talk fast, and I need you guys to act fast if you wanna get out of this. So pretty please, with sugar on top, clean the (expletive) car.

In the end, everything turns out all right. Jimmy and Jules dispose of both body and car, Jimmy's wife never finds out about the murder, The Wolf gets breakfast, and Jimmy receives several thousand dollars for a new bedroom set for his trouble.[2]

So, what does *Pulp Fiction* have to do with IT projects? In short, organizations in dire situations may need to "send in The Wolf." Distressed clients may need to turn to highly skilled and compensated hired guns at key points in a project in an attempt to solve major problems. Examples of situations requiring "The Wolf" include when the following occur:

- Essential setup decisions still need to be made.
- Reports or interfaces are well behind schedule.
- Testing is lagging and not manifesting issues in a timely manner.

If left unaddressed, these issues will result in missed activation dates and budget overruns. For the hired gun to be successful, all end users—even external consultants—need to fall in line, much like Jules and Vincent. The Wolf needs to have complete authority and cannot be bothered with knowledge transfer or ensuring that everyone is comfortable with the process. People need to quickly and comprehensively answer The Wolf's specific questions concerning anything—setup, testing, report requirements, and so on.

Although probably not quite as coarse as the Harvey Keitel character, the hired gun has one primary objective: to get the project back on track. The organization needs the hired gun to work his magic. To that end, excessive meetings, diplomacy, and hand-holding must go by the wayside. The Wolf is there to provide results, and everyone needs to follow his orders precisely.

The hired gun *cannot* guarantee a successful outcome. Some situations are so dire that they are beyond rescue, even for The Wolf. For example, no one person can configure and test an entire system in two days. Superman himself cannot completely validate an organization's general ledger or payroll setup at the last minute. Even a reporting guru cannot knock out 100 custom reports in a weekend. Still, for the project on life support, sending in a hired gun may be the only available option short of postponing the go-live date or scrapping the project altogether.

---

2. For a less vulgar equivalent of "The Wolf," check out George Clooney's eponymous character in the excellent 2007 film *Michael Clayton*. Clooney plays an attorney or "janitor" adept at cleaning up messy situations.

Summary

On IT projects, people need to lead, follow, or get out of the way, to quote Thomas Paine. Organizations lucky enough to have hybrids should take steps to ensure that they remain happy campers throughout the project and beyond. Followers may not have the skills that hybrids do, but at least they are on board.

Senior management should either not staff projects with problem employees or put them on short leashes from the beginning. This approach may seem draconian at first, and difficult people may eventually see the light. However, organizations that utilize employees with an axe to grind increase risk to the overall project and, ultimately, to the organization itself. As a last resort, bringing in a results-oriented hired gun may salvage a project and its go-live date.

Endnotes

i. http://instruct1.cit.cornell.edu/courses/ilrhr769/biosketch.html

Chapter 22

Intelligent Expansion

> We go out in the world and take our chances.
> Fate is just the weight of circumstances.
> That's the way that lady luck dances...
> Roll the Bones
> —*Neil Peart, Rush*

- Types of Future Enhancements
- Tate Case Study: Building on a Poor Foundation

O ne of my favorite board games is Risk.[1] In an attempt at world domina-
tion, players deploy their armies throughout the globe, roll the dice,
and conquer countries. To be sure, there is a huge luck component in the
game. However, the player who knows how to manage risk—specifically,
when to be aggressive and when to pull back—is at an advantage. That player
will not take unnecessary risks and, in the end, stands the best chance of win-
ning. Although no outcome is certain, intelligent strategy often overcomes
some bad rolls of the dice.

Most of the time, organizations go live with at least a few known and hopefully minor issues that will be addressed in the near future. (Remember
Voltaire's quote about perfect being the enemy of good.) Any thoughts of a
"pain-free" implementation disappeared long ago. Perhaps modules or features were intentionally tabled for budgetary reasons.

Depending on the severity of known issues, a project team may either push
them aside until Phase II or choose to live with them. However, as a general
rule, organizations should address the following issues well before even enter-
taining the thought of system expansion:

- Those that affect data integrity and reporting
- Those that affect system performance and stability
- Those that affect system security

This chapter focuses on expansion-related risks and the steps that organizations can take to ensure successful additions to the new system.

Types of Future Enhancements

To be sure, not all system enhancements and additions are equal—much like
all post-activation issues. For the organization to successfully realize the outputs of each enhancement, it must take into account the required and proportional inputs. This section presents each type of enhancement in ascending
order of *expected* difficulty and resources required.

---

1. According to the Hasbro Web site, about 50 years ago, an award-winning French film-
maker, Albert Lamorisse, created a revolutionary game he called La Conquete du Monde.
Loosely translated, this means "Conquest of the World." Two years later, in 1959, Parker
Brothers published the game we have all come to know as Risk. Risk pushed the envelope
and, depending on whom you ask, remains unmatched by any other game on the shelf,
quickly becoming a phenomenon with millions of copies sold throughout the world.

Enabling Additional Functionality Within a Module of an Existing System

Perhaps an organization's resources during Phase I were stretched. A few items originally slated for immediate activation did not make the cut. After a cooling-down period following system activation, organizations typically revisit those features, seeking to enhance their systems by adding functionality to existing applications. Examples include the following:

- Creating additional Web-based reports for an existing dashboard
- Turning on a new vacation plan within the currently used absence management application to track employee balances
- Increasing the number of government grants tracked

These types of enhancements tend to be the easiest to accomplish. Although design, documentation, planning, and testing are important, each enhancement is *incremental*. As a result, employees are typically already familiar with the system at this point. Thus, the new functionality simply represents an extension of that which is currently working.

Enabling Entirely New Modules

Aside from enhancing an application within the new system, organizations often activate new applications altogether. Examples include the following:

- Enabling asset management to leverage the value of fixed asset inventory and minimize the cost of tracking physical assets
- Enabling functionality to track employee vacation and sick accruals

These types of enhancements require significant resource commitments from organizations. Proper design, documentation, planning, and formal testing are essential. Although employees are already familiar with some of the applications in the system, they are *not* familiar with these new ones.

Integrating an Entirely Different System

The most expensive and time consuming of these enhancements is the third-party system integration. Organizations tend to go the best of breed (BOB) route for a number of reasons. First, right or wrong, management has confidence in the basic functionality, stability, and performance of the new system. Second, the BOB system offers superior functionality relative to the vendor's alternative, if one even exists. Finally, the organization believes that the BOB system addresses a compelling business need that justifies the additional license and support fees, integration costs, and departure from a unified systems strategy.

Examples of such projects include the implementation and integration of the following systems:

- Taleo's Talent Management for applicant tracking and recruiting
- Hyperion's business intelligence (BI) tool for enhanced reporting
- Kronos Workforce Central for employee timekeeping purposes

Often, organizations may have good reasons for doing this. I recommended this very approach a few years ago to a large hospital system that had great difficulty with a vendor's electronic recruiting application. That organization met the preceding criteria; it had tried the enterprise resource planning (ERP) vendor's alternative for years and still couldn't get it to work, resulting in a lack of qualified nursing applicants, excessive overtime costs, and a host of other issues.

> **NOTE**
> Before adding significant functionality or integrating another system, it is imperative that organizations ensure that their existing hardware, system infrastructure, and employees can handle the increased demands about to be placed on them.

The following case study illustrates an organization with a fascinating paradox: a powerful system and a simultaneous, complete dearth of a coherent strategy for how to use it. It not only routinely ignored opportunities to fix post-go-live issues; it actually exacerbated them by introducing an entirely separate system. It is a prime example of what *not* to do.

> **NOTE**
> This case also illustrates that, despite lip service to the contrary, some organizations simply do not want to "get better." Systems in these organizations are bound to fail. It's only a matter of time.

Tate Case Study: Building on a Poor Foundation

Publically traded Tate Apparel operates a chain of about 1,000 retail stores throughout the United States and Canada. About 10,000 employees work at Tate, although that number increases during the holiday season. Tate began its implementation of a new ERP system in 2000, ultimately going live in 2002. The enormity of the project called for a partial or phased approach.

Tate did not convert all regions throughout the organization to its new system. As a result, after activation, biweekly payroll needed to be processed from three different systems, a time-consuming and inefficient process fraught with risk. In most organizations, such arrangements tend to be ephemeral in nature. However, Tate management never did retire the other two payroll systems and consolidate everything in its ERP system.

During the project, Tate management made a number of critical mistakes. First, it did not upgrade its servers to handle the anticipated increase in the number of annual transactions that the ERP would generate. This problem was not immediately apparent after going live because Tate activated its system with minimal historical data. However, as the number of transactions continued to grow, system performance continued to exacerbate. A mere year after going live, employees noted a distinct decline in system performance with everything from entering basic information to running reports.

Second, Tate spent thousands of dollars implementing the ERP's native self-service product. That application would have allowed employees and managers to view key information, enroll in benefits, and enter important personal information updates—such as name and address changes. However, Tate never rolled it out. This is tantamount to getting all the buck for no bang. Instead, Tate built and attempted to integrate a separate system for store-based transactions with its relatively new ERP.

Post-Go-Live Issues

Tate faced a number of expected and significant issues in the months after going live. First, as mentioned, employee and financial transactions grew quickly. The existing server's lack of processing power—and management's unwillingness to buy more powerful boxes— made daily system processing and reporting glacially slow for employees. Management's stopgap solution was simply to purge important historical data from the PROD data area and move it to a different one on the same server.

This solution—and I use that term loosely—had two effects. System performance improved because PROD contained less data. However, on the flip side, an end user looking at employee compensation, benefit, or vacation history now had to look in two different data areas if the employee had been with Tate for more than one year. Also, from a reporting standpoint, reports would often need to be run twice, because no data area had comprehensive information, reinforcing Tate's inefficient business processes.

Tate's second major issue stemmed from the fact that data from its home-grown store system did not typically match the data in its ERP. Often, employees had to key information into both systems or did not know which system contained the correct information. HR and payroll clerks typically had to call individual stores and speak to managers to determine employee hire dates, rates of pay, and job titles.[2]

Tate was at a fork in the road. The dispersion, redundancy, and inconsistency of its data left it with two options: fix the problem or ignore it. Lamentably, Tate management chose the latter. A perfect example was its annual enrollment of employee benefits, a process for which Tate used the carrier's separate online application. Tate refused to use the ERP vendor's similar application because it would force the organization to clean up its data. The carrier's software could be used in relative isolation (sans data cleanup), although the data that the system generated would ultimately need to be imported into the ERP for employee deduction and interface purposes. The short-term solution of using a relatively independent application only exacerbated the long-term, underlying data and system problems.

Third, adding to the chaos, Tate suffered from extensive turnover at corporate headquarters. Many of its employees were relatively new to the system at any given point. Tate refused to train its staff properly and opted for an on-the-job approach. As a result of this lack of internal expertise, Tate end users made many errors in the system, adding more superfluous records and rendering many transaction-based reports essentially meaningless.

Finally and most important, Tate lacked both proper internal controls and a coherent system strategy. Collectively, these deficiencies caused inaccurate and inconsistent government reporting. Aside from financial discrepancies and irregularities, Tate also lacked the ability to track and properly audit transactions from its employee stock purchase program. Tate not only followed poor business processes, but the company could not even sufficiently document them. A few conscientious employees made executives aware of these issues in vain. Management did not even attempt to reconcile known differences, improve its processes, and create proper documentation. Ultimately, management would pay for its willful ignorance.

Misplaced Priorities and an Aversion to Change

Faced with major post-go-live issues, Tate attempted to address only one. It recognized that it needed more internal bandwidth and hired two knowledgeable and talented superusers: Sharon and me. Both of us had a great deal of previous experience with Tate's existing system and reported to Renee, the director of payroll and Human Resource Information Systems (HRIS).

---

2. Most large organizations have to do this *before* they spend millions on a robust system, not after.

Hiring "rock stars" will not automatically avert or correct a system failure. In this case, Tate did not use its new resources to optimize existing systems and stop the bleeding. Sharon and I *could* have helped address known issues, automate reporting, provide end-user training, and ultimately improve system performance and data consistency. On a larger scale, Renee could have deployed us on a system integration project, the intent of which would be to run payroll from one system, as opposed to three. Renee chose not to pursue either option.

Rather than address existing issues, Tate executives—at the behest of Laura, its senior VP of HR—decided to purchase and implement a BOB performance management system (PMS) at the cost of more than $1M. Although well aware of the status quo, Renee chose not to oppose this decision. Renee knew that Laura was not an "operations" person and would not appreciate Tate's current and future data challenges, much less care to fix them. Laura was hell bent on a new PMS and, as a result, Tate marched on with the third-party system. Renee put Sharon in charge of the project.

On the reporting front, Tate had deployed Web-based Crystal Reports to a limited extent. For the most part, however, it relied on old-fashioned mechanisms such as Microsoft Excel.[3] I immediately saw opportunities to improve Tate's systems, data, and business processes. I soon approached Renee and made my case for rewriting the company's reports to allow for automated scheduling and electronic delivery via Crystal. Renee would have none of it. She told me in no uncertain terms "that's not how we do things here." I would have to continue Tate's wholly inefficient process of manually cobbling together reports each month, a process requiring days of error-prone work.

Despite having superior reporting functionality and delivery mechanisms *already at its disposal*, Tate insisted on continuing the same antiquated methods for report generation and distribution. Aside from frustrating me, this decision had the additional effect of minimizing the time I could spend cleaning up the company's inconsistent and inaccurate data. As a result, Renee effectively minimized my contribution, negating my

- Extensive knowledge of the system on both the functional and technical ends

- Knowledge of best practices and system limitations based on my consulting background

- Strong desire to streamline manual processes

- Ability to clean up bad data

---

3. This is not to disparage Excel in any way. I love Excel and think it's amazing. However, it does have limitations.

As it turned out, Renee never wanted me to improve Tate's systems and data, although she preached the need to do those very things during my interviews. Despite her statements to improve Tate's systems, Renee knew that my work ethic and skill set would eventually unearth major data, configuration, integration, and processing issues. In fact, I was already uncovering such issues and attempting to address them within the ERP. To be blunt, Renee wanted no part of fixing them. Although Tate's systems were in disarray, from Renee's perspective, neither the organization in general—nor her boss in particular—was exactly in a hurry to fix them.

Rather than viewing me as an asset, Renee now saw me as a threat that could bring down the whole house of cards. If I made or attempted to make improvements to the system, I could expose the company's vast system and data inconsistencies, not to mention its complete lack of internal controls. Even with the lurking fear of a Sarbanes-Oxley audit, Renee continued to hide known issues. She certainly did not want me, or anyone else for that matter, discovering new problems and trying to fix them at their core. Renee and I soon decided that a mutual parting of ways was best for all concerned.

Outcomes and Lessons

Rather than improve its recently implemented ERP, Tate chose to spend more than $1M on a third-party BOB system. Tate management should have used the same resources to solidify its ERP and internal controls. Not a year after the PMS project began, Tate was the subject of a formal Sarbanes-Oxley (SOX) audit. In the end, Tate's misguided priorities, lack of internal controls, and poor systems directly—or indirectly—resulted in the following:

- The dispersal of even more organizational data to even more disparate places (including the newly implemented PMS), further compromising reporting and data integrity
- Core system issues remaining unaddressed
- A SOX audit that found material weaknesses[4] with respect to Tate's internal controls
- The restatement of three years of earnings
- The plummeting of its stock
- The departure of its CEO

---

4. A material weakness is a significant deficiency or combination of significant deficiencies that result in more than a remote likelihood that a material misstatement will not be prevented or detected. [Source: McGladrey & Pullen LLP Web site (http://www.mcgladrey.com)].

Although the PMS was certainly superior to the ERP vendor's equivalent, Tate was in absolutely no position to add a new system to its existing architecture. Tate's initial system activation resulted in a Forthcoming Failure. However, because management wantonly ignored major issues and actually created more after going live, Tate can be classified as an Unmitigated Disaster.

Summary

Systems are dynamic in nature. They change—hopefully, for the better—just like employees and organizations. As the Tate case study shows, organizations should enhance or expand their systems only on stable platforms with knowledgeable end users, proper testing, and coherent long-term IT strategies. If an organization has widespread system problems, it should absolutely not add more systems or functionality. Expansion for the sake of expansion is at best ill advised and, more often than not, just plain dangerous.

Organizations can certainly activate their systems without every feature under the sun, growing at later points. Organizations need not do everything at once. As a general rule, they should activate systems with critical functionality and with as many "desirable" features as is plausible. Organizations can and should revisit functionality dropped from Phase I in future phases, often after the dust settles from their initial activations and employees are more familiar with the new applications in a production world.

Chapter 23

Conclusions and General Rules of Thumb

Of course, that's just my opinion. I could be wrong.

—*Dennis Miller*

- Pre-Implementation
- Mid-Implementation
- Post-Activation

This book has been intentionally light on absolutes for two reasons. First, all projects are unique. No two organizations face identical challenges with respect to internal politics, system integrators (SIs), budgets, timeframes, issues, and end users. Second, even heeding all the advice in this book cannot guarantee a successful system activation. No text, consultant, or vendor can promise that an organization will not have major issues. To be sure, organizations benefit a great deal from skilled consultants, conscientious PMs, dedicated client end users, and responsive vendors. However, no one person or entity can guarantee a successful outcome.

> **NOTE**
> The best managed project may fail, whereas a horribly managed project may come in under budget, ahead of schedule, and do everything that the vendor promised at the onset. In reality, however, organizations are unlikely to find themselves in one of these extreme scenarios. On a fundamental level, successfully activating and utilizing a new system is about minimizing risk from day one until the end of the project and beyond. The organization that can do this stands the best chance of averting failure.

With that disclaimer out of the way, this chapter lists some of the book's more salient points and "relative absolutes" with respect to system implementations, broken into the following categories:

- Pre-implementation
- Mid-implementation
- Post-implementation

Pre-Implementation

Organizations that understand the importance of the following factors *before* starting IT projects tend to experience fewer problems and delays than those that do not.

Know Your Fields

Make sure to account for the *type* of project when budgeting, staffing, and planning the new system implementation. Greenfield sites pose *relatively* few obstacles and constraints because the organization often desperately needs some type of system.

Implementing a new system at a brownfield site is usually more difficult than its green counterpart. Brownfield employees tend to be a bit more ingrained in their ways and less open to change. These organizations are used to doing things in a certain way; the replacement system will mean that they will have to change certain business practices. What's more, the new system will often necessitate replacing hardware such as servers and databases. Plan and budget accordingly.

Consider All Alternatives

Rather than jump immediately into vendor selection among the usual suspects, take a long look at the offerings of SaaS and open source vendors. They are gaining greater acceptance and becoming more mature every day. Weigh the pros and cons of each before dismissing them as flashes in the pan.

Maximize Overlap of Client Constituencies from the Start

At their core, almost all IT projects involve three major client constituencies:

- Senior management
- Functional end users
- Technical end users

From the start of the project, minimize potential and real disconnects among these three groups. All too often, each of the three constituencies does not entirely understand the objectives, concerns, and limitations of the other two. Much can be lost in translation among the three parties, particularly between functional and technical end users.[1] This can be represented graphically in Figure 23.1.

From the onset of a project and continuing throughout its duration, each of the three groups should do the following:

- Understand the specific objectives, concerns, and limitations of the other two constituencies
- Effectively communicate to the other constituencies in a language that each can understand
- Ensure that each constituency does not make decisions inimical to the other two

The more the circles in Figure 23.1 are compressed, the greater the likelihood of a successful project.

---

1. Note that SaaS-based projects may require few, if any, client IT or technical personnel.

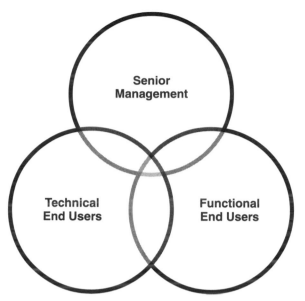

Figure 23.1 *The three key client constituencies on IT projects.*

Understand Trade-Offs in Advance

When implementing a new system, an organization must understand that it cannot expect to have its cake and eat it, too. As the Portnoy case study showed, no system can allow an organization to concurrently realize the benefits of integration and decentralization. By definition, more of one means less of another. Decide in advance the acceptable trade-offs, and live by those decisions.

Check the Engine and Tires Before Getting in the Car

Before even considering the implementation of a new system, an organization should honestly assess if it can do the following:

- Stomach the costs
- Remove significant internal political roadblocks
- Clean up its data
- Provide the requisite human and financial resources

An organization should overcome these obstacles before attempting an endeavor requiring such significant time and resources.

Don't Reinvent the Wheel

Organizations should stick to their knitting and purchase tested and proven systems rather than build them from scratch. The amount of time, money, and effort required to build a new system dissuades most executives. Undeterred organizations should consider that back-office systems present no sustainable business advantage. Those that want to reinvent the wheel better have enough bandwidth, documentation, and backup if and when the brakes fail.

Keep It Simple, Stupid (KISS)

Complicated systems face much greater chances of failure than simple ones. A system designed and configured intelligently—according to the best practices espoused by knowledgeable consultants—stands a much greater chance of withstanding the rigors of testing and the challenges of an implementation. Complex configurations increase the odds of encountering problems before, during, and after system activation. This is true in both the short and long term.

Bigger Isn't Necessarily Better

As Clint Eastwood said in *Magnum Force*, "A man's gotta know his limitations." In terms of systems, organizations should not overreach. Organizations need to view the alleged advantages of a new system within the context of the organization. If not tested and used properly, superior functionality from more costly applications does more harm than good. The organization that attempts to implement a critical system irrespective of that system's tier— needs to budget enough time and money to properly test that system. Spending $1M on a software license and support and $50K on its implementation is a recipe for disaster.

Know Your Organization

Organizations with old systems, old data, relatively high profit margins, and little competition are more prone to difficult IT projects. These organizations need to be aware of their own limitations and tendencies from the beginning of a project—while selecting a system and an SI, planning a project, and assigning timelines and resources. Management at a mature multisite health care organization should not delude itself into thinking that it can implement a system in the same time and within the same budget as a small telecommunications startup.

Take Vendor Promises with More Than a Grain of Salt

Vendor software demonstrations can be outright dazzling. Prospective clients will never hear the word "no" from salespeople in response to a question such as, "Can your software do this?" To be sure, the answer to this question may not be a complete misrepresentation of the truth. After all, anything is possible.

Prospective clients should ask a slightly different but much better question, "Does your software do this out of the box?" Should the salesperson answer in the affirmative, the follow-up question should always be, "Can you please show me now?" To quote from one of my favorite Rush songs, "Show me; don't tell me."

Vendor claims may or may not ultimately turn out to be accurate and justified. Do not take vendor claims as gospel. Look at their models "proving" the return on investment (ROI). Are the alleged outputs based on realistic inputs and assumptions? It is imperative to look at—and question—these assumptions from the beginning.

The success or failure of a new system hinges directly on the acceptance of that system by the organization's employees. Efficiency to senior management may mean job insecurity to a long-time employee scared about his future. Don't make the mistake of assuming that the project will take place without delays and cost overruns.

Get Everything in Writing

Organizations dealing with vendors or SIs should insist upon strict and comprehensive contract language. This is especially true if the organization is using either the vendor or the SI for the first time. Although time consuming and arduous in nature, such language serves as the ultimate insurance policy if a client's partner misrepresented items (not) covered during the sales cycle. In the unlikely event that the client ends up in court, it will be glad that it has extensive documentation.

More than a CYA (consultant-speak for "cover your ass") maneuver, a client's process of documenting its business requirements has the added benefit of helping it identify areas of potential improvement with the new system.

Find a Trusted Partner for Vendor Selection

Organizations that use SIs to assist with vendor selection should adhere to the all-or-nothing principle: find partners with experience in either multiple systems or no specific system—that is, vendor-agnostic organizations. An SI with a vested interest in the outcome tends to produce skewed findings.

Don't Skimp on Internal Staff

Organizations wanting to minimize the number of external consultants on an implementation first must ensure that their internal resources are devoted almost exclusively to the project. Beyond time, those internal resources must have sufficient expertise in that system—via training, previous experience, or both. Organizations should augment implementation teams with external talent, especially when current employees have no experience with the new system. Hybrid employees often cost a premium but, over the course of the project and beyond, more than justify their increased compensation.

Note that increased spending on IT projects has become more difficult to justify in recent years. Look at a contingency fund as a form of insurance: a multimillion dollar project with a potentially unnecessary $200K kitty may be a worthwhile hedge against such a large endeavor failing outright.

Not All Consultants Are Created Equal

Organizations should not make the mistake of assuming that all SIs and individual consultants are equal. By the same token, they should not choose a consulting firm solely on the basis of cost. More expensive consultants may in fact be worth a premium and save the client money in the long term.

The bottom line with consultants is that organizations tend to get what they pay for. A consultant's rate is a direct reflection of the experience brought to the table. All else equal, the organization that opts for the less expensive consultant should not expect the same level of performance that it would receive from a more seasoned—and expensive—one.

Build In Buffers to Combat Potential Project Delays from the Onset

The organization that adds buffers to its project plan (especially during natural breaking points) is in a better position to withstand invariable last-minute delays. One of my favorite bromides is, "Better to have it and not need it than need it and not have it." Assuming zero errors and a delay-free project is downright foolish.

In his comprehensive and well researched study *Patterns in IT Litigation: Systems Failure (1976 2000)*, Bruce F Webster looked at more than 120 IT projects over a 25-year period that dealt with some form of systems failure. His study yielded four recommendations for organizations embarking on major IT projects:

- Get expert legal and IT guidance before signing anything.
- Specify critical terms and articulate protections before agreeing to a sale of goods or services.
- Act quickly when problems arise.
- Remember that new technology entails risks.

Remember strategic, wild ass guesses (SWAGs) and Hofstadter's Law: "It always takes longer than you expect, even when you take into account Hofstadter's Law."

Mid-Implementation

Organizations that recognize the importance of—and deal with—the following factors during IT projects tend to experience fewer problems and delays than those that do not.

Listen to Consultants and Allow Them to Freely Disagree

Organizations that insist on complicated or cumbersome system configurations create problems down the road that can threaten entire projects. Consultants should guide the setup of the system such that it meets with best practices, lest the client be left with a system that it cannot easily support. Consultants able to challenge questionable client decisions can prevent or minimize long-term issues.

Be Afraid: Data Conversion Is Almost Never Easy

Vendors and consultants trumpet the ease of loading data into a new system via conversion programs. In all but the most severe circumstances, organizations will *not* have to hire temps to key 10,000 employees or 2,000 vendors into the new system. However, loading data is almost never as easy as clients believe. The conversion process involves much more than extracting old data and loading it into the new system. This crucial oversight has significantly derailed many project timelines and budgets. Implementation teams should kick the tires on data conversions as soon as possible, even if all individual configuration decisions have not been made.

When it comes to data quality, cleansing, and conversion, hope for the best but prepare for the worst. As a general rule, the older the legacy system and data, the more time that it will take to cleanse and convert it.

Allow Employees Sufficient Time to Play

Application exploration (AE) should focus extensively on items covered in the first phase of the project, but not at the risk of completely ignoring upcoming phases. Configuring the application with the knowledge that it will need to be substantially changed after go-live is ill advised. Also, employees should participate in training immediately before AE, because it will reinforce material that they learned in class. Technical users need to attend training before

AE, because their jobs mandate that they create data areas, set up security, and perform other tasks required to start the project in earnest.

Replacing an SI Is Not an Elixir

Many implementation issues stem from things such as overly ambitious vendor promises, bad data, and reluctance on the part of client end users to get on board. Simply changing SIs will in no way guarantee that a poorly conceived project will turn around anymore than Charles Barkley's buying a new driver will fix his horrible golf swing.[2] New consultants often tell clients virtually the same thing as their predecessors, simply in a different voice. In the words of Ernest Hemingway, "Never mistake motion for action."

Consider Postponing Sites and Functionality

System activation is not an all-or-nothing activity. Although organizations may want to concurrently activate new systems at all sites and with all applications, project delays may negate that impossibility. If a project has gone awry, organizations have options beyond blindly "powering through" or pulling the plug on the project altogether. Rather than forcing the issue and potentially causing an Unmitigated Disaster, organizations should strongly consider *partially* going live—that is, postponing functionality or certain sites until a later phase.

Consider Euthanizing Lost Projects

In May 2008, the IS Audit and Control Association, an independent IT governance group, reported that nearly half of all organizations (43 percent) surveyed had terminated an IT project prior to its fruition.[i] The five biggest reasons are listed here:

- The business needs changed.
- The project did not deliver as promised.
- The project was no longer a priority.
- The project exceeded the budget.
- The project did not support the business strategy.

Regardless of the reason, organizations should not rule out aborting projects with little to no chance of achieving their objectives. As Seneca The Younger once said, "To err is human, but to persist is diabolical."

---

2. I am surprised that this book contains so few golf references.

Post-Activation

Organizations that understand the importance of the following factors *after* implementing new systems (or upgrading from prior versions) tend to experience fewer problems and delays than those that do not.

Expand Cautiously

Before even considering adding functionality to a system, organizations must ensure that their existing systems and employees can handle the increased demands about to be placed on them in the short and long terms. Building on a poor foundation is never wise; shore it up before adding on. Remember the Tate case study.

Audits Work

Audits can be invaluable tools for organizations at many different phases, especially after system activation. When performed judiciously by knowledgeable and impartial resources, they can detect, avoid, and minimize issues that can derail an implementation or cause a potentially successful one to fail. Organizations should not view audits as superfluous; they typically more than justify their costs.

Shore Up Documentation

Upon going live, organizations should ensure that end-user documentation is accurate and comprehensive. Employees often intend to "get around" to documenting any last-minute tweaks in regular processing, interfaces, setup, and data entry. However, daily realities often cause this to fall by the wayside. When a key individual exits the organization, that opportunity may be forever lost.

Employee Backup and Succession Planning

After system activation, organizations need to identify or reassess critical roles. Those without suitable replacements pose the greatest risks and should be addressed immediately. Organizations should ensure that they have adequate backup in the event that a key end user decides to suddenly leave. Although a valuable source of talent, the external labor market is not a panacea to an immediate staffing crisis. Two organizations may run the same version of the same software, but replacement employees always have learning curves, especially when documentation is lacking.

Summary

Sixty percent of IT projects fail for all sorts of reasons. The examples and case studies in this book have revealed the different causes—and combination of causes—of many system failures. Differences aside, the activation of a new system is a major endeavor for any organization. Perils exist around every corner. Although the advice dispensed in this book cannot by any means guarantee success on a given project, one thing is certain: a new mindset is required for organizations to improve their batting averages on IT projects. As Albert Einstein once said, "We can't solve problems by using the same kind of thinking we used when we created them."

Endnotes

i. http://www.isaca.org/Template.cfm?Section=Press_Releases1&CONTENTID=423 36&TEMPLATE=/ContentManagement/ContentDisplay.cfm

Afterword

> The key to good decision making is not
> knowledge. It is understanding.
> —*Malcolm Gladwell*

Much has happened since the initial publication of *Why New Systems Fail* in February 2009—and even more since I sat down in May 2009 to expand the book. As expected in the technology world, things have continued to move at a rapid pace.

The Arrival of Enterprise 2.0

People are hearing and reading more about Enterprise 2.0, a term that means different things to different people. To hear some people tell it, Enterprise 2.0 is all about collaboration and utilizing social networks inside the organization. E-mail and intranets will go by the wayside because these new tools will allow employees, vendors, suppliers, and customers to work seamlessly across time zones and boundaries. Among the most prominent proponents of the collaborative view is the man who originally coined the term, Andrew McAfee. McAfee works as a principal research scientist at the Center for Digital Business in the MIT Sloan School of Management, and he's a fellow at Harvard's Berkman Center for Internet and Society.

In my view, Enterprise 2.0 is about so much more than mere collaboration. It is about taking IT to the next level. To this end, collaborative tools are an important but insufficient condition to do just that. Social networks and wikis alone will not fully unleash the power of so many exciting new technologies in the enterprise. Recent technological advents and advancements include master data management (MDM), business intelligence (BI), software as a service (SaaS), enterprise search and retrieval (ESR), cloud computing, open source software, mobility, and agile software development. Collectively, they represent an entirely new wave of possibilities and efficiencies. This is a broader definition of the term.

Without question, these new technologies offer myriad benefits to organizations, their customers, and their employees. The fundamental challenge facing organizations, however, is that relatively few are ready and willing to take the next step. Simultaneously seeing massive opportunity and chaos, I wrote *The Next Wave of Technologies* in 2009, an ambitious book that attempts to provide chief executives, IT practitioners, and academics with "GPS for the workplace." (As for writing so much in one year, I suppose there are benefits to a poor economy, an inability to sleep, good typing skills, and an inordinate number of opinions.)

I assembled a collection of experts who wrote about fundamental best practices, pitfalls, and next steps with respect to a variety of technologies already making inroads. My rationale was fairly straightforward. As *Why New Systems Fail* illustrates, well-understood systems and applications, implemented by experts, are continually plagued by a 60 percent failure rate. Against this backdrop, what are the odds that poorly understood technologies will have a better track record? To boot, throw in scarce resources stemming from a miserable economy and tight timelines. The results are twofold: a recipe for failure for those who don't get it and tremendous opportunity for those who do.

I truly hope—and believe—that my second book, like the one you just read, will help organizations do more than merely avert IT project failure. The book should assist organizations in truly garnering value, savings, and innovation from their IT dollar.

The Same Mistakes

As 2009 progressed, I realized that *Why New Systems Fail* struck a nerve with many of its readers. Random people contacted me via my Web site and told me similar stories of IT projects gone amok. Some attended my book signings and asked me if we had worked at the same company!

Aside from penning a second book, I continued to work on large-scale IT projects in a variety of industries in 2009. Although my experiences and challenges varied from client to client, I routinely saw organizations and individuals make the same mistakes detailed in *Why New Systems Fail*. The level of dysfunction at some of my clients' organizations continued to amaze me.

For instance, a hospital where I worked in 2009 was the very definition of an Unmitigated Disaster, one of my four types of system failures referenced in Chapter 2, "Why Organizations Maintain Legacy Systems." After being called in to do an initial project risk assessment and remediation plan, I started in earnest. Within minutes, I wondered how an IT project could go so awry in today's day and age. End users and senior managers seemed to disregard Project Management 101, continuing to find new and interesting ways to make a bad situation worse. The actions of a few exposed the organization to myriad problems, risks, lawsuits, and employee disaffection.

Although that hospital may have been exceptional, as a whole, most of my clients in 2009 fell into the same patterns that I had observed throughout my consulting career. On more than one occasion, I gave a copy of *Why New Systems Fail* to a senior executive and said something along the lines of, "Our problem here reminds me of a case study in my book." Part of me wished that seeing something in print would encourage these people to make better decisions. Unfortunately, I wasn't always right.

Let's just say that many organizations are entirely unprepared for newer technologies; they cannot even handle "older" ones.

It's the People, Not the Technology

All of this leads me back to the fundamental point of the book that you have just read: it's all about the people. If there's an enduring lesson in the book, that's it.

Whatever your definition of Enterprise 2.0, its tools and technologies are fundamentally different from those of the 1990s and early 2000s. However, there is one constant: the people making the decisions, using the applications, and running the projects. No technology, regardless of moniker, implements itself. Having written a second book about newer and less mature technologies, I am more convinced than ever of one thing: the management lessons in *Why New Systems Fail* are as true and valid as ever. Although I am well aware that technology books tend to have a limited shelf life, my hope is that this book has greater staying power.

I have seen nothing in "the next wave" of technologies that indicates otherwise.

Phil Simon
January 2010
Caldwell, New Jersey

Bibliography

Berkun, Scott. *Making Things Happen: Mastering Project Management*. Sebastopol, California: O'Reilly, 2008.

Brooks, Frederick P. *The Mythical Man-Month: Essays on Software Engineering*. Boston: Addison-Wesley Professional, 1995.

Callahan, David. *The Cheating Culture: Why More Americans Are Doing Wrong to Get Ahead*. Orlando, Florida: Harvest Books, 2004.

Carroll, Paul B. and Chunka Mui. *Billion-Dollar Lessons: What You Can Learn from the Most Inexcusable Business Failures of the Last 25 Years*. New York: The Penguin Group, 2008.

Champy, J.A. and Michael Hammer. *Reengineering the Corporation: A Manifesto for Business Revolution*. New York: HarperCollins, 2003.

Evans, Nicholas D. *Business Innovation and Disruptive Technology: Harnessing the Power of Breakthrough Technology for Competitive Advantage*. Indianapolis, Indiana: FT Press, 2002.

Hammer, Michael and James Champy. *Reengineering the Corporation: A Manifesto for Business Revolution*. New York: Harper Paperbacks, 2003.

Harrin, Elizabeth. *Project Management in the Real World*. Edinburgh, Scotland: British Informatics Society Ltd, 2007.

Hurwitz, Judith, Carol Baroudi, Robin Bloor, and Marcia Kaufman. *Service Oriented Architecture For Dummies, 2nd Edition*. Indianapolis, Indiana: For Dummies, 2009.

Levitt, Steven D. and Stephen J. Dubner. *Freakonomics: A Rogue Economist Explores the Hidden Side of Everything*. New York: Harper Perennial, 2005.

Mitchell, Doug. *Confessions of an Ex-Enterprise Salesperson* (e-book). Scribd, 2008. Available for download via http://createwowmedia.com/enterprise-confessions-e-book-available-for-download.html.

Patrick, John J. *SQL Fundamentals*. Upper Saddle River, New Jersey: Prentice Hall, 2008.

Peters, Thomas J. and Robert H. Waterman. *In Search of Excellence: Lessons from America's Best-Run Companies*. New York: Collins Business Essentials, 2004.

Plant, Robert and Stephen Murrell. *An Executive's Guide to Information Technology: Principles, Business Models, and Terminology*. New York: Cambridge University Press, 2007.

Stiglitz, Joseph. *Economics of the Public Sector (Second Edition)*. New York: W.W. Norton & Company, Inc., 2000.

Ward, Patricia and George Dafoulas. *Database Management Systems, Second Edition*. Boston, Massachusetts: Cengage Learning Business Press, 2008.

Webster, Bruce F. "Patterns in IT Litigation: Systems Failure (1976–2000): A Study by PriceWaterhouseCoopers," 2000.

Wohl, Amy. *Succeeding at SaaS: Computing in the Cloud*. Merion Station, Pennsylvania: Wohl Associates, 2008.

Yourdon, Edward. *Death March*. Upper Saddle River, New Jersey: Prentice Hall, 1997.

Glossary of Commonly Used Terms

AE. *See* application exploration.

application exploration (AE). AE is a phase of a system implementation in which end users and consultants sit down in front of the computer and explore the application. AE typically takes place in a training data area in which end users can perform dummy setup and processing without fear of "breaking anything."

application service provider (ASP). An ASP hosts an organization's systems, obviating the need for the client to handle many traditional IT functions. For example, ASPs tend to apply software patches and handle system maintenance. ASPs are no longer *de rigeur* and have been largely replaced with SaaS organizations. *See also* Software as a Service.

ASP. *See* application service provider.

batch program. Program within an application that creates or modifies data *en masse*. Examples include programs that automatically calculate employee overtime or match invoices—as opposed to end users having to manually perform these tasks. Although batch programs can save a great deal of time, they can cause serious problems if a system's design is incorrect, because they create many incorrect transactions.

best of breed (BOB). A BOB approach to enterprise systems involves purchasing applications from different vendors and stitching them together. For example, a company may purchase an HR/payroll package from one vendor and an accounting package from another.

BOB. *See* best of breed.

brownfield. An organization that already has some type of enterprise system. End users are accustomed to doing things in a certain way, and current IT infrastructure supports existing business processes. The implementation of a new system is likely to be much more time and resource intensive relative to a greenfield site. *See also* greenfield.

canned reports. Vendors ship their applications with many canned or standard reports that present data in a predefined way. Also known as standard reports.

commercial, off-the-shelf (COTS) application. A COTS application is delivered with a great deal of inherent functionality. An organization can replace a legacy system quicker with a COTS application than building a replacement from scratch.

COTS. *See* commercial, off-the-shelf application.

CRM. *See* customer relationship management.

custom report. A user-created report that presents data in a way the client requires; vendors do not ship their products with custom reports.

customer relationship management (CRM). CRM applications allow organizations to track their current and prospective clients.

data area. An instance of a new system with a specific purpose. An organization may conduct end-user training in TRAIN but build the new application in BUILD. Ultimately, all data resides in production (PROD) once the organization has gone live.

database trigger. Defines an action that a database should take when some database-related event occurs. For example, an AP clerk pays a vendor's invoice, an action that triggers an automatic e-mail to the head of AP.

database view. Take data from multiple tables and present it in a single database object, making reporting simpler than if the tables remained separate.

decommission. Software vendors typically retire or decommission older applications and versions of applications, essentially refusing to support them. Vendors almost always give their clients more than sufficient notice before pulling the plug.

EEOC. *See* Equal Employment Opportunity Commission.

end-user licensing agreement (EULA). A EULA covers how an organization can use its vendor's software. It is a legal document that largely absolves the vendor from responsibility if the software malfunctions or produces an undesirable result.

enterprise resource planning (ERP). An ERP system stitches together an organization's back office operations. Specifically, these systems create and store data related to the following types of transactions: manufacturing, supply chain management, finance and accounting, HR, and customer relationship management (CRM). Of course, this depends on what individual organizations choose to utilize.

Equal Employment Opportunity Commission (EEOC). The U.S. EEOC is a federal agency that fights discrimination against race, color, national origin, religion, sex, age, and disability in the workplace.

ERP. *See* enterprise resource planning.

ETL. *See* extracted, transformed, and loaded.

EULA. *See* end-user licensing agreement.

extracted, transformed, and loaded (ETL). A process by which data is extracted, transformed, and loaded into a data warehouse or database. ETL tools essentially move data from one system into another. ETL tools allow for additional integration among disparate systems, essentially allowing systems to "talk" to each other.

go-live. The date and event associated with activation of the new system.

greenfield. An organization lacking any type of enterprise system. Manual processes and spreadsheets act as a *de facto* system. The implementation of a new system at a greenfield is likely to be less time and resource intensive than for a brownfield site. *See also* brownfield.

Health Insurance Portability and Accountability Act (HIPAA). The U.S. Congress passed HIPAA in 1996 to protect the health insurance of displaced workers and to ensure the privacy of medical records.

HIPAA. *See* Health Insurance Portability and Accountability Act.

HRIS. *See* Human Resource Information Systems.

Human Resource Information Systems (HRIS). An HRIS tracks an organization's employees and related information, including payroll, vacation balances, benefits, and the like.

hybrids. End users who understand both the front end of an application and the more technical "back end." The latter includes tables, relationships, and data structures. Hybrids are usually able to solve functional and technical problems with equal aplomb, saving critical time on implementations.

index. From a database perspective, a table index is essentially a way of uniquely identifying each record on a table. A typical index might be an employee number. That way, an organization can employ 100 guys named Bruce Springsteen, but each would have his own unique identifier (employee number). This is a very good thing.

interface. An interface takes data from one system to be imported, exported, or updated by another system. On new system projects, interfaces from carriers or vendors typically have to be rewritten to reference the new system.

independent software vendor (ISV). ISVs make all types of software for all types of companies. Because organizations have increasingly sought the external expertise of ISVs in creating applications, it should not be surprising that ISVs have prospered.

ISV. *See* independent software vendor.

JOIN. An SQL JOIN statement is programming code that allows end users to retrieve data from multiple tables. There are several types of JOINs for different purposes. Suffice it to say, many complex reports and queries (and often some simple ones) require a JOIN statement to pull data from different tables.

legacy system. At one level, this is an organization's "old" system. A better definition of the term comes from *An Executive's Guide to Information Technology: Principles, Business Models, and Terminology* by Robert Plant and Stephen Murrell:

> A system needs to be considered in terms of its ability to support the current and future processes of an organization; an inability to support changing process requirements is now taken as the definition of a legacy system.

on-premise vendor. A software vendor that sells applications that organizations own, control, and host. This is in stark contrast to a SaaS vendor that offers to host and maintain its clients' applications for them.

open enrollment. Annual process by which organizations allow employees to sign up for benefits such as health and dental for the upcoming year.

open source software (OSS). OSS is another alternative for organizations to the traditional on-premise model. Organizations can download applications for free, get under the hood, and modify them to meet their business needs. OSS has been gaining ground in many private and government organizations.

OSS. *See* open source software.

parallel test. In a parallel test, identical data is loaded or entered into two disparate systems for testing purposes. The results are then compared. In theory, the output should be similar, if not identical. Legitimate system differences often persist, however, because no two systems are the same.

postmortem. A process by which an organization evaluates the successes and failures of a recently completed project. This is a unique opportunity for an organization to learn about what went right and wrong and why, often with the help of external consultants.

pre-implementation audit. A process evaluating the potential risks that could hinder the success of a forthcoming IT project. These risks may include data, internal politics, end-user documentation, resource availability, and the like.

production environment. After activating its new system, an organization enters a "live" or production environment. From this point forward, the new application is the system of record, responsible for all data entry, transactions, and reports.

Sarbanes-Oxley Act (SOX). In 2002, U.S. President George W. Bush signed the SOX into law in response to a number of highly publicized accounting scandals involving large U.S. companies. The bill was designed to increase corporate responsibility and auditing requirements. SOX was named after sponsors Senator Paul Sarbanes (D-MD) and Representative Michael G. Oxley (R-OH).

scope creep. Scope creep takes place when the project initially sets out to accomplish X. However, based on a number of factors, the project now must accomplish X, Y, and Z. For projects sold as fixed bids, the system integrator (SI) will avoid scope creep like the plague.

Service-Oriented Architecture (SOA). SOA essentially allows for application development as a series of building blocks that can be integrated more easily than previous methods.

shelfware. A term for software that organizations have purchased but not implemented/activated. This results in organizations paying support and maintenance fees for unused applications.

SI. *See* system integrator.

SOA. *See* Service-Oriented Architecture.

Software as a Service (SaaS). SaaS is an alternative to the on-premise application model. Rather than purchase and maintain applications, organizations "rent" applications, paying a per-transaction or per-seat license fee. As such, organizations need not host SaaS applications, reducing the need for traditional IT involvement.

software tiers. A means of categorizing different vendors' offerings. Large, international organizations with revenues north of $100M use Tier 1 applications. Much smaller organizations use Tier 4 applications.

SOW. *See* statement of work.

SOX. *See* Sarbanes-Oxley Act.

standard reports. *See* canned reports.

statement of work (SOW). A SOW is an agreement between a client and system integrator (SI) defining the scope of the project. SOWs are meant to avoid scope creep. They detail the specific work products that the SI will provide throughout the project.

strategic, wild ass guess (SWAG). A SWAG represents an estimate by either consultants, vendors, or senior managers about how much time, money, and effort are required to undertake a massive endeavor. Because the guess involves so many factors, it is impossible to predict any of these with any degree of certainty.

Structured Query Language (SQL). SQL is a simple but powerful programming language that allows for selecting, updating, adding, and deleting data from tables.

SQL. *See* Structured Query Language.

sunk costs. Costs that cannot be recovered. Think of a movie ticket as a sunk cost. Economists would argue that you should always leave a bad movie after paying because you can't get your money back. You can at least recover your time. On IT projects, senior managers often forget this principle and throw good money after bad.

SWAG. *See* strategic, wild ass guess.

system design. Phase of system implementations in which consultants and end users configure the system to meet the organization's business needs.

system integrator (SI). A consulting firm that specializes in migrating clients from one system to another.

TALC. *See* Technology Adoption Life Cycle.

Technology Adoption Life Cycle (TALC). The TALC shows that most organizations wait until a technology is mature before adopting it. Only a few "early adopters" jump at the chance to use a new technology from the get-go.

test scripts. During testing, end users complete these comprehensive sets of directions designed to see if the system does what it is intended to do.

Y2K. See Year 2000.

Year 2000 (Y2K). The Y2K problem resulted from a great deal of software code written with a two-digit year field instead of a four-digit one. Companies spent billions of dollars tweaking code to ensure Y2K compliance.

Index